How you can have lovely plants and…

GARDEN FLOWERS

Color photos
Marion Nickig

Drawings
György Jankovics

Oriental poppy
(Papaver orientale).
Gorgeous flowers, later
replaced by decorative
seed capsules.

Bernd Hertle/Peter Kiermeier
Marion Nickig

How you can have lovely plants and...

GARDEN FLOWERS

Portraits of favorite garden flowers
and ornamental grasses and ferns,
with instructions for their care

With plans and ideas for large
and small gardens

500 color photos and
150 how-to drawings

Consulting Editor:
Dennis W. Stevenson
Administrator, Harding Laboratory
The New York Botanical Garden

BARRON'S

Even in a bed of extremely diverse perennials, there is always room to add a few accents—for example, plants in handsome containers.

Walking in the Garden

is an experience all its own, whatever the time of year. The various colors and forms of the flowers, depending on the season, can conjure up quite different moods and impressions (see photos, page 57, as well as pages 58–59).

Iris sibirica 'Celeste'

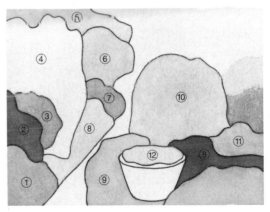

A magnificent array of flowers in June:

1 *Stachys byzantina*
2 *Geranium clarkei* 'Kashmir White'
3 *Salvia officinalis* 'Aurea'
4 *Iris barbata-elatior* hybrid
5 *Centranthus ruber* 'Albus'
6 *Salvia nemorosa*
7 *Salvia officinalis* 'Purpurascens'
8 *Viola cornuta* 'John Wallmark'
9 *Viola cucullata* 'Alba'
10 *Gillenia trifoliata*
11 *Corydalis*
12 *Sempervivum* hybrid

5

CONTENTS

Siberian iris

Trumpet lily

Collarette dahlia

Gardens with yellow ribbons of coneflowers

The Authors

Bernd Hertle, graduate engineer, Technical Director of the Weihenstephan Demonstration Garden. Scientific Assistant at the Institute for Perennials and Woody Plants. Numerous publications.

Professor Peter Kiermeier, Ph.D., Director of the Institute for Perennials and Woody Plants at the Weihenstephan Professional School, Director of the Demonstration Garden. Numerous publications.

Marion Nickig, a prominent photographer of plants, became well known for her unusual photographs of gardens and flowers in the magazine section of the *Frankfurter Allgemeine Zeitung*. Her work has appeared in noted gardening and interior design magazines for more than a decade.

Perennial sunflower

Garden lupine

Pompon dahlia

Important: To keep your pleasure in your hobby untarnished, please read the information on page 62 and the **Important Notes** on page 240 carefully.

FLOWERS FOR YOUR GARDEN

A Preface

Spring flowers usher in the gardening year.

Just what is it that makes flowers so beautiful? With their pyrotechnic display of colors, forms, and scents, they repeatedly tempt us into making unplanned purchases and planting our impulsive selections—not always to mutual benefit, as subsequent events often prove, because garden flowers develop their full splendor only if the right plant is in the right site in the right surroundings.

Your very own garden full of beautiful plants—a dream that you can make a reality. If you want to create a garden that is an oasis for relaxation and enjoyment, Barron's plant guide will accompany you faithfully through every season of the year.

Forms and Colors, the introduction and design section, will show you what a gaily colored tribe the name *garden flowers* conceals and what a variety of magical feats you can accomplish with them. A short course in the basics of design will teach you what to look for when choosing colors, what role is played by growth forms and flower and leaf shapes, how to group flowers for eye appeal, and how to keep your garden in bloom throughout the year. Examples of stunning gardens shown in breathtaking full-color photos and accompanied by clearly drawn planting diagrams will encourage you to try your hand at duplicating them.

Planting, Care, and Propagation is the title of the section on gardening techniques, including practical advice on planting, proper feeding and watering, and preventing or controlling pests and diseases. How-to pages with step-by-step drawings in color will tell you how to propagate flowers correctly.

The Plant Portrait and Tips on Care section presents more than 500 of the loveliest garden flowers, arranged in groups: annuals, perennials, bulbs and tubers, and—as companions for them—ornamental plants like grasses and ferns. Each plant is portrayed in a brilliantly colored photograph with detailed information on appearance, growth, blooming season, site, care, and propagation. Also included are tips on suggested use and plants that make good companions.

The authors and the editors of Barron's series of plant books wish you a garden full of the most beautiful flowers you've ever seen.

Hybrid tulips, with their lively colors, add cheerful spots of color to spring gardens.

Whether double- or single-flowered—Chinese peonies make a strong statement in your garden. Here, the single, pure white Paeonia lactiflora 'Jan van Leeuwen'

FORMS AND COLORS

What kind of color scheme do you want in your garden: cool tones, or a combination that uses warm colors?

This section of the book presents the different groups of garden flowers and discusses the elements of garden design. Learn to see forms and colors in a new way! A short basic course suggests methods to guide you in choosing appropriate flower colors, while keeping in mind the growth form, bloom times, and foliage.

Color photos of stunning gardens whose effects you can duplicate, along with lists of plants, will help you achieve your goal.

WHAT ARE GARDEN FLOWERS?

Garden flowers next to the house provide a beautiful transition between outdoors and indoors. Here, colorful hollyhocks (Alcea rosea hybrids).

For thousands of years, people have brought plants from near and far to grow close to home. What would a garden be without trees and shrubs, without the enormous variety and beauty of garden flowers—flowering perennials, annual or biennial summer flowers, bulbs and tubers, and grasses and ferns?

Buildings, hedges, and single specimen woody plants form garden "rooms" and thus create the setting that perennials and annuals decorate.

Trees and shrubs are long-lasting, lignified garden plants, so-called woody plants. They produce aerial shoots that withstand cold and frost. Over the course of the year, leaves, branches, and flowers develop from leaf buds and flower buds.

Garden flowers, including perennials, annuals, and bulbs and tubers, do not form wood. These herbaceous plants droop and die back in the fall.

What Are Perennials?

Perennials are long-lived herbaceous plants, some or all of whose above-ground parts die in fall after they have stockpiled reserves of nutrients and water in their underground storage organs (rhizomes, fleshy tubers, storage roots, or runners). These storage organs bear the rudimentary buds for the season ahead. In spring the perennials shoot forth again. New York asters, for example, survive with short creeping shoots that hug the ground. The rudimentary buds of delphinium, monkshood, and peonies lie on the surface of the soil, and for that reason these plants are also called "ground-huggers."

The long-lived grasses (see page 224) and the ferns (see page 228) also are not woody, and they last for several years; they too are classified as herbaceous perennials.

What Are Bulbs and Tubers?

Strictly speaking, bulbs and tubers (bulbous and tuberous plants) are herbaceous perennials, as they also produce underground storage organs and their aerial parts live for only one vegetative period (growth period or growth season). Because they display a few peculiar features, however, these plants are discussed separately here.

The shoot buds of bulbs and tubers are farther below ground than the storage organs of the perennials, grasses, and ferns. For

Bleeding heart (Dicentra spectabilis) is a perennial that dies back soon after the bloom finishes.

this reason bulbs and tubers are also called geophytes (plants with underground buds). They include our early harbingers of spring—for example, crocuses, tulips, snowdrops, and hyacinths, as well as many summer-blooming plants like lilies, gladioluses, and dahlias. Last of all is the autumn crocus, which blooms in late fall.

We distinguish between winter-hardy bulbs and tubers—spring-blooming plants like narcissuses, daffodils, and crown imperial, which are set out in late summer—and nonhardy tubers, the summer-flowering gladioluses and dahlias, which are planted from May onward. Their tubers are frost-tender and have to be taken out of the ground in fall, so that they can survive the winter dry and free from frost.

Why Do We Plant Perennials?

Perennials are planted to have the dazzle of brightly colored flowers in our garden, to admire the infinite variety of leaf shapes and colors, to know the fragrance of blossoms and the aroma of leaves, to watch the insects, to experience the up and down of the seasons, and to provide a counterbalance for everyday stress and strain.

What Are Annual Flowers?

Annual, or summer, flowers are short-lived herbaceous plants that bloom for a single summer and die after seed formation. Included here are true annuals, which are sown in spring and bloom, bear fruit, and die within the same year (snapdragons and zinnias, for example) and biennials, which are sown in early summer, spend the winter in the seedling stage, and bloom, bear fruit, and die the fol-

lowing year (pansies and wall-flowers, for example).

Finally, the category of annual flowers also includes the tropical woody plants or herbaceous perennials that live for years, even decades, in their native regions, but fall victim to the winter conditions of temperate areas and die. They necessarily become annuals in those areas and have to be raised anew every year.

Turkestan onion (Allium karataviense) is one of the winter-hardy bulbous plants.

Why Do We Plant Annuals?

Annuals are planted to set up color contrasts and color sequences with the perennials, to have cut flowers to fill our vases, and, even more than in the case of the perennials, to experience afresh each year a tremendous variety of flowers and forms.

Where Do Annuals Come From?

A great many annual flowers were discovered in South America. A large number of them were used as garden flowers among the Incas—groups of South American Indian peoples—and among the Aztecs in Mexico. The Spanish conquerors, enthusiastic about the exotic, richly colored blooms of the free-flowering plants, sent the seeds of nasturtiums, sunflowers, marigolds, and zinnias to Europe with the first ships, as early as the sixteenth century. South American flowers with such lush blooms of bright orange or scarlet were unknown in Europe at that time. Interestingly, most were introduced to North America by European settlers.

Later, European plant collectors overseas searched quite systematically for other beautiful flowering plants. They found them principally in the southern United States. From there they brought sunflowers and coneflowers, beardtongue, scarlet sage, and verbenas back to Europe.

Some annual flowers come from tropical Africa. These plants, which include impatiens and spiderflower, are quite sensitive to cold.

Only a few annuals are native to Europe, including the original forms of daisies, pansies, and forget-me-nots.

Can Annuals and Perennials Be Mixed?

Many annual flowers have perennial cousins—for example, annual sunflowers (*Helianthus*) and perennial sunflowers or the coneflower species (*Rudbeckia*).

The similarity of annuals and perennials in terms of their flowers and shapes often allows us to plant them together in a border without any difficulty. Because many annual flowers come from sunny countries, however, they can be combined only with perennial plants that like sun.

Good coordination becomes critical when annual flowers with a foreign air—with brilliant or even gaudy, exotic blooms—are combined with the subdued colors of woodland perennials or with mountain flowers in a rock garden or a border. Then the colors clash. The neon-light effect of the red sage species, the orange blooms of Mexican sunflowers, and the pink-violet verbenas would drown out and fade the modest perennials next to them.

Annual flowers with strikingly colored or shaped blooms should not be mixed with perennials. It is better to keep some distance between them.

If the border is intended less to supply a lasting effect in summer than to provide a source of cut flowers, don't worry about mixing the various annuals and perennials—but do keep in mind their site and space requirements!

Midsummer—the Peak Season for Annual Flowers

In using annual flowers, remember that after you bed them out (after the last frost date in May), weeks will pass before the first blooms appear in July. Most annuals are at their prime in midsummer; others don't display their abundance of blossoms until September. If it is a sunny, warm autumn, they will continue to bloom well into October. Their splendor will be gone, however, after the first cold night. Experience shows, nonetheless, that a good many frost-free days and nights are still to come, and the flowers can keep on blooming if you protect them in time by covering them with burlap or plastic sheeting before the first night frosts.

In an autumn garden annuals can continue to add spots of color until the gardening year really is at an end.

Salvia viridis

Underground Parts of Plants
① *Shallow roots*
② *Rootstock (rhizome)*
③ *Taproot*
④ *Bulb*

The purpose of plant life is to propagate and thereby maintain the species—that is, to grow, to flower, and to bear fruit.

The Flower: An Enticement
For us humans, flowers are for the most part what motivates us to grow plants in the garden, in tubs, and on the balcony. But for plants, flowers are nothing more than sexual organs that serve exclusively to propagate the species. For that to occur, the pollen from the stamens—the male part of the flowers—has to reach the female parts, so that it can pollinate them and ensure seed formation. This can be achieved either with the help of the wind or by insects.

Wind-pollinated flowers are usually inconspicuous. Flowers that are pollinated by insects, however, have to be showy. They have developed all possible strategies for calling attention to themselves and enticing the pollinating insects: vividly colored petals, strange flower shapes, intense perfume. All these features ensure that insects are lured to the flowers and, moreover, take pollen away with them to spread. The insects let themselves be drawn not in order to perform a

Structure of a Flowering Plant
① *Flowers*
② *Buds*
③ *Leaves and stalk*
④ *Rootstock (rhizome)*

A BOTANY LESSON

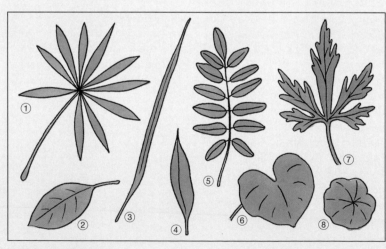

Various Leaf Forms
① *Digitate (lupine)* ② *Ovate (garden phlox)*
③ *Linear (grasses)* ④ *Lanceolate (asters)*
⑤ *Pinnate (Jacob's-ladder)* ⑥ *Cordate (Siberian bugloss)*
⑦ *Palmately divided (cranesbill)* ⑧ *Shield-shaped (lady's-mantle)*

courier service, but because they suspect that behind the flowers' ballyhoo there is some food—sweet nectar and nourishing pollen.

While they look for food, the insects incidentally pick up pollen and carry it to the next flower. The more insects a flower attracts, the greater the chance of pollination.

Pollinated blossoms have fulfilled their reason for existence—they turn to seed formation and wither. Many garden perennials and annuals will keep blooming considerably longer if you remove the spent flowers regularly. Deadheading stimulates the plants to continue producing new blooms.

Flowers come in a great many shapes and colors (see photos, pages 6–7), but in their basic composition they are largely identical (see drawing above, Structure of a Flower). On the receptacle—the uppermost, broadened part of the flower stalk (pedicel)—are found the sepals, which form the outer floral envelope (calyx). Attached to them are the petals, acting as an inner floral envelope (coralla). Collectively the calyx and coralla are known as the perianth. Next come the stamens and the carpels.

The stamens, the male part of the flower, are usually quite numerous. A stamen consists of a more or less long stalk, the filament, and a thicker part attached to the top of it, the anther, in which the pollen ripens.

The carpels, the female part, are located in the center of the bloom. They are intergrown to encircle a hollow space in their midst, the so-called ovary. It usually supports an elongated stalk, the style, at whose end is found a sticky surface called the stigma, which receives the pollen. Flowers may be borne singly or in various types of clusters called inflorescences (see drawing at right, Diagram of the Major Inflorescences).

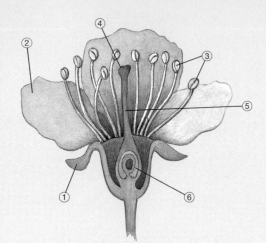

Structure of a Flower in Cross Section
① *Sepal*
② *Petal*
③ *Stamens*
④ *Stigma*
⑤ *Pistil* (Gynoecium)
⑥ *Ovary with ovule*

The Leaf: A Supply Facility

If flowers are to develop at all, the plants must photosynthesize and develop. This is enabled by the leaves, with the help of the green pigment known as chlorophyll.

Leaves vary greatly in their shapes and colors. Nature has developed an enormous profusion (see drawing at left, Various Leaf Forms). Many garden flowers are chosen to adorn gardens solely for their picturesque leaves.

The Roots

Roots are below-ground parts of plants (see drawing at top left, Underground Parts of Plants) that anchor the plants in the soil, are responsible for supplying water and nutrients, and are able to store spare foodstuffs. In addition, rhizomes, bulbs, and tubers serve as storage organs.

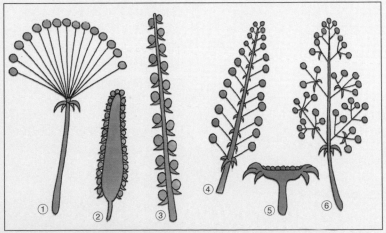

Diagram of the Major Inflorescences
① *Umbel (Astrantia major)*
② *Spadix (Kniphofia)*
③ *Spike (Lythrum salicaria)*
④ *Raceme (Aconitum napellus)*
⑤ *Head (Aster)*
⑥ *Panicle (Astilbe)*

17

SITES AND NATURAL ENVIRONMENTS

Geranium pratense 'Mrs. Kendall Clark' thrives in damp, open areas. In this kind of habitat, meadow geranium can grow wild and live to a ripe old age.

Site requirements are paramount in determining the way we use garden flowers today. First we choose flowers that meet those fundamental requirements. Only then can we proceed to considerations of mature plant size, color, blooming season, leaf shape, or scent. Over decades of trial and error, we have learned that choosing the loveliest and widest variety of colors and forms is useless if the plants' specific habitat requirements are overlooked.

Originally only diversity of color and form was decisive in our choice of perennials. In the last few decades that has changed considerably, as a result of scientific study of herbaceous perennials.

That research showed that within the huge realm of perennials and annuals for garden use, there are certain areas of agreement in the demands that plants make of their site.

For example, a great many perennials from the Alps need stony or gravelly, permeable, but well-drained to moist soils in a sunny situation. Mountain perennials from the Canadian Rockies and perennials from the Himalayas or mountainous districts of northern China have identical, or at least very similar, needs. The same site requirements were also found to exist in the case of woodland perennials from the mixed deciduous forests of eastern North America and the Caucasus and the deciduous forests of the moderate climate regions of China and Japan.

Natural Environments
If you classify perennials according to similarity of needs, eight different groups emerge.

Today, all commercially available perennials have been assigned to certain habitat preference groups by the Work Group for Classification of Herbaceous Perennials. They are as follows:
- Woodlands
- Edges of groves or woods
- Open areas
- Rock garden
- Alpine garden
- Bed
- Wetlands
- Water

Many catalogs of perennials supply this information on the various types of preferred natural environments. This makes it easier for laypeople to choose perennials for specific sites.

Of course, all these types of environments overlap in a number

Transitional domain between woodland perennials (hosta, center) and perennials from the woods edge (Geranium x magnificum and cranesbill, foreground)

of ways. The classification is intended merely as a tool to assist you in choosing plants.

Woodland Perennials

This habitat group includes all perennials that have close bonds with the woody plants. They need the protection of the woody plants, in whose shade they grow best. Many of the woodland perennials also need the leaves that fall on them in autumn and protect them from cold. Sweeping fallen leaves away from them is not good for their roots.

For woodland perennials, it is irrelevant whether the protection they receive is supplied by a single tree, a group of trees and shrubs, or a park-like grouping. These plants are also known as shade-tolerant perennials.

In newly laid-out gardens or portions of gardens, you may have spots where large trees or shrubs already exist. Beneath very old trees, fussier perennials will grow poorly because they are in competition with the strong tree roots. Appropriate here are less demanding forms, such as plants that naturally stay small.

Many woodland perennials use early spring as a time for growth, before the woody plants have leaves. They stretch toward the sun, and soon they start to bloom. Examples are anemones, lungwort, and sweet woodruff. Many spring-flowering bulbs and tubers—including daffodils, snowdrops, and winter aconite—also grow well beneath woody plants.

Examples: *Cardamine trifolia* (bittercress), *Epimedium* (epi-

medium), *Hosta* (hosta), *Tiarella cordifolia* (Allegheny foamflower), *Vinca minor* (lesser periwinkle), *Waldsteinia* (barren-strawberry)—*Carex morrowii* (Morrow's sedge) —ferns—*Anemone nemorosa* (European wood anemone).

Perennials from the Edges of Groves or Woods

These are plants whose preferred natural environment is the open edge of stands of woody plants, where they grow in sites with light shade or shifting patches of shade. They also are known as semishade-tolerant perennials. Sites near the edge of groves are always difficult if the branches of the woody plants hang down to the ground. That, and the dense foliage in summer, allow very

The regal lily (Lilium regale) is a form resulting from select breeding, and thus a typical bedding perennial.

few garden flowers to gain a footing for any number of years. Woody plants with upright or slanting branches, like shadbush or hazel, are fine.

Perennials at the edge of woody plants have a predilection for ducking under the shrubs and trees in order to catch the sun, while being protected from wind and cold. If they have shade some of the time or grow in a bright place, they will do equally well. Again, many spring-flowering plants are suited to the woods' edge.

Over time, many of these perennials form dense, extensive mats of flowers and leaves in which they are intermingled as in a mosaic. Once such a thick carpet of perennials has been created, don't dig or hoe in it. Only if the wind has amassed heaps of leaves there is it all right to remove the excess.

Examples: *Astilbe* (astilbe), *Buglossoides purpureocaeruleum* (European bugloss), *Ceratostigma plumbaginoides* (blue ceratostigma), *Geranium endressii* (Endres cranesbill)—*Molinia arundinacea*—*Chionodoxa* (glory of the snow).

Perennials from Open Areas

Perennials from unsheltered areas are the "sun children" among the herbaceous perennials. These meadow and steppe plants grow in open places far from shade-dispensing woody plants and are exposed to sunlight and weather. They cannot endure competition from larger woody plants, but tolerate dwarf shrubs and subshrubs that are similar to herbaceous plants.

A great many of these open-area perennials are warmth-loving or, in some cases, heat-tolerant plants, and many typically develop silvery gray foliage or a bluish waxy coating on their leaves to protect against the effects of strong sunlight. Some of them have aromatic leaves—for example, lavender, marjoram, some species of mint, and sage. They release their scent particularly in hot, dry places. In shady locations the leaves fade and the perfume is far less intense.

Examples: *Anaphalis triplinervis* (pearly everlasting), *Salvia officinalis* (garden sage), *Stachys byzantina* (lamb's ears), *Verbascum bombyciferum* (mullein), *Yucca filamentosa* (Adam's needle)—*Pennisetum alopecuroides* (fountain grass)—wild tulips.

Rock Garden Plants

These are perennials that occur in close proximity to rocks; it is irrelevant to the plants whether the rocks are natural or artificial (concrete, plastic). The leaves of these garden plants enjoy the warmth reflected by the rock, while the roots like the coolness of the cracks and joints in the stone. They do not tolerate rich soils and damp; in those conditions they generally rot.

Examples: *Aethionema* (stone cress), *Alyssum saxatile* (goldentuft), *Aubrieta* hybrids (rock cress), *Campanula carpatica* (Carpathian bellflower), *Sempervivum* (houseleek)—*Festuca cinerea* (fescue)—*Crocus flavus* (Dutch crocus).

Alpine Perennials

Alpine perennials also occur in conjunction with rocks. They usually are hard-to-grow, specialized plants from extreme mountain habitats. In lowland gardens they can thrive only with the aid of special cultural procedures.

Examples: *Gentiana acaulis* (stemless gentian), *Leontopodium alpinum* (edelweiss), *Saxifraga* x *apiculata* (saxifrage).

Bedding Perennials

This category includes the popular border and garden perennials, high-quality plants improved through cultivation and sold in a wide-ranging assortment. They need well-tended garden soils and require regular maintenance. There are virtually no prototypes in nature for these hybridized perennials; they are not wild plants, but are man-made innovations.

Because they are more demanding, bedding perennials should not be mixed with wild perennials if at all possible. The bedding plants like open ground; competition from ground covers, flowery meadows, and low-limbed woody plants disagrees with them. They suffocate in such sur-roundings. Unlike wild perennials, bedding perennials have more abundant flowers, a long-lasting bloom, and often double flowers.

Examples: *Aster novi-belgii* (New York aster), *Chrysanthemum indicum* hybrids, *Delphinium* (delphinium), *Helenium* hybrids (sneezeweed), *Paeonia lactiflora* (Chinese peony), *Phlox paniculata* (garden phlox)—*Miscanthus sinensis* (eulalia grass)—improved forms of tulips and narcissuses.

Wetland Perennials

This group includes the perennials that grow at the edges of ponds and in shallow-water zones, swamps, and bottom land. They require wet soils and tolerate having their roots under water.

Frequently the tenacity and vigor of these plants from the water's edge are underestimated. If you have planted too many, in a short time the entire pond and shore landscape will be overwhelmed by their exuberant growth. Some even develop so profusely that the water surface is soon hidden from view. It is advisable to begin with a small number of plants in your pond, so that you can see how vigorously they grow at the designated spot. Gradually, you can add more and experiment with new forms.

Examples: *Caltha palustris* (marsh-marigold), *Iris kaempferi* (Japanese iris), *Lythrum salicaria* (purple loosestrife), *Polygonum bistorta* (snakeweed)—*Molinia caerulea*, *Leucojum aestivum* (summer snowflake).

Water Plants

These plants always occur on or under water. For their culture, you need ponds, pools, or troughs.

Examples: *Nymphaea* hybrids (water lilies).

To Help You Choose

Classifying these plants according to the type of natural environment they prefer is meant only as a way to help you choose plants based on site requirements. Because the preferred habitats overlap at many points—for example, perennials from woodlands and those from the woods' edge—there is no need to adhere slavishly to a single category in your choice of plants.

Saxifraga x apiculata

Water as an element of design—a host of marvelously beautiful garden flowers are suitable only for damp to wet sites.

An Oasis: The Garden Pond

This garden setting beside a pond demonstrates a highly successful transition from a bank habitat to a water habitat. Many water and swamp plants tend to grow rampant. Consequently, don't put in too many plants at the beginning; otherwise, you'll soon be unable to see any light reflections or any relected plants and water movements.

The contrast between the narrow, grassy leaves of the various irises *(Iris)* and the round, floating leaves of the water lilies *(Nymphaea)* is exceptionally picturesque.

Iris kaempferi, the Japanese iris, grows up to 40 in. (1 m) tall and likes damp, nutrient-rich sites. Here, the hybrid 'Royal Banner'

IDEAS FOR LANDSCAPE DESIGN WITH GARDEN FLOWERS

Hostas (Hosta) need very little care.

All of us who take an interest in flowering plants, especially herbaceous perennials, have in mind some ideal image of how we want the planting to look someday. We probably are thinking not only of specific cultivated varieties for our garden, but also of beautiful flowering plants that we have seen while hiking in the mountains, in flowering meadows, or in the forest undergrowth.

Such "flower daydreams" can be made a reality in relatively large or fairly small spaces, but only if we know and respect the basic needs of the individual plants, including the amount and kind of care they require.

There are perennials for every need: for sunny or shady places, nutrient-rich or nutrient-poor soils, dry or moist soils. There are low-growing ground covers and bushy plants that grow several feet tall, plants that need a great deal of care and plants that are far less work to tend.

High Maintenance or Easy Upkeep?

The first question amateur gardeners need to ask themselves is this: How much time do I want to invest in taking care of my garden? Where does pleasure stop and unpleasant duty begin?

All plantings for which growth and colors should remain consistent for years are care-intensive, for example. Maintaining a uniform appearance at all times requires constant supervision and regular pruning. Appropriate for such plantings are the magnificent, selectively bred plants from the commercially available stock of perennials, although they must have care if they are to develop their full beauty and have maximum life expectancy.

Every plant species has its own individual needs. The greater the number of different species you combine, the more time-consuming it will be to tend the planting.

Gardens are relatively easy to maintain only if, after the initial planting, you let the perennials grow as they wish: in an orderly way, in disarray, dominating the landscape, or scant and sparse. That kind of combination corresponds to the conditions found in nature, and it is best achieved with wild species.

Many Plants, or Just a Few?

Dense, luxuriant beds and borders are especially attractive and effective. The denser the first planting, the faster the bed will be filled in, but watch out. The pressure of competition among the plants will become faster, too. Fast-growing perennials spread

June is the principal blooming season—after that time, leaf shapes and growth forms are important.

quickly, covering and shading slower-growing ones and preventing them from developing further.

A Bed Needs to Develop
Rarely are the selection and laying out of perennial plants so successful from the very beginning that no change of any kind is necessary. Even when you have chosen the plants with extreme care and gathered extensive information on their needs, there are always some failures. Moreover, a few plants may spread out at the expense of others. This is not a disaster, however, because vacant places give us an opportunity to add new spots of color, try new cultivars, or fill in the gaps with annuals.

However well prepared you are, you still have to experiment to see how the perennials do once they are in the ground, how they behave with each other, and what interplay of forms and colors they produce over the course of the year.

Small and relatively large "revisions" in your plantings will be needed over and over. No planting of herbaceous perennials is perfect from the start and for all time to come.

Gorgeous Flowers Throughout the Year
To have splendid flowers in your perennial beds all year long, you need large areas. With small borders, it is best to concentrate on one main blooming season. In choosing the perennials, pay attention both to the form and color of the individual plants and to their blooming seasons. Don't limit yourself to summer-flowering plants; include early summer and fall bloomers as well. If your choice is well thought out, even floral compositions with very different colors can be achieved.

Designing with Colors

Most plants affect us primarily through the colors of their flowers. Whether in a motley array, in shades of a single hue, or in matching tones, color gives life to the garden. By successfully combining and grouping the various shades, you can create totally different garden scenes.

Green is the predominant color in the plant kingdom; it is produced by the chlorophyll found in plants' stems and leaves. Not all greens are alike, however. The delicate green of linden trees, the fresh green of grass, the dark green of moss, and the dull green of olive trees give some indication of the broad spectrum in which the color green presents itself in the vegetable kingdom.

The other colors appear primarily in the plants' petals—and not without reason. Richly hued flowers are intended to be a focal point and to attract insects and other animals for the purpose of pollination.

Playing with Flower Colors

Extremely beautiful displays of color can be achieved with flowering plants. Moreover, planting brilliantly colored flowering plants in a great variety of combinations gives each garden its stamp of individuality. Here, there are no limits to your imagination.

If you are at all unsure of yourself, use the theory of colors as a guide. By following the rules for using the color wheel, you will quickly gain experience in dealing with colors. You can then make your garden a highly personal work of art, whether it be a garden with a great variety of colorful flowering plants, a bed with perennials in matching tones, an elegant all-white border, or several beds with lively color contrasts or blending shades.

The Color Wheel

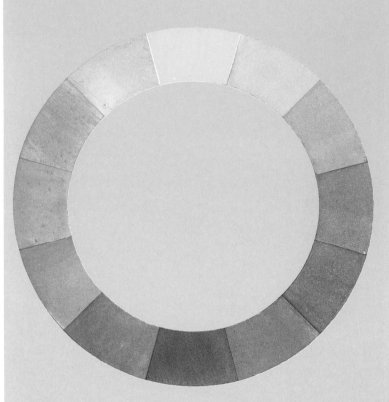

On the color wheel, all the colors of the rainbow are arranged systematically. Each of the three primary colors—yellow, red, and blue—dominates one-third of the wheel. Between two primary colors lie the colors obtained by mixing them—for example, orange between yellow and red, purple between red and blue.

The tones from yellow to red are called "warm" colors, while those from blue to green are known as "cool" colors.

Because white and black are not true flower colors, they are not represented on the color wheel. White is produced when many tiny air inclusions in the petals reflect all incidental sunlight unchanged—like a highly polished mirror.

List of Flower Colors

<u>Scarlet</u>: Maltese cross (*Lychnis chalcedonica*), scarlet sage (*Salvia coccinea*), dahlias (*Dahlia*)

<u>Orange</u>: Chinese globeflower (*Trollius chinensis*), yellow cosmos (*Cosmos sulphureus*)

<u>Golden yellow</u>: Day lily (*Hemerocallis* hybrids), rough heliopsis (*Heliopsis scabra*), French marigolds (*Tagetes patula* hybrids), Moesia crocus (*Crocus aureus*)

<u>Yellow</u>: Yarrow (*Achillea* hybrids), bearded iris (*Iris barbata-elatior* hybrids), narcissus (*Narcissus*), common sunflower (*Helianthus annuus*)

<u>Yellow-green</u>: Lady's mantle (*Alchemilla mollis*), spurge (*Euphorbia polychroma*), tobacco plant (*Nicotiana* x *sanderae*)

<u>Light blue</u>: Jacob's-ladder (*Polemonium caeruleum*), Siberian iris (*Iris sibirica*), ageratum (*Ageratum houstonianum*),

Complementary Colors

Color Triads

Colors That Blend

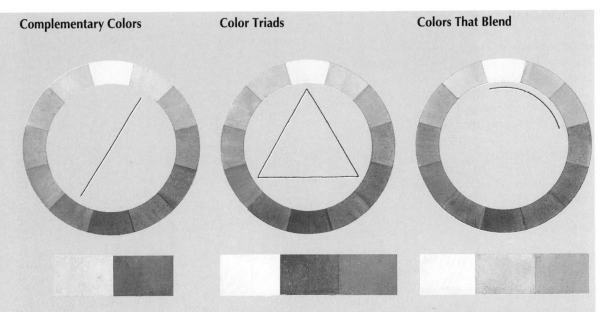

A straight line joins two opposite colors on the color wheel, the so-called complementary colors. They form the greatest possible contrast to each other. If you turn the straight line like a compass needle, it will show you new color contrasts each time.

Plantings in complementary colors, like ultramarine delphinium and golden yellow yarrow, have a particularly vivid effect. Complementary colors sometimes are found on the same plant, as in the poppy with its bright red flowers above green leaves.

If you put an equilateral triangle inside the color wheel, the colors at its points form combinations of three highly contrasting hues. By turning the triangle, you get a new variation each time.

One such triad is made up of blue, yellow, and red, which in your garden can convert to delphinium, yarrow, and Maltese cross. This color combination, which some people find garish, is expressed more pleasingly if lighter versions of these colors are chosen. For example, you could combine pale pink geraniums, linden-green lady's mantle, and sea-blue Jacob's ladder.

As indicated above by the curved line, any sector of the color wheel shows gradually blending tones. You can put together small groups of plants by using the colors of one-fourth of the wheel, while larger plantings can be arranged in the colors of half the wheel. Lively groupings can be produced by warm colors—for example, golden-yellow rough heliopsis, velvety red sneezeweed, and orange marigolds. Cool color groups result in a scene with restrained charm—for example, lilac-colored moss phlox, purple rock cress, and blue dwarf iris.

glory of the snow (*Chionodoxa luciliae*)

Blue: Delphinium (*Delphinium* hybrids), gentian (*Gentiana dinarica*), large-flowered hyacinths (*Hyacinthus orientalis*), gentian sage (*Salvia patens*)

Dark blue: English monkshood (*Aconitum napellus*), bearded iris (*Iris barbata-elatior* hybrids), grape hyacinth (*Muscari armeniacum*), edging lobelia (*Lobelia erinus*)

Lilac: True lavender (*Lavandula officinalis*), Italian aster (*Aster amellus*), verbena (*Verbena bonariensis*), Tommasinian crocus (*Crocus tommasinianus*)

Violet: Columbine (*Aquilegia vulgaris*), New York aster (*Aster novi-belgii*), allium (*Allium aflatunense*), heliotrope (*Heliotropium*)

Pink: Garden phlox (*Phlox paniculata*), Chinese peony (*Paeonia lactiflora*), tulip (*Tulipa*

hybrids), garden cosmos (*Cosmos bipinnatus*)

Crimson: Bee balm (*Monarda* hybrids), astilbe (*Astilbe arendsii* hybrids), corydalis (*Corydalis cava*), spiderflower (*Cleome spinosa*)

Monochromatic White Garden

Plant list:

① *Chrysanthemum corymbosum*
② *Shrub rose* 'Schneewittchen'
③ *Artemisia ludoviciana,* 'Silver Queen'
④ *Chrysanthemum corymbosum*
⑤ *Verbascum chaixii* 'Album'

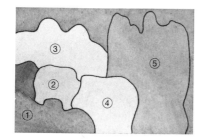

Spots of Color in Large Colored Areas

A few dots of color in contrasting shades enliven areas of uniform color.

Plant list:

① *Salvia lavandulifolia*
② *Anthemis tinctoria*
③ *Geranium* x *magnificum*
④ 'Fireking', *an Asiatic hybrid lily*
⑤ *Salvia pratensis*

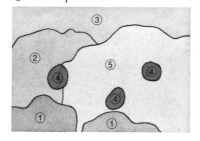

In monochromatic gardens, the growth forms are especially sharp and clear.

Isolated spots of color attract attention.

Color Effects

Nature's rich palette of colors offers amateur gardeners unsuspected possibilities for playing with the effects of the colors and with their combinations.

In order to design a bed or even an entire garden as an integrated whole, it is advisable to think about which colors you want to predominate. The other flower and leaf colors have to harmonize with them. Proficiency in choosing colors is not demonstrated by a gaudily colored garden drowning in a multitude of hues; rather, it is a combination of a few well-considered, perfectly coordinated complementary colors that reveal the true master.

The four photos on these pages show the varying effects of perennial beds planted in different colors.

A planting that is limited to primarily one color is an especially good way to show the plants' shapes to best advantage. Combinations using only a few similar

Even two complementary hues can create a lively planting.

Complementary Colors
Complementary colors produce an intense contrast.
Plant list:
① *Alchemilla mollis*
② *Salvia nemorosa*

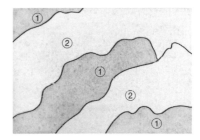

Closely related colors blend harmoniously.

Color Sequence with Warm Tones
Typical summer colors—a combination of yellow, orange, and red
Plant list:
① *Helenium* hybrid 'Moerheim Beauty'
② *Heliopsis helianthoides* var. *scabra*

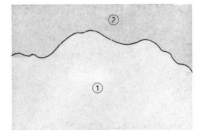

colors are particularly pleasing because of the subtle color nuances. Spots of color sprinkled through a fairly large uniform expanse of color are extremely eye-catching, and multicolored beds full of contrast create a lively, cheerful effect.

In choosing and distributing colors, always keep in mind the light conditions, because sun and shade contribute greatly to the color effect. Although flowers in dark hues are splendidly bright in full sun, they often look dull and flat in shade, at twilight, or on gloomy days. White, cream-colored, and light yellow compositions are effective at dusk, and they can brighten darker areas of the garden.

A "white" garden is lovely, especially if you have chosen sweet-smelling perennials for it and have installed indirect lighting for evening use. Plants with white or light-toned flowers are often visited by insects that are active at twilight or at night; consequently, these plants are full of life in the evening.

29

Flower Colors in Matching Tones

Lilac-pink and purple-violet are engaged in a rendezvous here. The colors of the old garden roses are nicely complemented by perennials in similar hues. Even the geranium in the large pot fits in with the colors in this picture. Every nook and cranny of this garden is in bloom in late June and early July. After that, attractive perennials with ornamental foliage maintain eye appeal.

View of the inside of a foxglove flower (Digitalis purpurea)

Plant list:
① Salvia lavandulifolia ssp.
  hispanica
② Lavandula angustifolia
③ Geranium x magnificum
④ Pelargonium hybrid
⑤ Stachys grandiflora
  'Superba'
⑥ Digitalis purpurea
⑦ Delphinium x cultorum
⑧ Geranium psilostemon
⑨ Roses 'Celsiana' and 'Rose
  de Rescht'

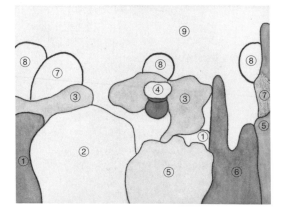

An intoxicating array of flowers in cool pink and violet—all calculated

to bloom precisely at the same time as the roses.

Triad in Yellow, Blue, and White
This color triad can easily be varied—for example, by replacing blue with violet or yellow with orange. White, however, needs to be present, and amply represented.
<u>Plant list</u>:
① *Apium sodiflorum*
② *Trollius* hybrid
③ *Iris sibirica*

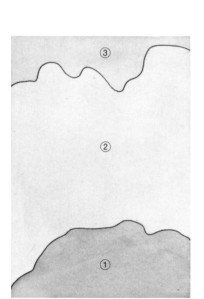

One of the best triads is the classic combination of white, yellow, and blue.

Color Combinations

Through careful combination of various colors, you can achieve new color effects repeatedly in beds or borders.

Clear, strong colors always have a lively effect, while lighter colors are more subdued. The green of the leaves and stems accentuates the flower colors and creates a background in a neutral color. Flowering plants with white, yellow, pink, or light blue blossoms bring light and a friendly atmosphere into the garden, even in shady corners.

Red, crimson, violet, and dark blue have a particularly heightened impact in full sun; in the afternoon and evening they tend to look dull and somber.

The greater the number of colors that are juxtaposed in a bed, the harder it is to create harmony and the more jarring the overall picture will be. If you are not willing to do without various triple and quadruple chords combined in a single planting, then

32

White complements these three tones, which are adjacent on the color wheel.

Foursome in Purple-red, Violet, Lilac, and White
<u>Plant list</u>:
① *Centranthus ruber* 'Albus'
② *Delphinium elatum* hybrid
③ *Campanula medium*
④ *Malva sylvestris*
⑤ *Digitalis purpurea*
⑥ *Campanula medium* 'Einfach Weiss'
⑦ *Campanula medium*

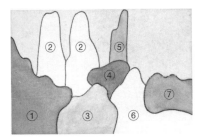

Threesome in Red, Yellow, and Blue
The three primary colors juxtapose sharply.
<u>Plant list</u>:
① *Lychnis chalcedonica*
② *Delphinium elatum* hybrid
③ *Delphinium elatum* 'Abendleuchten'
④ *Lysimachia punctata*

Pure colors are sharply delineated.

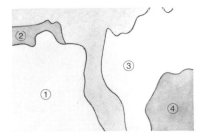

improve the groupings and the overall view. This can be done either by adding a great many perennials with decorative foliage or by creating neutral zones with plants that have white flowers or silver-gray leaves.

The smaller a planting is, the less appropriate it is to allocate space to flowers of widely differing colors. The safest are the lighter shadings. Pink with light blue, pale greenish-yellow, or even delicate lilac is a better combination than intense crimson with cool blue and strong golden yellow. Here too, as always, white plays the supporting role of the neutral partner. This function can be assumed equally well by ornamental foliage plants with silvery, gray, or even white-variegated leaves.

Designing with Forms

Along with the color of the leaves and flowers, the growth form also has a profoundly decisive influence on the appearance of every plant.

To loosely quote the philosophers Kant and Hegel, color is a stimulus to the senses, while form is the foundation of beauty. Only form, acting as the vehicle of color, gives true expression to both elements.

The diversity of a plant is revealed in numerous details, ranging from the contours of the plant as a whole to the shapes of the leaves and flowers.

Different Growth Forms

The growth form of a plant, or its silhouette, is most apparent against the light. By skillfully using a variety of growth forms, you can design a planting as effectively as by combining a variety of colors. Different configurations can support the coloration of a planting.

Clump-forming plants that bend over as they grow, for example, agreeably loosen the stiff, formal look of a group of one-stemmed plants. Frothy forget-me-nots dance around austere tulip stalks and add fullness to a bed in spring. Upright clusters of red-hot pokers or single-stemmed plants like mulleins give variety and excitement to a monotonous carpet of chickweed flowers.

Flower and Leaf Shapes

If you turn your attention to beauty on a smaller scale, you will be surprised what a wide range of forms the plants produce in their leaves and flowers as well: large, striking flower shapes alternate with small, frothy, loose ones; flowers with velvety hairs alternate with blossoms that have a waxy shine or a subdued, matte look. Some corollas have a complicated structure, while others have a simple, radial one; single inflorescences grow alongside composite and multibranched ones.

The leaves of the flowers also present themselves in myriad forms, often apparent only at second glance. Leaf sizes and contours play as important a role as the leaf surfaces or undersides. Coarsely veined, strongly ribbed, or wrinkled leaves are, so to speak, the rustic representatives while sleekly smooth, pruinose, tomentose, or fine-veined leaves are members of the elegant delegation.

Designing with Growth Forms

In designing a border, it is a good idea to take advantage of the different growth forms, because they stay visible for a long time, possibly even throughout the entire gardening year—in contrast to the flowers, which make a grand but fleeting appearance on the scene.

In certain plant groups, the growth forms play an unmistakable leading role—for example, in plantings where a single flower color predominates.

Quite often, leaves supply the flowers with a harmonious frame. They are the tray on which the flowers are served. Additionally, their varying forms, sizes, and surfaces give a planting added contrast and expressiveness.

Grasses and Ferns

In the rivalry between the leaves and the contours of plants' configurations, ornamental grasses and ferns are of great importance. Although these plants generally have inconspicuous flowers (grasses) or none at all (ferns), they are welcome guests in the garden.

The leaf shape of the grasses is quite uniform. All grasses have linear, relatively narrow blades—a shape that is less common among the other garden plants.

Tall, imposing grasses are considered the keepers of order in a planting. Stiffly upright shapes like those of eulalia grass or reed-grass can organize borders effectively. Frequently grasses bend downward and arch as they grow. They have a knack for mediating among diverse growth forms and linking them together.

Ferns are predominantly plants for light shade, where their fine foliage and striking shapes underscore and accentuate woodland perennials with light-colored flowers.

The ferns put on their main show when the spring-flowering perennials have already vanished. Many ferns are noted for their fresh green color and the filigree pinnation of their leaves. Moreover, their funnel-shaped growth is often fascinating.

The Growth Forms

Different types of growth forms are created by the set of interrelated elements that includes the flowers, leaves, stems, and growth directions of the shoots. The seven form types that reappear every year are unmistakable, and are typical of the respective species and cultivar.

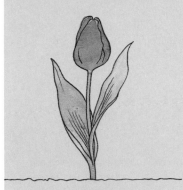

Une-stemmed plants
have basal leaves and only one stem, which supports the flowers.
Examples: Tulip, foxglove, mullein.

Clump-forming plants that grow erect
consist of a large number of shoots stiffly ascending into the air and growing in a loose or compact group.
Examples: Delphinium, New York aster, eulalia grass.

Clump-forming plants that bend over
consist of many shoots that are more or less drooping, arching in soft, graceful lines.
Examples: Bleeding heart, day lily, ferns.

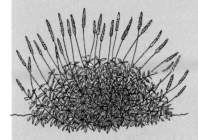

Cushion-forming plants
are low-growing, hemispherical, compact plants whose common name often contains a term describing their growth form.
Examples: Ground pink, cushion bellflower, true lavender.

Mat- or carpet-forming plants
spread their shoots directly over the ground and form more or less dense ground covers—hence their names.
Examples: Bugle, chickweed, barren-strawberry.

Rosette plants
arrange their leaves in a compact circle or spiral around a central point without rising to any significant height.
Examples: Houseleek, sedums, saxifrage.

Thickets
are created when shoots and stems grow haphazardly from the ground, close together or widely spread, and present a relatively untidy picture.
Examples: Loosestrife, garden bamboo species.

Contrasting Leaf Color and Leaf Size
An exciting confrontation between red fall foliage and green leaves.
Plant list:
① Dwarf bamboo
② *Darmera peltata*

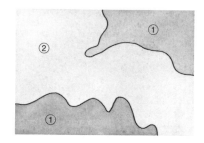

Noteworthy contrast between coarse and fine foliage

Contrast Produced by Different Leaf Surfaces and Undersides
A lively ornamental foliage planting based on varying colors and forms.
Plant list:
① *Briza media*
② *Ligularia dentata* 'Othello'
③ *Phalaris arundinacea* 'Picta'

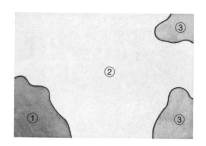

The tracery of the leaf veins makes the leaf blades more eloquent.

Leaf Colors and Leaf Shapes

In choosing perennials, also keep in mind the period when the plants are not in full bloom, when only the growth form and leaves have an impact.

Simply by selecting different leaf shapes, sizes, and colors, you can create interesting effects. Silvery, red, white-edged, yellow-edged, blue-green, or variegated leaves can replace flowers altogether. Moreover, they display their beauty far longer.

With ornamental foliage plants that have been set out in well-chosen places, a bed becomes vivid when the flush of new growth begins in spring, even before the main blooming season, and it will continue to present an attractive display of forms well into fall.

Ornamental foliage plants can also be used quite deliberately to create resting points for the eye as it travels between individual plants or plant groups.

The planting acquires additional appeal from the alternation

Unusual contrast between broad and filigree leaves

Contrast between Different Leaf Forms

All the foliage here is gray. Nevertheless, the very fine *Artemisia* leaves and the coarse *Macleaya cordata* leaves are combined in an extremely effective way.

Plant list:
① *Artemisia* 'Powis Castle'
② *Macleaya cordata*

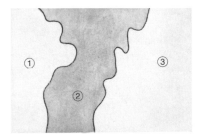

Designing with Blue-green

Diverse leaf colors make perennials worth looking at even after the bloom.

Plant list:
① *Hosta fortunei* 'Aurea'
② *Hosta* hybrid
③ *Alchemilla mollis*
④ *Epimedium* x *rubrum*
⑤ *Helleborus* hybrids

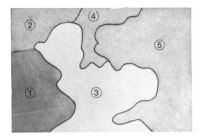

Very different green shades in a wide range and contrasting leaf forms

of different leaf shapes. Combinations of fine-leaved plants with broad- and coarse-leaved plants are highly expressive. Smooth-leaved plants placed next to conspicuously veined plants have a similarly exciting effect. Other impressions are created by contrasts between linear, pinnate, and round or whorled leaves. In certain plant juxtapositions, leaf contrasts are much more important than the ephemeral flowers. It is no accident that combinations of delicate sedges (*Carex*) with coarse-leaved hostas or sturdy Christmas roses look so good.

These groupings, which are rich in contrast and extremely valuable in the design of plantings, are found in all types of habitats preferred by perennials. For example, striking combinations in the category of sun-loving plants from open areas include eryngo (*Eryngium*) and fescue (*Festuca*), or baby's-breath (*Gypsophila*) and irises (*Iris*).

Designing with Various Mature Heights and Blooming Seasons

In designing a bed, the mature heights of the individual perennials and their varying blooming seasons play a considerable role. By arraying the flowers according to size, you create a variety of possibilities for the planting.

In addition, if you take into account the successive blooming times of the plants, you can arrange it so that something in the bed is in bloom throughout long stretches of the year.

Layout Based on Mature Height

The colorful bevy of flowers in all their glory is most effective if the plants are arranged in tiers according to their height at maturity. To show all the "faces" in the best light—as in a group photo—put the tallest flowers in the back, the smallest at the front.

Layout Based on Height

Lectern-like arrangement In front of a wall, the side of a house, or a group of woody plants, or on the opposite bank of a pond, flowers are seen from one side only. Viewed from the side, a sloping, tiered arrangement should be discernible.

Shallow conical arrangement Beds in the middle of the garden, along the patio, or in the front yard are visible from all sides. Put the tallest flowers in the center, with the lower-growing plants in succession toward the edges.

In cross-section, the silhouette is a shallow cone shape.

Staggered Layout

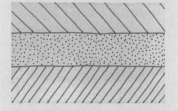

Seen from the front, plants rigidly organized according to mature size have a monotonous effect.

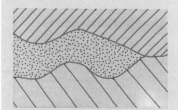

A gracefully flowing line will make the full-grown plants seem more expressive.

This lectern-shaped structure (see drawing above) with its sloping surface view optically enlarges the visual field, and a great deal more of the flowers is visible.

The picture becomes more interesting if, in place of a rigid, precisely calculated arrangement, you interrupt the anticipated lines of the mature heights with several plants that grow slightly taller or lower (see drawing at left). A species noted for beautiful color or form—a lily or a bearded iris, for example—is more conspicuous in the front, where it will rise above the low-growing plants like a sculpture. Similarly, smaller plants can be shifted farther to the back for a change, particularly if their flowering is quickly finished.

Layout Based on Blooming Seasons

If a planting is to call attention to itself constantly from spring to fall, you must take into account the length of time the plants are in flower.

Intervals between individual blooming seasons are probably unavoidable. During this time you can find pleasure in the finer points of the growth forms and leaves.

Spring bloomers like European wood anemone, crown imperial, and bleeding heart die back soon after they flower or wither completely and leave gaps. It is best to place such species in the center or back of the bed, planting them singly or in small groups among other species. The profusion of spring blooms will be especially noticeable among neighboring plants that are just beginning to shoot forth, and later the vacant spaces will be filled by these neighbors' leaves and flowers.

Species like alyssum, purple rock cress, and candytuft are quite a different matter, however. Their cushion of leaves retains its good looks even after the bloom is finished, and they definitely belong near the edges of the bed.

Early summer bloomers begin to flower sometime in late May or early June. They too often vanish after the bloom is ended. Oriental poppy, globeflower hybrids, and painted daisies, like spring bloomers, belong in the middle or at the back of the planting. Because most of them leave obvious gaps, use them rather sparingly—that is, either singly or in groups of three. Even in smaller numbers, their often brilliantly colored, large flowers are effective.

For the summer bloomers like yarrows and rough heliopsis, the blooming season begins approximately in late June and lasts for weeks. Summer bloomers will give the bed long-lasting beauty;

consequently they can be grouped in the bed solely on the basis of color distribution, design, and mature size.

Small late-summer and fall bloomers like bushy asters, dwarf hostas, and saxifrage species, which always look handsome, need to be set in the foreground, where they give the bed a resting point for the eye. Tall species like New York aster, sneezewort, and giant daisies, on the other hand, belong in the central and rear portions. Before the bloom, their leaves underscore the flowers of the other plants; later, as the gardening year draws to a close, they appear in their own colorful garb.

Early blooming bulbs like tulips, snowdrops, and bluebells should be distributed among the other plants to give the bed some color once winter is past. Do the same with the other bulbs and tubers—lilies, for example—to give the bed the look it needs.

Woody plants as the finishing touch. At the back of the graduated tiers of perennials, you can put ornamental shrubs—mock orange (*Philadelphus*), beauty bush (*Kolkwitzia*), or butterfly bush (*Buddleja*), for example—that complement the colors of the perennials. An alternative is the neutral green of clipped hedges, as a backdrop against which the colors and forms of the perennials will show up well.

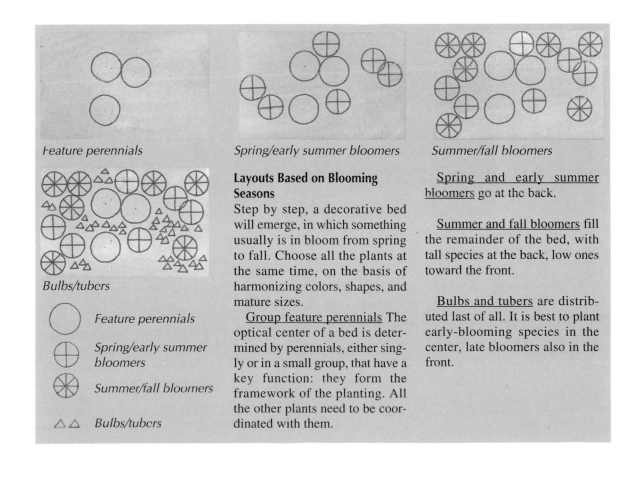

Feature perennials

Bulbs/tubers

◯ Feature perennials

⊕ Spring/early summer bloomers

✳ Summer/fall bloomers

△△ Bulbs/tubers

Spring/early summer bloomers

Summer/fall bloomers

Layouts Based on Blooming Seasons
Step by step, a decorative bed will emerge, in which something usually is in bloom from spring to fall. Choose all the plants at the same time, on the basis of harmonizing colors, shapes, and mature sizes.

Group feature perennials The optical center of a bed is determined by perennials, either singly or in a small group, that have a key function: they form the framework of the planting. All the other plants need to be coordinated with them.

Spring and early summer bloomers go at the back.

Summer and fall bloomers fill the remainder of the bed, with tall species at the back, low ones toward the front.

Bulbs and tubers are distributed last of all. It is best to plant early-blooming species in the center, late bloomers also in the front.

Arrangement by Mature Size
Garden flowers that are planted in tiers according to mature size complement one another.

Plant list:
① *Hosta undulata* 'Undulata'
② *Myosotis sylvestris*
③ *Viridiflora* tulip 'Spring Green'

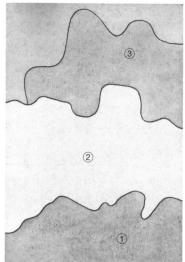

A successful arrangement based on mature size, with fine color harmony

Layouts
Garden plants should put their best foot forward at all times. For this reason, arrange them so that each individual plant is shown to its advantage.

A decidedly boring effect is produced when plants of the same size grow just anywhere and everywhere in the bed. It looks better if perennials and annuals are deliberately placed according to their mature size. The tallest plants are best at the back, where they provide an attractive backdrop for the lower-growing species. However, they can also be put in the middle of the bed where they help create a pyramidal structure for the bed.

The later the blooming season, the closer the plants may be set to the front of the bed. Then the "flower zone" will gradually shift toward the forward edge of the bed as spring moves toward autumn.

Disposition is a decisive factor for most plants, not only for flowering perennials. The lectern-like

A lectern-shaped array of perennials

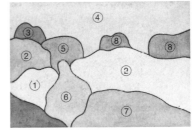

Asymmetrical Arrangement
Plant list:
① *Geranium endressii*
② *Centranthus rosea*
③ *Centranthus ruber* 'Albus'
④ Park roses and *Buddleja alternifolia*
⑤ *Lysimachia ephemerum*
⑥ *Polygonum bistorta*
⑦ *Ligularia dentata*
⑧ *Chrysanthemum macrophyllum*

Pyramidal Arrangement
Plant list:
① Asiatic hybrid lily 'Fireking'
② *Euphorbia griffithii* 'Fireglow'
③ *Eremurus ruiter* hybrids
④ *Salvia officinalis*

Arrangement by mature size, with heights increasing toward the center of the bed

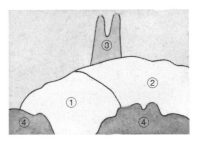

arrangement is equally applicable to perennials with ornamental foliage and other plants that are characterized by a decorative structure. The leaf mosaic of the low perennials in the foreground is complemented by that of the next-taller tier behind it. Again, shrubs or hedges can offer a quiet background for the lively interplay of lines and forms.

The effect of a graduated arrangement is heightened by planting elevated areas of the terrain, such as slopes and rises in the garden. The largest perennials should be at the highest point or at the upper edge, the lower-growing plants logically at lower spots.

This will produce an extremely impressive plant composition. This practice is known as "super-elevating the elevations."

Designing by Creating Groups

Just as a painting has a focal point that catches and holds the eye of the observer, a bed also derives an optical center of interest from one or more conspicuous perennials, known as feature plants or guiding plants. They are characterized by a long life span, an imposing or extraordinary growth form, and a rich profusion of blooms. Delphinium, asters, sneezeweed, sunflowers, eulalia grass, or male fern can serve as feature perennials.

These dominant plants need the right companions to complement or support their beauty. The companions should be coordinated in terms of color, form, mature size, and blooming season. Their pur-pose is to accentuate the keynote plants without in any way trying to compete with them. The more of a showpiece a feature plant is, the less conspicuous its companions may be—and vice versa.

Solitary Plants

Some unusual perennials are not suited for use in a group; they deserve a spot of their own, where they can display their beauty freely. For the most part they stand apart in a garden, as so-called solitary plants. Eulalia grass, *Eupatorium fistulosum*, and *Rudbeckia nitida*, for example, hold their own by virtue of their imposing growth and prolonged attractiveness of appearance; they can add unique accents as solitary plants on a lawn, at bends in a path, or in connection with a sculpture.

Forming Groups

Many plants, on the other hand, show their best side only when placed together in more or less large groups to form a plant unit.

Towering perennials like delphinium, phlox, bearded iris, and New York asters should be used in little groups made up of a small number of plants, ideally an uneven number of three, five, or at most seven individual plants.

The smaller and more modest the individual plants, the larger the groups may be. Ground covers like bugle and chickweed are even used two-dimensionally in large numbers. Such a massed planting acts as a carpet, becoming truly lively only when larger plants are sprinkled through it.

Some elements need to thread through a bed, though in a harmonious pattern of distribution. Such elements can include individual plants or even small plant groups that may vary in size or composition.

Additional variety is supplied, for example, by small groups, each composed of different cultivars of a single plant species, such as light pink, rose-pink, and dark red phlox.

A similar kind of linking effect is obtained by repeating a certain flower color several times in a bed—for example, delphinium, bellflower, and perennial sage, all in the same bright blue.

Space Requirements

In planting a bed, it would be very convenient if we could say how many of each perennial we need to set per square yard (square meter). Unfortunately, such data can be given only within limits. In poorer sandy soils, for example, you need more perennials. In nutrient-rich, loamy soils, fewer are required. With fast-growing wild perennials, it doesn't matter if the individual specimens become in-

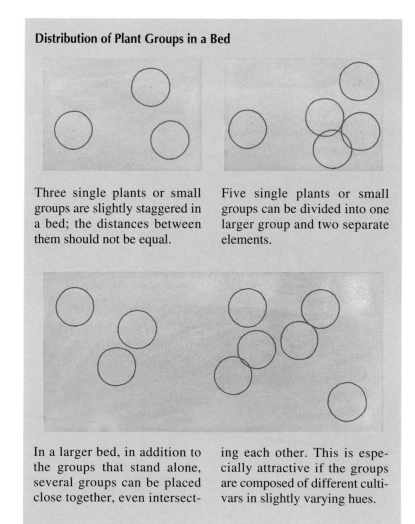

Distribution of Plant Groups in a Bed

Three single plants or small groups are slightly staggered in a bed; the distances between them should not be equal.

Five single plants or small groups can be divided into one larger group and two separate elements.

In a larger bed, in addition to the groups that stand alone, several groups can be placed close together, even intersect-ing each other. This is especially attractive if the groups are composed of different cultivars in slightly varying hues.

tergrown because they were set too close together in the first place, but with fine, top-quality cultivated varieties it would be a pity for them to suffocate in a crowded thicket of plants.

The figures at the right are based on practical values. They are intended only as reference points, so that you have something to go by.

Creating Spaces with Flowers

Many gardens are scarcely conceivable without the beauty of flowering perennials. With their many colors and forms, they fill the green frame created by the woody plants and lawn, cover up walls or fences, act as a focal point, or divide areas.

The diversity of color and form is so vast that gardens can be designed in a great variety of ways, with no garden like any other. To keep a planting decorative and long-lasting, it is essential to make the right choices when selecting species and cultivars. Other important prerequisites are skill in planning, proper planting techniques, and appropriate care.

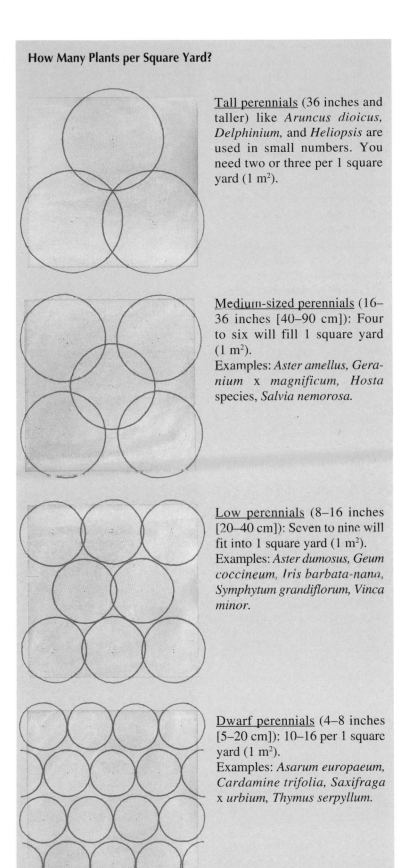

How Many Plants per Square Yard?

Tall perennials (36 inches and taller) like *Aruncus dioicus*, *Delphinium*, and *Heliopsis* are used in small numbers. You need two or three per 1 square yard (1 m²).

Medium-sized perennials (16–36 inches [40–90 cm]): Four to six will fill 1 square yard (1 m²).
Examples: *Aster amellus*, *Geranium* x *magnificum*, *Hosta* species, *Salvia nemorosa*.

Low perennials (8–16 inches [20–40 cm]): Seven to nine will fit into 1 square yard (1 m²).
Examples: *Aster dumosus*, *Geum coccineum*, *Iris barbata-nana*, *Symphytum grandiflorum*, *Vinca minor*.

Dwarf perennials (4–8 inches [5–20 cm]): 10–16 per 1 square yard (1 m²).
Examples: *Asarum europaeum*, *Cardamine trifolia*, *Saxifraga* x *urbium*, *Thymus serpyllum*.

A Variety of Growth Forms

A successful arrangement of perennials with different growth forms can produce a bed as splendid as the one shown here.

Towering over low cushions of *Artemisia* and *Salvia* are broad, rounded, compact cushions of *Saponaria* x *lempergii* and loose clumps of *Aster* x *frikartii*. The neon-light effect of the *Kniphofia* spikes is intensified even more by the stiffly erect growth of the clump. The colorful ensemble is framed by a virtual thicket of *Achnatherum calamagrostis*, which richly deserves its common name, "silver spike grass."

Plant list:
① *Kniphofia* hybrid
② *Achnatherum calamagrostis*
③ *Artemisia schmidtiana* 'Nana'
④ *Saponaria* x *lempergii* 'Max Frei'
⑤ *Salvia lavandulifolia*
⑥ *Aster* x *frikartii*

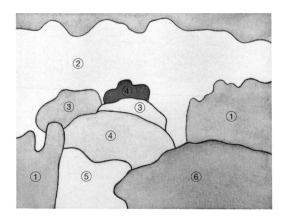

Rhythmic repetition of rigidly erect and gracefully curving outlines is

the design behind this planting.

What to Keep in Mind When Planning

Before you start choosing the garden flowers, you need to have a clear picture of the existing situation. Where do you want to put what planting? What is the background? Should it be concealed or tied into the planting? What plantings are already in existence? What kind of style do you want for the garden? Do you want a country garden, an elegant, contemporary style garden, or a natural garden? Where do you want the beds, the borders, the individual plants? What are the site conditions?

Choose the plants on the basis of the living conditions that you can offer them. Already existing plants such as trees, hedges, or well-established perennials provide a frame with which the new planting has to be coordinated. A house wall, a fence, stairs, or other man-made structures also have to be taken into consideration when choosing the plants. Finally, all the areas of the garden need to become part of an overall picture, with the plants in harmony with all the other elements.

The Character of the Planting

Before it's time to choose the plants, you need to decide on a specific direction for your design. Considerations of coloration are just as vital here as the personality that emanates from a plant.

The amount of care you want to provide will determine whether you plant bedding perennials and new cultivated varieties or vote in favor of wild perennials. As a rule, the former need more upkeep.

The Garden Plan

Drawing a planting plan is quite helpful in gaining a better overview, and it will make choosing the plants easier. Begin by measuring the bed area and transferring it, true to scale, to paper. Graph paper is best for this purpose, because the regularity of the pattern makes the job easier.

First, decide what scale you want to work with. All the measurements will have to be drawn to that scale. A scale of 1:20, whereby 2 inches (5 cm) on the plan corresponds to 40 inches (100 cm) in the bed, is a good choice for planting areas that are not overly large.

All the lengths that are measured in the garden have to be reduced to that scale and transferred to paper. Beginning with the edges of the beds, first draw the outline of each proposed bed. Then add all the existing plants, as well as any woody plants or flowers next to the bed.

Make several copies of this plan, so that you can create several designs. Using the example on page 39 as a guide, gradually fill the plan with plants, sketching them in on the basis of their approximate space requirements. Ideally, also work with the colors of the flowers you've picked out; then you can readily estimate the color effect.

Choosing the Plants

In choosing and combining the species and cultivars for the individual plantings, differences in order of importance play a major role. Start with the dominant plants, the feature perennials, then move on to the companion plants, the harbingers of spring, the latecomers, and the filler plants, adding plant after plant to your plan and, later, to your bed.

Feature or Keynote Perennials

Using the previously listed criteria, first choose the keynote perennials that you want to be eye-catching and to dominate the bed by their shape (see page 42). The feature plant determines the principal blooming season and the dominant color.

Companion Plants

Next, choose one or more partners for the feature perennials. They need to bloom at the same time, either in the same color, in shades of that color, or in a contrasting color. Their mature size ought to be markedly smaller. In addition to coordinating the colors, you also need to choose among various forms at the same time (see pages 34–35).

Filler Plants

If there still are any gaps between the plants, stop them with filler plants in colors as neutral as possible—for example, white-flowering species or ornamental foliage plants like grasses and ferns.

Hollyhocks (Alcea rosea hybrids) with flowers that seem to be made of tissue paper

Planting

Once the garden plan has given you an approximate picture of the bed or border, it's time to acquire the plants you need and to get ready for planting.

First, lay the plants out on the bed, following the design of your garden plan, to get some idea of its eventual look. Now there is still time to make changes—for example, if the spacing is too close or if one group turns out to look better in another place after all.

At the beginning, the planting very rarely is the way we have imagined it. It takes time to develop and to reveal its strengths and weaknesses.

Check List: A Step-by-Step Guide to a Perennial Bed

• Check the site conditions (light and shade, soil).
• Decide what the character of the planting is to be.
• Put together a garden plan drawn to scale.
• Take into account existing elements and plants.
• When choosing the plants, always keep in mind the site conditions, and make sure the plants fit into the overall picture of the garden.
• When combining plants, always remember the rules for selecting colors and forms, arranging the plants in tiers, and creating groups.

• Choose the feature perennials.
• Choose companion plants in suitable colors and shapes.
• Choose early and late bloomers.
• Close gaps with filler plants.
• Set bulbs and tubers as accents.

PLANTING AND CARING FOR GARDEN FLOWERS

The long-lived Christmas roses (Helleborus hybrids) are among the garden perennials that need little tending.

Once we know what plants are to be planted where in the garden and in what groupings, and whether the plants we have chosen are suitable for the given site conditions, half the battle is won. It is worthwhile to make a note of your initial experiences with meeting the plants' needs, so that you can gradually put together some kind of schedule or calendar for tending them. Possibly you will be able to see at a glance how much maintenance is necessary for individual plantings. Then you can decide whether to keep unusually labor-intensive beds or to disband their components.

With respect to the subsequent amount of attention necessary, it is a good idea to put species with identical needs and identical competitive abilities in the same planting area. Then you will have no need to protect one plant from being overgrown by another. Moreover, the entire planting can be given similar treatment when you water and fertilize.

It is preferable to plant the entire area in one working cycle, so that plants bursting into leaf are not continually disturbed during their early development by more planting on your part.

Preparing the Soil

It is extremely important to work the soil before you plant, because the prospective area will serve the perennials as a basis for life for years. Preparing the soil does not mean that the soil ought to be completely altered. After all, the plants were chosen on the basis of the available soil.

In any event, the soil has to be well loosened, in order to eliminate any compacted areas that could cause water to accumulate, and to allow the roots to penetrate to a sufficient depth and take hold.

Chronic weeds absolutely have to be removed before you plant! Especially the resistant, tough, well-rooted weeds like goutweed, bindweed, horsetail, and nettle have to be carefully dug out with a garden fork. Once they have grown into the cultivated plants' matting of roots, it is almost impossible to eradicate them.

Loosening the soil also goes hand in hand with weeding. Working coarse sand, fine stone chips, pumice, expanded clays, or other fine-grained rock matter into the soil loosens it and helps water move more easily if the soil is heavy. This prevents the surface from rapidly becoming muddy after heavy rains. To improve light, sandy soils, work in some well-aged horse or cow manure. These substances also

Helleborus hybrids, as well as snowdrop bulbs (Galanthus nivalis), need to be planted in late summer.

benefit the crumb structure of heavy soils.

The different plant groups require different types of soil preparation:

Bedding perennials and annual flowers need a loose, fine-crumbed soil structure and good nutrient supply; consequently, add a slow-release organic fertilizer when you loosen the soil.

Shade-tolerant perennials prefer loose, humous soils; consequently, work plenty of leaf mold and aeration materials into the area to be planted.

Perennials for rock gardens require soil with good water drainage that promotes the formation of these plants' usually deep-reaching roots.

Perennials that like dry conditions (xerophytes) are, like many rock garden plants, deep-rooted;

they must have a well-aerated site that permits water to flow freely.

The Right Time to Plant

In general, if you plant on days with full sun or on hot or very windy days, the plants will transpire too much water and will not yet be able to compensate for that loss by increasing their absorption of water from the soil. Planting in very wet areas is also not desirable. The soil can become too compacted, and work would proceed slowly. Otherwise, these rules are applicable to the various plant groups:

Annuals are extremely frost-tender and should not be set out before the last average frost dates (in temperate areas this is usually in mid-May), when late frosts are no longer expected.

Biennials should be set out in

early fall and left outside over the winter.

Perennials today are cultivated predominantly in pots (containers). With few exceptions (see below), they can be planted in frost-free weather—in many areas, this is from March to November.

If the soil is heavy, it is best to plant from mid-April to October, because the ground warms up very slowly and freezes hard at the first signs of frost.

Sandy soils can hold little water, so planting in midsummer is not at all wise—you can't keep up with the watering!

For underplanting woody plants with perennials, early fall is the best time. The roots of the woody plants are already decreasing their activity perceptibly, and as far as competition is concerned, the sit-

51

The same garden setting in the same shades in spring…

…and in late summer.

uation becomes more tolerable for the perennials—they are better able to strike root.

Some fall bloomers, including Japanese anemones, New York asters, *Chrysanthemum indicum* hybrids, and a number of perennials sensitive to damp winters, such as Italian aster, red-hot pokers, and mauve catmint, should be planted only in spring.

It is best to transplant existing perennials in spring or fall. Transplant spring and early summer bloomers in late summer and early fall, so that they still have a chance to become firmly rooted. Midsummer and fall bloomers are replanted in spring.

Grasses and ferns, if at all possible, should not be brought out until spring. In fall their roots have almost ceased all activity, and they do not become well established.

Dahlias and gladioluses are extremely frost-tender, and for this reason the tubers shouldn't be put in the ground too soon—ideally, not before late April. About three weeks will pass from the time they are planted to the time when the first green parts appear.

Spring-flowering bulbs and tubers are put in the ground in fall, while fall bloomers (for example, *Crocus speciosus* and *Crocus sativus*) are planted in midsummer.

How to Plant Perennials Properly
Lay out the perennials according to your garden plan—the grouping needs to be checked once more. The spacing may need to be corrected slightly, or you may decide that some groups really would be better in a different spot.

Don't let the plants lie there too long: their roots will dry out!

Container plants
Before setting container-grown perennials, water them well once more by submerging their pots in a tub of water until no more air bubbles rise.

Often the container-grown plants develop roots so vigorous that they grow out of the holes in the bottom of the pot. In some cases they are so dense and strong that you can't get the plant out of its container.

It is all right to cut off these roots. Alternatively, you can cut open the side of the pot or break it, then carefully extract the root ball from the container. Usually the roots are tightly meshed and closely wound against the sides—the places where they could find no way out of the enclosing pot. With such root-bound plants, it is advisable to gently tease the matting loose or untangle it with somewhat more force. You can cut off some portion of the outer roots, because such surgery will stimulate the root system to send out new growth.

Mosses, algae, or weeds on the surface of the potting soil need to be removed, as does any encrusted material.

Avoid pulling a container-grown plant out of its pot by the stalk or trunk. Instead, holding the pot upside down, tap the rim of the pot against the edge of a wall or a table, so that the soil ball will slide out. If the ball does not come out easily, cut open the container on one side.

Planting
It is best to dig the planting hole with a hand spade. It needs to be large enough to hold the root ball without bending it, but do not set the plant deeper than it was originally in the pot or in the soil. The basal buds need to lie just below the surface. Long roots can be pruned to a length equaling the width of your hand. Taproots (or main roots), however, need room in the planting hole to accommodate their full vertical length.

Next, fill in soil around the sides of the root ball, tamping it down gently with your hands so that the plant is vertical, firmly in

place, and completely surrounded with soil.

Start planting in the center of the area and move backward toward the edges. Then the compacted areas in the soil where you have stepped can easily be loosened again. In addition, you will run no risk of treading on and crushing plants you have just set.

After planting, it is time for a thorough soaking with water. Supplying water is only the secondary purpose of that activity, however. The soaking is intended primarily to wash fine soil from around the root ball, so that the roots have good ground contact and can become established and continue to grow normally.

Using a watering can or a hose, water the plants individually.

After watering, mulch the planting area with a layer of straw or leaf mold to keep the surface of the soil from becoming crusted and to improve moisture retention. A layer of mulch 1.2 to 2.4 inches (3–6 cm) deep is recommended. Too shallow a mulch layer will let weeds grow through; too deep a layer will create soggy zones, in which the young plants may well suffocate or rot.

If you don't mulch, loosen the surface of the soil soon after planting.

Naturally, you need to water your new plants regularly—during heat waves, daily.

How to Plant Bulbs and Tubers Properly
With a few exceptions, bulbs and tubers need to be planted in holes three times as deep as the bulbs and tubers are tall. Set crown imperials and some lilies at a depth of 10 inches (25 cm), desert candles roughly 12 inches (30 cm) deep. With dahlias, let what remains of last year's stalks just barely protrude from the ground. For some tubers that originally were woodland plants—European wood anemones, for exam-

ple—it is enough to remove the mulch layer under the woody plants, lay out the tubers, then cover them with the same material you removed.

Particularly in heavy soils, give bulbs that are sensitive to damp a drainage layer of fine rock fragments or coarse sand in order to prevent rot.

Care

It doesn't matter whether you have a natural garden or an ornamental one, every kind of garden needs some care! This applies not only to watering and feeding. You also have to consider whether to let an extremely vigorous species keep spreading or to reduce its size with your space; whether spontaneous seedlings enhance a planting or should be removed. Taking care of the plants requires that you repeatedly make decisions on the basis of the current situation.

Weed Control

The greatest danger of weed growth occurs immediately after planting.

Weeds that spread by rooting have to be removed with a digging fork as quickly as possible. Weeds that spread by seeds need to be removed before germination, so that they cannot set seeds and spread.

It is best to pull weeds when the soil is moist (not wet!). In dry ground the roots are quite apt to break off, and the plants will force their way through again. While you are loosening the soil, you can easily gather up weeds. Some weed species like dandelion or creeping thistle form very deep-reaching taproots. When you try to pull them or remove them with a hoe, the roots usually tear, and the plants soon grow back. For these you will have to use a spade or digging fork and dig out the weeds.

Mulching

Mulching is not only a safeguard against severe evaporation of the ground water and muddying of the soil surface, but is also a means of preventing weeds from growing—provided your choice of mulching material is on target.

Watering

The water needs of the various garden flowers have an extremely wide range. The following is a basic guide to watering.

• If at all possible, use rain water for watering. In many areas, it is "softer"; that is, it has a lesser mineral content than tap water. Also, rain water usually is warmer and closer to the temperature of the air than tap water.

• In warm weather, cold water has a real "shock effect" on various plants. For this reason, when possible, water only in the early morning hours or in the evening, when less moisture is lost through immediate evaporation. You also will avoid burns caused by the magnifying glass effect of drops of water.

• Generally it is better to water thoroughly and deeply than to keep sprinkling the surface with small amounts of water. If the plants receive a regular supply of water at the surface, they will tend to develop roots in the upper layers of soil. The drawback is that the plants often wilt if even a short period passes between irrigations, because the deeper soil layers, still well supplied with water, have not been penetrated by roots.

At the same time, by keeping the soil surface constantly moist, you provide ideal germinating conditions for weeds that spread by seeds.

• Loosening the soil means less watering! When the surface of the soil dries out, the earth shifts, and any channels in the soil that have formed are destroyed. This is particularly critical in new plantings without a mulch layer, before the

plants have had time to cover the ground completely with their leaves. The water is not drawn to the surface of the soil through capillary action, but is retained in the ground. Loosening the soil also prevents the surface from crusting over.

• It is better (and more water-efficient) to apply water to the individual plants directly, using a sprinkling can or hand-held hose, than to spray large volumes of water over them.

Fertilizing

In addition to water, plants also draw from the soil the nutrients they need for growth. In soil where plants grow continually, the nutrients would in time be depleted unless they were replenished in some form.

In accordance with their importance to plants, nutrients are classified as primary elements, secondary elements, and trace elements. The primary elements are nitrogen (N), phosphorus (P), and potassium (K). The percentages of them present in commercially available fertilizers are listed on the package label, always in the order given above. The secondary elements are magnesium, calcium, and sulfur. The trace elements—iron, manganese, molybdenum, zinc, copper, and boron—are needed only in minute quantities. As a rule they are present in the soil in sufficient measure; only in extremely sandy soils do deficiencies occasionally appear.

To know exactly what nutrients are contained in your soil, it is best to have a soil analysis made. Once the results are known, you can provide the right types and amounts of fertilizer.

Plants with different needs require especially careful tending.

When to Fertilize?

You can feed perennials to give them a boost as they start to grow and just as they are preparing to bloom. Stop applying fertilizer to perennials in late August; otherwise, their shoots will not harden sufficiently, and the plants will be easily killed by cold weather. Exceptions to this rule are peonies and spring-flowering bulbs. For annuals, work an organic fertilizer or a compound fertilizer into the soil before planting. After this basic application, it is best to fertilize with a weak concentration once each month until September.

The amount of fertilizer applied is determined by the plant species in question. Basically, garden flowers that grow tall need more nutrients than lower-growing ones.

Organic Fertilization

Organic fertilizers improve the humus supply and promote plant growth in the soil. These fertilizers include commercially available horn shavings, blood meal, bone meal, compost, and animal manures (horse or cow). Animal manure can be worked into the soil only if well seasoned; when fresh it contains too much ammonia, which can cause plant injury.

Inorganic Fertilization

Most inorganic fertilizers provide readily available plant nutrients, although some fall into the category of so-called slow-release fertilizers. Because they act quickly, inorganic fertilizers are especially valuable when plants show symptoms of deficiency. When using these fertilizers, be sure to take into account the doses of organic fertilizer applied previously! Overfeeding will lead to instability and render the plants more susceptible to disease.

Tying and Staking

Some tall garden flowers frequently prove wobbly and unstable, especially in wind and rain. For this reason it is advisable to give them some support early on, Free-standing perennials can be kept upright by bare twigs stuck into the ground around the clumps. Alternatively, put a bamboo or iron stake next to the clump, tie a string to it, and wrap it around the stems. Special kits for staking perennials are also available at garden centers. Usually made of green plastic, these materials are fairly inconspicuous. Tall stalks have to be tied individually.

Whatever you do to support your plants and keep them upright, make certain that their natural form is not lost in the process. Tightly pinched clumps of perennials look even uglier than clumps that have flopped over.

Pruning

When pruning perennials, proceed on a case-by-case basis.
• With quite a few perennials, completely cutting back after the blooming season will induce new growth and a very attractive second bloom (for example, delphinium and fleabane).
• Some perennials can easily be mowed or cut down after their blooming season. They will respond by putting forth again. As a rule, this results in a second, less intense, floral display (for example, lady's mantle, cranesbills, purple loosestrife).

• Repeatedly cutting or breaking off spent flowers stimulates the production of new flower buds. Deadheading extends the blooming season of most annuals and certain perennials by several weeks.
• Spent flowers that remain on a plant will begin to form seeds, usurp stored nutrients, and weaken the plant, so that it produces fewer flowers the following year.
• Some perennial species (New England aster, sneezeweed, phlox) become noticeably sturdier and less wobbly if the clumps are cut back by half before flowers form. It will delay the blooming season, however.
• To keep growth compact, subshrubs like true lavender, garden sage, and lavender cotton, as well as various cushion-forming plants for rock gardens, can be cut back after the bloom to about two-thirds of their original height, in order to stimulate new growth close to the ground and to induce branching.
• To keep the bare twigs from getting in the way of the new growth, cut perennials back to the ground in late fall or spring.

Should the Soil Be Turned?

There is a long tradition behind the practice of cutting back perennials each fall and then turning over the soil between the plant clumps with a spade or digging fork.

If you recall, however, that almost all perennials produce new buds at the edges of their clumps, it is easy to see that the task of turning the soil is unnecessary. The digging will injure or even destroy the young buds.

Lifting Older Perennials

Although annual flowers have to be started or bought anew each year, perennials can stay in place for several years. The life spans of the individual species vary greatly, however. When the perennials lose their vitality, produce fewer flowers, or begin to lose their foliage at the center, it is time to divide the plants. You simply dig them up, divide them into small pieces, and replant them elsewhere. Rejuvenated in this way, they regain their vigor and wealth of flowers.

The light blue early summer garden (see pages 4–5) displays heavy red and gold tones in fall.

Winter Protection

Many evergreen garden perennials suffer from the winter sun, which causes them to transpire water on windy, radiation-rich days. Because the soil is frozen, however, and the roots are unable to absorb water, damage caused by dryness ("frost dryness") results.

Damage of that kind can be prevented by loosely covering the evergreen perennials in sunny and snow-free sites with boughs or burlap. At the same time, this prevents the plants from rapidly putting forth on the first warm days of early spring. They would soon fall victim to the frosts still to come.

Some perennials are not completely hardy, especially while young. For this reason, protect them from heavy frosts with a loose layer of dry leaves covered with evergreen boughs (so that the wind doesn't blow the leaves away). With red-hot pokers and pampas grass, tie the evergreen tufts of leaves together and cover the root zone with dry leaves, held in place with boughs.

Often our intentions are too good, and we cover our plants too well and far too soon. They certainly will not freeze, but they will lose vigor and suffocate under the well-meant winter protection or rot for lack of ventilation. You can easily wait until the first heavy frosts to cover them.

In spring, remove the winter cover, but leave the boughs near the plants they protected, so that if need be you can cover them again if there are frosts late in the season.

A great many garden perennials suffer from wet winters. The best protection is to ensure that the drainage is good at the planting site before you plant.

A garden has a different face for every season (see pages 4–5 and 57). With a sugar-coating of frost, the leaf shapes,

growth forms, and seed structures are highly effective.

FIRST AID FOR YOUR GARDEN

Ladybugs, which destroy aphids, are beneficial insects.

If you read about the vast number of diseases that can affect plants, you could soon lose all interest in gardening. In practice, however, the situation is not as bad as it first appears. With a few exceptions, most of the garden flowers presented in this book are not—or at least not appreciably—affected by pests or diseases.

Don't worry about a few aphids! They don't automatically condemn the plants to lingering disease and death. There is no need to reach immediately for insecticides. Aphids in small numbers can definitely be tolerated or crushed with a paper towel. Energetic efforts to suppress them, however, will also decimate the natural enemies of the pests. The decision to mount a campaign against pests or disease depends on the severity of the attack. You need to weigh the pros and cons of pest control and to carefully think through all the possible methods of control. Admittedly, you won't always be able to avoid taking action. The appearance of very high numbers of pests or a severe onslaught of disease demands appropriate countermeasures, if you want to save your cherished plants. If you see that some plants are chronically diseased or pest-ridden, ask yourself whether it might be better to replace them with other cultivars or species.

Preventive Measures

Disease and pest prevention begins early—at the time you are planning the planting and choosing the optimum site and plants. A good, balanced supply of nutrients keeps the plants healthy and boosts their resistance to disease. Too much nitrogen, however, makes the tissue spongy and thus vulnerable to fungi. An appropriate water supply also helps keep your plants in good health. In addition, make sure that the plants are properly spaced and that you don't have too many plants of one species growing in a crowded area.

First Diagnosis—Then Control

Diseases and pests are not always responsible for symptoms of plant injury. Often leaf damage or even wilt are caused by inadequate or unbalanced plant nutrition, dryness, or poorly

In the right site, plants usually stay healthy and flourish splendidly.

drained soil (see Physiological Damage, page 62). It is important first to make an accurate diagnosis, then to treat the cause of the plant injury. The how-to pages (see pages 64–65) will help you search for the cause. If you still have doubts about your ability to identify the cause of the injury, consult the Agricultural Extension Service or your local botanical garden.

Methods of Control

Don't always resort to the strongest preparations; in many cases "benign" tactics also will help.

<u>Mechanical control</u> is sufficient if the problem is not serious. It includes:

• Removing affected or diseased plant parts and/or removing entire plants.

• Removing the animals by hand, by either picking or brushing them off the plant. Also, by washing them off the plant with water or a solution of soft soap and water.

<u>Chemical controls</u> are used only if other methods have failed or if the plants are so valuable that no amount of damage is acceptable.

• Insecticides affect insects and can be sprayed or poured on.

• Acaricides are used to kill mites, which are members of the arachnid family. Many commercially available pesticides are effective against both insects and arachnids.

• Molluscicides are used to curb slugs. These products, in the form of small granules, are fairly long-lived, even in the rain.

• Fungicides are effective against fungi.

• Bactericides are dangerous and are not approved for use in some countries, e.g., Germany.

There are no agents that are effective against viral diseases.

Delphiniums (Delphinium hybrids) and Canterbury bells (Campanula medium)

Important Dos and Don'ts!
- If at all possible, avoid using toxic materials.
- Don't use materials that are harmful to bees. If you feel you can't avoid their use, employ them only late in the evening.
- Follow the instructions for use and the recommended dosages to the letter.
- To protect the environment, avoid using sprays with propellant.
- Don't breathe in any of the mist of pesticides or insecticides.
- Observe the recommended precautions (wear gloves, respirator, etc.).
- When handling pesticides, never eat, drink, or smoke.
- Always keep pesticides in the original package, out of the reach of children and household pets, stored separately from groceries and pet foods, and closed securely.
- Discard leftover materials (most products are quite short-lived); don't put them in your household trash, but take them to a special collection site.
- Clean containers thoroughly after use. Sprinkle the water you use to wash them between the plants that were treated—don't pour it down the drain or on your compost pile.

Physiological Damage
The health of your garden flowers is ensured only if the given site factors, including temperature, light, humidity, and soil structure, are suited to the needs of the plants. If that is not the case, physiological damage will occur. At the same time, the plants will become more disease-prone. Controlling physiological damage is possible only within limits, and that is accomplished through improving the growing conditions.

Frequent types of physiological damage:

<u>Wilt</u> due to lack of water: Water plants adequately.

Root rot due to standing water: Replace plants with others not sensitive to damp. Possibly improve site by adding a drainage layer to the soil.

Chlorosis (pale leaves) due to nitrogen or iron deficiency: Test soil, then compensate by addition to fertilizer.

Etiolation (greatly elongated, spindly stems) and chlorosis (pale leaves) due to insufficient light: Site suitable only for shade-tolerant plants.

Reddening or yellowing of leaves and leaf damage due to excessive light: Site suitable only for sun-hungry plants.

Stunted growth due to compacted soil: Deep, thorough loosening of soil.

Frost damage: Choose microclimatically favorable sites for frost-tender plants—for example, in the shelter of walls. Use winter protection (see page 57).

Reduced flowering due to unbalanced nitrogen supply: Don't feed for prolonged period; test soil.

Fungal Diseases

Fungal infections are triggered by fungus spores, which are spread by wind, rain, animals, and humans. Once spores find their way onto a plant, the state of the plant's development and health determines whether an infection results. Factors that favor a fungal infestation include overfertilization with nitrogen, high atmospheric humidity, wet, cold weather, and dryness.

Eradicating fungal diseases often proves difficult because it means controlling a plant (the fungus) that is parasitic on another plant (the host plant). For this reason, special agents (fungicides) are used to destroy fungi. If you want to combat a fungal disease, start as soon as possible after an accurate diagnosis has been made. Otherwise the mycelium (filamentous elements) of the fungi will be so

deeply interwoven with the host that any efforts at control are doomed.

On page 64 you will learn how to recognize specific fungal diseases, what plants are susceptible, and what the best remedies are.

Pests

The term "pests" refers to all animals that cause injury to cultivated plants. Only in this sense can we apply the word "pests" to the creatures that are such a nuisance for gardeners and plant fanciers. These creatures are a part of nature too, and they perform an important task in nature's system of housekeeping (in the food chain, for example). Whether and how you should manage the appearance of plant-damaging beetles, aphids, leaf bugs, or other animals depends on the severity of the infestation. Sometimes external factors promote the increased incidence of pests: for example, dry air, dry soil, a long spell of humid, warm weather, soil humidity, mild winters, use of unbalanced, nitrogen-heavy plant fertilizers, and use of many plants of a single species. Wherever you can prevent an invasion of pests by choosing an optimum site and providing the best care, you should do so. Those precautions, however, are no guarantee of damage-free plants. On page 65, you will learn how to recognize specific pests, what plants are susceptible, and what the best controls are.

Bacterial and Viral Diseases

These diseases affect only a few garden flowers. Because they can't be controlled chemically or otherwise, the affected plants need to be removed and destroyed at once in order to keep the disease from spreading. In addition, do not set the same plant species in the affected spot

immediately after removal of a diseased plant.

Viral infections that occasionally appear in garden flowers are:
• Ring spot in dahlias: Distorted leaves with mosaic-like spotting; dwarfing.
• Mosaic virus in lilies: Light, yellowish-green spots on misshapen (contorted) leaves.
• "Fire" disease in tulips: Deformed plants, leaves with light-colored spots.
The following bacterial diseases occur from time to time:
• Soft rot in iris: Pulpy, rotting rhizomes and roots.
• Bacterial blackspot disease in delphiniums: Black, irregular spots on leaves.
• Leafspot disease in marigolds: Burned-looking plants that later die.

The Most Common Diseases

Powdery Mildew
Symptoms: Whitish, powdery deposit on leaves, shoots, and flowers. Contributory factors: Dryness, intense sunlight, too much nitrogen in fertilizer.

Susceptible plants: Aster, phlox, lupine, delphinium, daisy, forget-me-not.
Remedy: Apply fungicide early, repeat at short intervals.

Downy Mildew
Symptoms: First yellowish, then brown spots on the leaf surface. Whitish-gray deposit on underside of leaf. Contributory factor: High atmospheric humidity.

Susceptible plants: Pansies, forget-me-not, hellebores.
Remedy: Remove diseased plants.

Rust
Symptoms: Leaf surface—Light-colored, yellowish spots. Underside of leaf—light brown, orange, or rust-colored pimples.
Susceptible plants: Hollyhocks, dandelions, bellflowers, sweet William, peonies.
Remedy: Use fungicide only with perennials during the first half of the year. Remove annuals altogether.

Botrytis (Gray Mold)
Symptoms: Soft, rotten places with mouse-gray mold on shoots, leaves, or bulbs.
Susceptible plants: Peonies, dahlias, gladioluses, hyacinths, lilies, tulips.

Remedy: Control by fungicide good only for peonies. Remove all other kinds of diseased plants. Avoid using site for same species for two to three years.

Septoria Leafspot Disease
Symptoms: Round, dark (brown or purple) spots, sometimes with white center, on leaves. Affected leaves die.
Susceptible plants: Chrysanthemums, phlox, peonies.

Remedy: Use fungicide for peonies, as stems are also infected. For other plants, removal of affected leaves suffices.

Wilt Disease
Symptoms: Plant wilts despite good water supply.
Susceptible plants: Common in China aster, sometimes appears in perennial asters, lupines, stonecrop.

Remedy: Destroy diseased plants. Use site for different plants for several years.

Bulb Rot
Symptoms: Light brown, sunken places; bulb rots. Inside chocolate brown in color.
Susceptible plants: Narcissuses, tulips.

Remedy: Destroy affected bulbs at once; avoid using site for bulbs for several years.

The Most Common Pests

Slugs
Symptoms: Traces of damage and trails of slime on leaves.
Susceptible plants: Marigolds, hostas, delphinium, ligularias, asters, bellflowers.

Remedy: The only lasting means is repeated strewing of slug grains. Trapping slugs under boards or damp cloths is of limited effectiveness.

Aphids
Symptoms: Colonies of black or greenish lice; sticky, deformed leaves and shoots. Contributory factors—poor water supply, overfeeding with nitrogen.

Susceptible plants: Monkshood, max daisies, dahlias.
Remedy: Wash shoots off with water or soft soap, or cut them off. Use insecticide for severe infestation.

Leaf Bugs (Plant Bugs)
Symptoms: Injuries (holes) visible on buds, leaves, and young shoots caused by sucking insects.
Susceptible plants: Chrysanthemums, dahlias.

Remedy: With fairly severe infestation, control with insecticides.

Spider Mites
Symptoms: Small, light-colored mottled areas on leaves caused by sucker punctures. Leaves (usually the undersides) covered with a fine web, later turning yellow. Contributory factors— dry, warm weather.
Susceptible plants: Chrysanthemums, ageratum, hollyhock.
Remedy: Use insecticides promptly.

Nematodes
Symptoms of stem nematodes: Shortened or thickened shoots, curled, twisted leaves.
Susceptible plants: Phlox.
Remedy: Dig up and destroy plants.

Symptoms of foliar nematodes: Yellowish brown, later black leaf spots outlined by heavy veins.
Susceptible plants: Asters, chrysanthemums.
Remedy: Remove and destroy diseased leaves.

Voles
Symptoms: Damage done to stem modifications.
Susceptible plants: Bulbs such as crocuses, lilies, tulips (exceptions: crown imperial, allium species, narcissuses) and perennials such as day lilies.
Remedy: Set traps. (Be careful with special baits; they contain toxic substances that also can harm other animals!)

Lily Beetles
Symptoms: Notched, streaky feeding sites on leaves of lilies.
Susceptible plants: Lilies, crown imperials.

Remedy: For mild infestations, it is enough to pick off the beetles and larvae regularly. For severe cases, control by insecticide is necessary.

PROPAGATING GARDEN FLOWERS SUCCESSFULLY

Single flowers hold food ready for bees and butterflies.

Today, amateur gardeners can raise most garden flowers themselves, and many commercially available aids make their task easier. Of course plants vary, but with a minimum of equipment quite a few of them can be propagated successfully and cost-efficiently. A spade, for example, is all you need for dividing numerous perennials into several plants. The propagation of perennials in your garden can become an exciting hobby. Trying it out, watching, and hoping; seeing how and whether new plants come into being; having a chance to swap flowers with like-minded gardeners and plant fanciers—all these make gardening a richer experience.

The tools and equipment you need for propagation depend on the method of propagation you use and on the number of young plants you want to obtain from the parent. In the simplest case, a spade is all you need. For more intensive division and for taking cuttings, sharp knives are necessary. To make sure that the young plants develop well, however, a number of other important accessories are also needed.

Nurseries for Plants

Many perennials can easily be divided outdoors, and each portion can be replanted immediately. With some garden flowers, too, seeds can be sown directly at the site. Most plants, however, have to be started in a place shielded from the influence of the weather. Here a hotbed is useful. Various models are available commercially, but you can also build one yourself:

Hotbed: The simplest design is a frame about 16 to 20 inches (40–50 cm) tall, made of wood, asbestos cement, or concrete blocks, and capable of being sunk partially into the ground. Cover it with glass windows, or stretch plastic film over the wooden frame.

Glass or plastic film houses without heating offer the plants more air space than a hotbed and have the further advantage of allowing you to step inside.

In small and mini-hothouses with heating, garden flowers can be propagated professionally.

On a bright window sill and in a conservatory, you can raise a smaller number of plants. Here, too, light and warmth are—as always—prerequisites for successful propagation.

Ornamental grasses like the imposing pampas grass (Cortaderia selloana) are propagated by division in spring.

The Right Containers

Garden centers offer a host of different containers for germinating garden flower seeds. Amateur gardeners, however, can also recycle discards from their own household—yogurt or ice cream containers, for example—for sowing, transplanting, or potting. Even shallow fruit crates with a one-piece bottom are ideal for starting seeds and for transplanting seedlings. With all containers, make sure there are sufficiently large holes in the bottom, so that excess water can drain off quickly.

A few tips on containers:

Shallow pans make good seedbeds, because seedlings do not produce any long roots.

Weatherproof containers are necessary if you sow cold-temperature germinators (see page 69). Clay or sheet-metal containers are suitable.

Multipot flats consist of a large number of small pots connected together. They are available in a range of individual pot sizes. One flat holds between 24 and 96 young plants. They are extremely well suited
• for transplanting seedlings
• for holding cuttings
• for sowing individual seeds that are relatively large.

The young plants develop a compact, strong ball, and the root systems of two neighboring plants have no chance of becoming interwoven. With some special flats, all the plants can be lifted out at once.

Clay pots are heavy, hence quite stable, but hard to stack.

Plastic containers can be stacked easily and take up less space. The sturdier types can be reused several times.

Pots made of recycled waste paper or peat can be planted along with the flowers.

Soil Mixes

Garden plants in various stages of cultivation need soil mixes that conform to their state of development.

Seedlings, for example, need only a small amount of food, but have to be kept moist at all times. For this reason, choose a low-nutrient soil mix that holds water well for starting seeds.

Cuttings need to produce an abundance of roots, so their growing medium needs to aerate well. Nutrients are not yet necessary at the outset, because the plant is meant to search for food with its newly formed roots.

67

Consequently, cuttings will produce roots better in a loose, extremely nutrient-poor soil mix than in a firm, nutrient-rich one.

Growing, transplanted plants need more nutrients. The growing medium for transplants needs to contain a modicum of nutrients, while the potting soil needs much larger amounts.

Important Properties of Soil Mixes

There are two choices: either you make whatever soil mix you need, or you buy the commercial mixes. All good mixes should have certain characteristics:
• They must retain water and nutrients well.
• They should aerate well and have a stable structure, so that they don't collapse when you water.
• They should be free from weed seeds, pathogens, and pests.

With commercial products, peat or fermented bark compost ensures that the mix can hold water and nutrients well. With some mixes, this function can be performed also by well-rotted compost, especially leaf mold. Coarse sand, fine rock fragments, expanded clays, pumice, perlite, and other fine rock or rocklike materials provide good aeration, drainage, and structural stability.

Commercial Soil Mixes

The basic ingredient of commercially available growing media is peat. Attempts are being made to replace at least a part of the peat with other substances such as bark compost, wood fibers, rice husks, or coconut fiber in order to reduce the cutting of peat.

Well-tried growing media include these:

Peat growing media.
• Seed-starting mix: Modicum of nutrients added; used for germinating and transplanting.
• Potting soil: More nutrients added, including slow-release fertilizer; used for potting.

All-purpose soil mixes. Their chief components are peat and noncrumbling clay. Depending on the addition of inorganic (mineral) fertilizer, the following types result:

1. An all-purpose soil mix that is truly suitable for all purposes. It has extra calcium, but no additional inorganic fertilizer. The nutrients are to be added according to the plant's state of development.

2. An all-purpose soil mix that is a medium for transplants, contains added fertilizer, and is also suitable for germinating.

3. An all-purpose soil mix used in propagation that contains a small percentage of inorganic fertilizer and perlite, which makes its structure more stable. It is suitable for germinating, transplanting, and seedling propagation.

4. An all-purpose soil mix, with large amounts of added fertilizer, is a potting soil.

Bark growing media. These are potting soils that contain a high percentage of bark humus (30 to 40 percent).

In addition, there are many other equally suitable commercial mixes (including seed-starting soil, garden mold, and potting soil).

Different Methods of Propagation

There are two ways to obtain new plants: sexual propagation (see HOW TO, pages 70–71) and asexual propagation (see HOW TO, pages 72–73). In the individual plant descriptions (see pages 74–229) you will learn which method of propagation is best for each plant species and cultivar.

What You Need to Know About Seeds

Propagation by seeds, also called sexual (generative) propagation, is used extensively for reproducing common annuals. These seeds are readily available in places such as local seed stores, garden centers, and nurseries. If you want to grow somewhat more unusual flowers from seeds, you will have to contact special suppliers (see sources, page 238).

Collecting Seeds Yourself

If you already have flowers in your garden, you can also remove seeds from them—from bellflowers and columbine, for example. Keep in mind, however, to remove seeds only from healthy plants and only in dry weather. The ideal time for seed harvesting is the moment when the first seeds are dispersed. With annuals, harvesting seeds is worthwhile only for a few species (like marigolds and sunflowers), because in the resulting flowers the color frequently is no longer stable. Moreover, other advantageous properties (resistance to disease, stem rigidity) are lost.

How to Do It:

Clip off the seedheads, put them in a paper bag, and note the plant's name and the collection date on the bag. Then store the seeds in a dry, airy, cool place, where any immature seeds can continue the afterripening process. Except for the species that are best sown right after harvesting (see Difficult Germinators, at right), you can wait until winter to clean the seeds.

Cleaning the Seeds

Remove all extraneous portions (fleshy fruit wall, pods, capsules, dried leaves), so that only the seeds remain. It is best to pick out or sift out coarser debris; small, light particles can be removed by shaking the seeds to and fro in a bowl and blowing on them gently. Separate seeds from fleshy fruits such as berries by washing. Once the seeds are clean, store them in an airtight, tinted glass jar. Alternatively, seal them in foil or plastic film. Always remember to label!

Differences in Germinating Behaviors

Not every seed germinates readily and easily. Although most annuals can be grown effortlessly from seeds, with some perennials you will find repeatedly that without special treatment the seed will not germinate as you wish. These plants fall into the following groups:

Normal germinators (such as primrose and centranth) are not problematic. Germination occurs at temperatures of roughly 59°F (15°C) about two or three weeks after sowing. It is best to sow the seeds in winter or spring, so that the young plants can be set the same year.

Rapid germinators (such as flax and Maltese cross) germinate only a few days after they are sown. Because the seedlings grow very quickly, don't wait too long to transplant them.

Difficult germinators (such as prickle nuts) need to be sown right after seed collection; then, as a rule, they germinate after two to six weeks. If they fail to do so, treat them as cold-temperature germinators. Sometimes it still takes them a long time to germinate.

Cold-temperature germinators (such as sweet woodruff and lily spiderwort) have to be chilled for several weeks, so it is best to sow them in early winter. Immediately after sowing, put the containers in a warm place for about two weeks and keep them moist, so that the seeds will imbibe water. Then they need temperatures between 32° and 41°F (0–5°C) for the next six to eight weeks: put them outdoors or in the refrigerator. After the cold-temperature treatment, the seed generally should germinate at temperatures around 54°F (12°C).

Potting

Once the transplants (see page 71), tip cuttings (see page 73), or root cuttings (see page 73) are well developed and have produced enough roots, the young plants need to be potted in larger containers. Because the plants now require more nutrients, give them a more heavily fertilized growing medium like an all-purpose soil mix, or a 1:1:1 mixture of compost soil/peat/sand with added fertilizer. After potting, put the plants in the hotbed on a cloudy day. Shade them at first when in blazing sunlight, and on cold nights cover them with a cold frame or plastic film. Gradually acclimatize them to outdoor conditions. Make sure they have a good water supply, but don't let the plant balls stay dripping wet the entire time. Species that prefer dry ground in the garden (see Plant Portraits, pages 74–229) will rot quickly in wet soil. If you do not plant for some time, fertilize young plants occasionally with a weak concentration. If a plant becomes root-bound, it will have to be repotted in a larger container.

Propagating Bulbs and Tubers

Propagation by seed is also possible with some bulbs and tubers (such as *Allium*), although it takes patience to wait until you can plant bulbs that will grow and flower. Often it takes years before plants grown from seed finally flower! Normally this plant group is propagated by specialized breeders, because the attempt rarely succeeds without special propagation equipment.

Some bulbs and tubers (such as narcissus and grape hyacinth), however, form large numbers of offspring that you can dig up and replant elsewhere. These are known as brood bulbs or brood tubers. The same is true of species (such as winter aconite and cyclamen) that readily reproduce by seed on their own and thus increase their numbers.

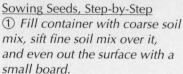

Sowing Seeds, Step-by-Step
① Fill container with coarse soil mix, sift fine soil mix over it, and even out the surface with a small board.
② Sow the seed grains evenly and not too close together.
③ Over coarser seeds, sift a layer of seed-starting medium the thickness of one good-sized seed grain.
④ Using a spray bottle or mister, spray the seeds well with water.
⑤ Lift the cover periodically to prevent fungal infestation.

Chinese lantern plants have decorative orange-red seed coverings. They can be propagated by seed, but it is even simpler to remove the runners, which appear in large numbers.

PROPAGATION FROM SEEDS

Plants that are grown from seeds obtained through sexual propagation are usually more vigorous and more resistant than plants grown by vegetative (asexual) propagation. Sexual propagation results in new plants that frequently have different traits. When propagating cultivated varieties, however, breeders want to obtain offspring identical to the mother plant. For this reason, only species and so-called "true-breeding" cultivars are suitable for growing from seeds. Those that do not breed true have to be propagated by vegetative (asexual) means.

Preliminary Care of Seedlings
Most garden flower seeds cannot be sown in a permanent location (direct seeding); they have to be started in a hotbed or small hothouse, or on the window sill. They can be planted out in the garden when they are large enough and their root systems are sufficiently well developed.

How to Do It:
Seeds that are large or germinate easily can be placed singly or in small quantities directly into their final pots, to avoid the labor-intensive job of transplanting (see right) and potting (see page 69) them. Most seeds are sown in special seed-starting containers. The size of the container depends on how many plants you want:
• Sift the soil mix (seed-starting mix or a 1:1:1 compost soil/peat/sand mixture) through a fine sieve.
• Place what remains in the sieve, adding some rock fragments or gravel, in a well-cleaned seedling container with drain holes for use as a drainage layer. Fill the container to one-third of its depth.

- Add the second layer of seed-starting mix, filling the container to the rim. Tap the container sharply against the table and draw a small board across the top to remove any excess soil. Then tamp the soil lightly to create some head space for watering (see Drawing 1).
- Sowing straight from the seed package or using a folded piece of paper (see Drawing 2), sprinkle the seeds evenly and not too close together.
- After sowing, cover larger seeds with a layer of seed-starting mix to a depth equal to the thickness of the seeds, spreading the mix through a screen (see Drawing 3). Tamp lightly with a small board. Very small seeds should not be covered, merely pressed in lightly.
- Water the seeds well with a fine spray nozzle or sprinkler (see Drawing 4), then keep them moist (not wet!) (see Drawing 5). To water very fine seeds, set the container in a pan of water; by capillary action the water will work up from below, and the seed will not be washed away by overhead watering.
- On the seedling container, stick a label giving the full name of the plant, the origin of the seed, and the sowing date.

Subsequent Care of the Seedlings

Large seeds that were sown directly into their final pot can be kept in the same container until large enough to be set out.

With containers of scattered seeds, the seedlings often become crowded soon after they start to grow. They may need to be thinned so that they have more room in which to develop.

Transplanting
Drawings 6 to 9

The Right Time: Transplant the seedlings after they have grown "true" leaves, which follow the "seed" leaves (expanded cotyledons). More room means that the seedlings will have more nutrients, water, and light available and can develop better. Wider spacing also reduces the risk of disease.

The Right Container: For transplanting, it is best to use multi-pot flats (see page 67). Alternatively, you can relocate them to pans, spacing the seedlings 1 to 2 inches (3–5 cm) apart. Seedlings that grow very rapidly can be set in pots (singly or also in groups). You won't need to pot them later (see page 69), but you will need somewhat more space.

How to Do It:
- Fill the transplanting container to the brim with all-purpose soil mix 2 or a 1:1:1 compost/peat/sand mixture that has a small amount of added fertilizer (0.05 ounce [1.5 g] of compound fertilizer per quart [1 L] of soil mix).

- Loosen the soil mix in the seedling container. With a small wooden transplanting stick (dibble), carefully take the seedlings out of the container (see Drawing 6) and lay them on light-colored cardboard or on a piece of glass (see Drawing 7).
- Take a single seedling (or, with slow-growing plants, a small tuft) in one hand. Using the other hand, poke a hole with the dibble (see Drawing 8).
- Guide the seedling into the planting hole so that the plant is buried up to the point where the "seed" leaves begin (see Drawing 9). Do not bend the roots. Gently press the soil around it with the dibble.
- Attach a label to the finished transplant container, giving the full name of the plant and the transplanting date.
- Using a fine spray nozzle or sprinkler, water the transplant container well.

Direct Seeding
Only a few plant species can be grown by direct seeding at the chosen site in the garden. These include sunflowers, nasturtiums, pot marigolds, and lupines. Here's how to go about it:

Sowing Seeds Singly. Put large seeds individually into a previously loosened and weeded patch of fine, crumbly soil and cover them lightly.

Sowing Quantities of Seed. Very fine seeds should be sprinkled over the prepared sites. Do not sow too close together. If too many seedlings sprout, you need to thin them out. Remove individual seedlings in order to give the others more room to develop properly.

Important: Don't let the seeds dry out; if the weather is dry, they have to be watered.

It is best to mark freshly sown spots with small stakes, so that you don't plant something else later in seemingly vacant areas.

Transplanting, Step-by-Step
⑥ Loosen soil mix with dibble.
⑦ Lift out seedlings and carefully pry them loose.
⑧ With the dibble, first make a planting hole, then insert the seedling, leaving the seed leaf above ground.
⑨ Press the soil mix down lightly.

① *Division* is a suitable method of propagation for many perennials. Dig up the plants in early spring or in fall, and divide the plant clump with two garden forks placed back to back.

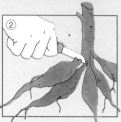

② *The root tubers* of dahlias can be cut with a sharp knife. Important: Each piece needs to have several eyes capable of sprouting.

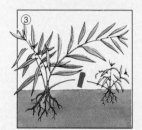

③ *Layers* are aerial, already-rooted shoots of the parent plant (here, Buglossoides pur-purocaerulea). They can be removed and replanted at once.

VEGETATIVE PROPAGATION

If your goal in propagation is not to obtain large numbers of plants, vegetative (asexual) propagation is often an easier, and usually faster, way to grow young plants. Moreover, if the plant species do not set seeds or do not breed true—that is, do not produce identical offspring—vegetative propagation is the only way possible.

Cuttings need humid air to keep them from wilting. To retain humidity, simply put a clear plastic bag over an arching wire structure and tie it securely.

Division
Drawing 1

Division is perhaps the easiest, quickest, and often most appropriate technique, for propagating perennials. Not all species can be divided, however. Plants with taproots or a woody rootstock, for example, are not candidates for this type of propagation.

Here's How:
• Dig up the plant in early spring or in fall (in fall, also cut it back).
• With your hands or with two garden forks placed back to back and/or a sharp spade, separate the clump into several portions, each about the size of the palm of your hand.
• Plant the new divisions, and water immediately.

Portions of larger plant clumps can be cut off in the same way, without lifting the entire plant out of the ground.

If you want more new plants, perennials can be separated into even smaller pieces. Once the plant clump has been lifted, divide it into egg-sized pieces with a knife. Each piece should have at least one well-developed eye (bud capable of sprouting).

Small Plant Segments
Propagation by small plant segments is possible with all plants that have a creeping root system or cushion-like growth (such as bushy aster, moss pink, and lungwort). Simply pull off very tiny pieces from the edge of the plant, making sure they include a shoot and a piece of root, and pot them.

④ *Basal cutting. Along with the shoot, cut off a small piece of the woody rootstock.*

⑤ *Tip cutting. Cut off shoot tips about 1–3 in. (3–7 cm) long, each with two or three leaf pairs.*

Cuttings

Spring is the best season for taking cuttings for most plants. Evergreen and woody perennials or subshrubs (such as alyssum and wall rock cress) and some annual flowers (such as shrub marguerite and beard-tongue) are best propagated by cuttings taken in the fall.

Herbaceous (Softwood, Green) Tip Cuttings
Drawing 5

• Fill containers (multi-pot flats, shallow wooden boxes, or flower pots) with a moistened rooting medium that conducts water well and is low in nutrients (peat/sand in a 1:1 ratio).

• Take cuttings about 1 to 3 inches (3–7 cm) long from the tips of the shoots of the mother plants, including at least two or three pairs of leaves, and place the cuttings in a dampened plastic bag.

• Bring the cuttings to a place that is bright but does not get full sun.

• First remove the lower leaves, then make a fresh cut straight across the cutting just below a node.

• Stiffer cuttings can be stuck directly into the medium; for softer shoots, first make a hole with a dibble.

• Insert the cutting and gently push the surrounding soil into the hole.

Basal Cuttings
Drawing 4

Basal cuttings can be taken from perennial plants with hollow stems (like delphinium and sneezeweed) when they experience their flush of new growth. Remove not only a shoot, but also a small piece of the woody rootstock in the soil, using a sharp knife.

Further Care (see drawing, page 72 bottom).

Now the cuttings need air as humid as possible. Use sturdy wire to create an arching framework over the container, stretch a dampened piece of transparent plastic film over it, and tie up the "head" so that it is airtight. Put the cuttings in a bright place. A few weeks later, once they have produced enough roots and new leaves, remove the "hood." Now it is time to pot the young plants.

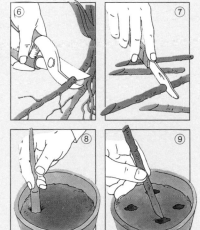

⑥ *To stick root cuttings: Separate roots about the thickness of a pencil from the clump.*
⑦ *Cut them into pieces about 2 in. (5 cm) long. Cut the upper end straight, the bottom end at a slant.*
⑧ *With the dibble, make a planting hole.*
⑨ *Stick the pieces of root, slanted end downward, into the medium.*

Root Cuttings

This propagation technique can be used for perennials whose roots are capable of producing new growth.

Lift the plants for taking cuttings in late fall. Depending on the plant species, the root cuttings are either inserted straight up in the medium or simply scattered over its surface. Perennials with tap-like roots (such as Oriental poppy and globe thistle) put forth only at the upper end of the root (polarized roots); consequently the root cuttings have to be planted vertically, with the end nearest the parent pointing up. Other perennials (such as Japanese anemones and creeping barren-strawberry) produce new growth over the entire length of the root (unpolarized roots).

Sticking Root Cuttings
Drawings 6 to 9
Method for polarized roots:

• Cut roots the thickness of a pencil into pieces 2 inches (5 cm) long, making a slanting cut to mark the lower end and straight cut across to designate the upper end, where the new growth will occur later.

• Plant the pieces, the slanted end on bottom, in a pan or a wooden box filled to a depth of about 3 inches (8 cm) with permeable medium.

• Sprinkle some of the medium lightly over the root cuttings.

Scattering Root Cuttings
Method for plants with unpolarized roots:

• Cut the roots slightly over 1 inch (3 cm) long. Scatter them—not too close together—in a bowl filled with medium, and cover them with medium to a depth of about half an inch (1 cm).

Further Care
The containers of root cuttings should not be kept overly warm; about 53.6°F (12°C) is sufficient.

The colors of the attrac-
tively shaped flowers of
the bearded iris range
widely, including all
shades but scarlet. Here,
a portrait of the Iris
barbata-elatior hybrid
'Amethyst Flame', seen
from an insect's
perspective.

PLANT PORTRAITS AND TIPS ON CARE

A brilliantly colored kaleidoscope of the most beautiful garden flowers, with a gorgeous array of blooms for every season, dazzling on every page. In addition, a selection of attractive ferns and grasses to combine with the flowers is given. Every plant profile includes a color photo of the plant and a description of its flowers, leaves, and growth form. You will also find information on the plant's place of origin and data on appropriate sites, propagation techniques, and year-round care requirements.

The Most Beautiful Garden Flowers and Their Care

In the plant portraits that follow, you will become acquainted with the most popular garden flowers, along with attractive grasses and ferns that make stylish companions for them. The color photos will familiarize you with the plants' individual growth habits and with the wide-ranging palette of flower and leaf colors. The descriptions give background information on each plant's place of origin and botanical particulars, along with pointers on year-round care. Moreover, the authors also supply valuable suggestions on design, explaining how each plant can be used in the garden and listing good partners for it. These recommendations are supplemented by tips on particularly gorgeous or healthy cultivars and relatives.

The Four Groups in the Plant Portrait Section

All the garden flowers described here are arranged by their physiological characteristics into one of these four groups:

■ Annuals (see pages 78 to 95), red bar.

■ Perennials (see pages 96 to 191), blue bar.

■ Bulbs and tubers (see pages 192 to 221), yellow bar.

■ Grasses and ferns (see pages 222 to 229), green bar.

Sequence within the Groups. The garden flowers belonging to a group appear there alphabetized under their botanical name. If you want information about a garden flower but know only its common name, use the index (see pages 230 to 235) to find the plant.

The Symbols and Their Meanings

They provide information on the blooming season, mature height, and light requirements of each garden flower. You can see at a glance whether a plant yields good cut flowers and whether it is poisonous.

Important: For improved readability, there are just three symbols explaining the plants' light requirements. For each plant, you will find more detailed information in the accompanying descriptive text.

The months of the blooming season are given.

H 16–48   Gives the mature height of the plant being described in inches (centimeters), but also includes the height of all the cultivars and relatives listed.

◯ The plant needs a site with full sun to sun.

◖ The plant needs a site out of the sun or light to partial shade.

⬤ The plant tolerates shade.

✂ The plant provides good and long-lasting cut flowers.

☠ The plant is poisonous or contains skin irritants.

Structure of the Plant Portraits

All the plant descriptions are arranged in a clear, well-organized structure. Headings ensure that information about each plant is available quickly. Because all the descriptions follow the same format, making comparisons between individual plants is easy.

The English common name appears in large, easy-to-read type above each description, because it is more familiar to many plant fanciers. If a garden flower has several common names, the most important ones are given.

The botanical name is placed directly below the English one. Because it is internationally accepted, it determines the alphabetical sequence of the plant descriptions. The botanical name usually has two parts: The genus name (for example, *Phlox*) appears first; then follows the species name (for example, *Phlox paniculata*). Both names are italicized, unlike those of the cultivated varieties (cultivars), whose names are in Roman type and enclosed in single quotation marks (for example, *Phlox paniculata* 'Flamingo').

The shaded bar where the symbols are displayed contains basic information at a glance. Found in each profile below the color photo and above the plant description, it is consistent in format (see explanations of symbols, left).

Explanation of the Headings

Each description is preceded by a brief characterization of the plant.

Flower: For many plant fanciers, it is the most important part of the garden flower. The flower color, shape, and size and the head are described (see page 17 for terminology). Remember, however, that hues are never constant; they depend on the weather and the soil.

Leaf: Here the shape, color, and other particulars of the leaves are noted. "A Botany Lesson" (see HOW TO pages 16 and 17) provides information on different leaf forms.

Growth: Here you will find special information about the growth form, need for staking, and urge to spread.

Origin: This paragraph gives the plant's place of origin and preferred natural habitat.

Site: The required light and temperature conditions and the optimum soil factors (for technical terms, see explanation in table at right) are given.

Care: This heading supplies information on important gardening techniques ranging from planting through watering to fertilization. Major pests and diseases are listed.

Propagation: You will learn whether the plants spread by sowing seed on their own. The most common methods of propagation are also listed. The chapter on propagation will tell you how it's done (see pages 66 to 73).

Use: Valuable information derived from the authors' experience on the best ways to use each plant is given.

Good partners: Under this heading are listed the species and cultivars that are a good match for the given garden flower. They are arranged in this order: annuals; perennials; bulbs and tubers; woody plants.

Technical Terms Used in This Book

Light intensities: In the site information we distinguish among the following degrees of exposure:
• full sun = a completely unshaded site, lit by the sun from morning to evening
• sun = a place usually in the sun, with light shade in the early morning or late evening
• out of the sun = a growing site unsheltered from above, not struck directly by the sun but almost as bright as a sunny site, without the build-up of heat caused by the sun
• light shade = a bright shade produced by a light growth of branches and leaves of woody plants, with fairly long phases of intermittent sunlight
• partial shade = pronounced shade caused by somewhat denser growth of woody plants, with patches of sun occasionally moving over the plants
• shade = dense growth of woody plants lets the sun penetrate only rarely for brief periods; predominantly dark areas of shade

Soil type: In the text, reference is made to various categories of soils ranging from light to heavy:
• sandy soil
• loamy sand
• sandy loam
• loam
• heavy loam
• clay

Soil humidity: An important criterion for many plants. These gradations exist:
• dry
• moderately dry
• well-drained (= normal)
• moist
• very moist
• wet

Degree of soil acidity: (increases as the pH decreases):
• extremely acid = pH below 4.5
• acid = pH 4.5–6
• slightly acid = pH 6–6.5
• neutral = pH 6.5–7
• slightly alkaline = pH 7–7.5
• alkaline = pH 7.5–8
• extremely alkaline = pH over 8

Data on frost-hardiness and frost damage in garden flowers:
• moderately frost-hardy = damage to buds, with evergreens also to leaves
• frost-tender = frost damage is regularly observed, but usually heals completely

Cultivars/Relatives: To help with your shopping or just for your information, well-known cultivated varieties or related species are listed according to flower color, always going from the lightest shade to the darkest.

Warning: This heading appears if the plant contains toxins or skin irritants. Plants thus designated can be harmful or even lethal to adults, children, or pets if poisonous plant parts are ingested or come into contact with the skin or eyes.

ANNUALS—FLOWERS

This successful planting of annual grasses and sunflowers is full of variety.

FOR A SINGLE SUMMER

What Are Annual Flowers?

Annuals are plants that within a single vegetative period grow from seed, produce foliage and shoots, flower, and bear fruit. After seed is formed, they die.

Because all of them bloom for no more than a single summer, they are commonly known also as summer flowers. Although they are short-lived, these flowers have extremely resistant seed and therefore can withstand unfavorable weather conditions; in our country, that means the winter—in warmer regions, frequently prolonged periods of drought. Thus the annuals ensure their continued existence through bountiful seed production.

How the Flower Portraits Were Chosen

In the following selection, you will find, along with the true annuals, plants with a slightly different rhythm of growth whose flowers are especially beautiful and abundant.

Plant list:
① *Tagetes tenuifolia*
② *Rudbeckia hirta* 'Marmalade'
③ *Rhynchelytrum repens*
④ *Tithonia rotundifolia*
⑤ *Penstemon* hybrid 'Southgate Gem'
⑥ *Verbena bonariensis*
⑦ *Rudbeckia hirta* 'Marmalade'

Annual coneflower

Long-lived shrubs and herbaceous perennials from warmer regions are treated as annuals in this country because they are not sufficiently winter-hardy; they have to be raised again each year. These species survive if overwintered in frost-free quarters, and for this reason they occasionally are used also as container or tub plants.

Biennials are plants that are grown from seed sown in early summer and are set out in late summer or fall. They survive the winter in the rosette stage, then bloom the following spring. They also are known as winter annuals.

Tips on Use: All the flowers in this group produce lush, abundant flowers over a period of weeks, many even for months at a time. The possibilities for combining them are extremely varied. Coordinate the shades with great care, so that you will have a harmonious scene in summer, not a jumbled confusion of colors.

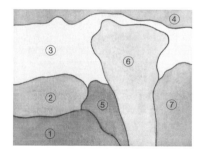

Ageratum, Flossflower
Ageratum houstonianum

Ageratum houstonianum

July–October ○ ✄
H 4–28 in. (10–70 cm)

A wide range of cultivars of different heights.
Flower: Soft medium blue to sky blue or white, some cultivars also old-rose color. Many single flowers in broad, terminal, umbrella-shaped false umbels (cymes).
Leaf: Ovate, margins crenate, vivid green.
Growth: Depending on cultivar, low, broad and bushy, or erect. Clump like with copiously leaved stems.
Origin: Mexico.
Site: Sun, warm. Soil well-drained, nutrient-rich. No water-logged soils!
Care: Moderate nutrient and water supply. Low cultivars are prone to rot. Always deadhead spent flowers.
Propagation: From February to March sow indoors, from May on plant out in beds. Alternatively: Propagate by cuttings from overwintered plants.
Use: In flower beds with other annuals. Also pretty with yellow and white perennials in borders.
Good Partners: *Cleome, Cosmos bipinnatus, Verbena,* or as contrast for the warm colors of *Cosmos sulphureus, Calendula, Tagetes, Helianthus decapetalus, Heliopsis, Helenium, Rudbeckia.*
Cultivars/Relatives:
• 'Schnittstar White', pure white, 24 in. (60 cm).
• 'Schnittwunder', soft medium blue, 28 in. (70 cm).

Hollyhock
Alcea rosea Hybrids

Alcea rosea hybrids

July–September ○
H 64–88 in. (160–220 cm)

Popular plant in country gardens.
Flower: Pink, raspberry, purple-red, white, also bicolored and double. Mallow-like flowers in candle-shaped heads.
Leaf: Broad-oval to round with crepe paper-like surface, matte green.
Growth: Erect, stately biennial.
Origin: Very old cultivated plant, supposedly from the Orient.
Site: Sun, warm. Soil dry to well-drained, permeable, nutrient-rich.
Care: Plant in early fall; flowers bloom the next summer. Good nutrient supply. Pick off the frequently appearing jumping fleas. Combat mallow rust disease only if plants are severely attacked.
Propagation: Sow indoors from April to June.
Use: Singly or in small tufts. Pretty next to south walls, in borders, and in country gardens.
Good Partners: *Cleome, Cosmos bipinnatus, Verbena bonariensis—Delphinium, Phlox*—old, double rose cultivars.
Cultivars/Relatives:
• 'Himbeer', raspberry-red.
• 'Nigra', extremely dark velvety red.

Snapdragon
Antirrhinum majus

Antirrhinum majus

June–September ○ ✄
H 8–40 in. (20–100 cm)

Well-known garden flower with innumerable color variations.
Flower: Almost all colors except blue, also bi-colored in candle-like inflorescences.
Leaf: Narrow ovate, pointed at the tip, grass-green.
Growth: Erect, bushy.
Origin: Southern Europe, where it is a perennial.
Site: Sun. Soil well-drained, nutrient-rich, loose.
Care: Good supply of nutrients and water. Deadhead spent flowers.
Propagation: Sow indoors from January to April, plant out in bed from late May on. Self-sowing.
Use: In beds, with white- and blue-flowered partners.
Good Partners: *Chrysanthemum frutescens, Cosmos bipinnatus* 'Unschuld', *Lobularia maritima, Salvia uliginosa.*
Cultivars/Relatives: Various hybrid groups designated by the color of the given cultivar, for example:
• Sonnet F1 hybrids bloom early and long, 20 in. (50 cm). 'Sonnet Dark Red', 'Sonnet Yellow'.

Wax Begonia
Begonia semperflorens Hybrids

Begonia semperflorens hybrid

May–October ○
H 6–10 in. (15–25 cm)

Undemanding, with a long-lasting bloom.
Flower: Pink, salmon, orange, crimson, scarlet, white. Saucer-shaped flowers.
Leaf: Broad oval, fleshy, margins slightly saw-toothed. Depending on the cultivar, dark green, brownish green, or purplish bronze.
Growth: Compact, low, clump-forming plant.
Origin: Cultivated form.
Site: Sun, warm. Soil well-drained, loose, nutrient-rich. No wet or cold sites!
Care: Plant out in winter; otherwise, it has trouble taking root.
Propagation: Sow seeds indoors in winter. Do not cover the very fine seeds with growing medium. Cover rooting container with glass. Shade seedlings and accustom them slowly to light.
Use: In small groups in the front of beds; for grave plantings, balcony boxes, and bowls.
Good Partners: White-flowered summer flowers like *Cosmos bipinnatus* 'Unschuld', *Lobularia*, *Salvia farinacea* 'Argent'.
Cultivars/Relatives:
• Jewel F1 hybrids bloom early and freely, foliage green.
• Diable F1 hybrids free-flowering, foliage dark.
• *Begonia*-tuberous begonia hybrids: large, usually double flowers in brilliant colors. Biennial plants for partially shady sites.

English Daisy
Bellis perennis

English daisies make good cut flowers.

March–May ○ ◐ ✂
H 6–8 in. (15–20 cm)

Spring bloomer, heavily laden with double flower globes. The original ancestor is the common daisy. In cultivation, the cultivars are "biennial" (winter annuals).
Flower: Depending on the cultivar, white, pink, crimson, or scarlet. Pompon flowers on short stems.
Leaf: Spatulate, vivid green.
Growth: Compact leaf rosettes.
Origin: Europe to Asia Minor. In meadows and grass. The cultivators are old cultivated plants.
Site: Sun to partial shade. Plant is sensitive to heavy frosts. Soil well-drained to moist, nutrient-rich and well loosened.
Care: After planting in fall, protect with evergreen boughs in winter. Tidy plants in spring. Good nutrient supply.
Propagation: In July, sow in seedbeds or in hotbed; in fall transplant to desired site. Alternatively, sow seeds in hotbed in summer, overwinter there, and plant out in early spring.
Use: In beds, on graves, and in bowls.
Good partners: *Myosotis sylvestris*, *Viola wittrockiana* hybrids, *Hyacinthus*, tulips, or white narcissus.

Cultivar 'Roggli Weiss'

Cultivars/Relatives:
• 'Pomponette Weiss', white.
• 'Pomponette Rosa', pink.
• 'Pomponette Rot', red, all with many double flowers in the colors of the cultivar names.
Free-flowering with long flower stalks, hence also good as cut flowers.

Pot Marigold
Calendula officinalis

'Cutting and Bending Mix'

June–September ○ ✄
H 12–28 in. (30–70 cm)

Very old healing plant; survives by self-sowing without coaxing.
Flower: Yellow, orange, or apricot flowers resemble daisies; usually double on long stems.
Leaf: Oval, fresh green.
Growth: Erect, clump like.
Origin: Mediterranean region.
Site: Sun, warm. Soil well-drained to moderately dry, nutrient-rich and loose.
Care: Good nutrient supply. Deadhead faded flowers regularly.
Propagation: With direct sowing outdoors in April or May, the pot marigolds will start to bloom in late July. Alternative: Sow seeds indoors in February or March, plant out in bed in May, then they will bloom earlier. Self-sowing.
Use: In beds of summer flowers, in gaps in perennial borders, in country gardens.
Good Partners: *Ageratum, Salvia farinacea, Tagetes— Delphinium, Heliopsis, Rudbeckia—Calamagrostis.*
Cultivars/Relatives:
• Kablouna series, with many double cultivars. Cut flowers.
• Pacific series, semidouble.

China Aster
Callistephus chinensis

Callistephus chinensis hybrid

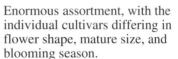

July–September ○ ✄
H 8–36 in. (20–90 cm)

Enormous assortment, with the individual cultivars differing in flower shape, mature size, and blooming season.
Flower: Depending on the cultivar, violet, blue, lilac, pink, velvety red, crimson, purple red, white, or pale yellow. Flowers single, semidouble, double, or pompon-shaped. The individual petals range from narrow and elongated tubular to tongue-shaped.
Leaf: Lanceolate to obovate, margins coarsely toothed or incised, grass-green.
Growth: Depending on cultivar, low, spreading, and bushy or erect and clump like.
Origin: The original, rather inconspicuous species, not in cultivation, comes from China.
Site: Sun, warm. Soil well-drained to moist, nutrient-rich. No soils that dry out easily!
Care: Good water and nutrient supply. That is also the best way to prevent the commonly occurring aster wilt, which causes the plants first to look limp. The base of the stem and the root neck then turn blackish-brown from dead tissue. Once that happens, the diseased plants need to be removed at once and destroyed (don't add to your compost pile!). It is best to avoid planting China asters for several successive years in locations where aster wilt has occurred. In selecting cultivars, give preference to generally wilt-resistant breeds.

Cultivar 'Mylady Melange'

Propagation: From February to April, sow indoors; plant out in late May. Alternatively, sow directly in the bed in May.
Use: In borders and in country gardens; also as a cut flower.
Good Partners:
Chrysanthemum frutescens, Lobularia, Salvia farinacea.
Cultivars/Relatives:
The following groups are available:
• Low bedding and pot asters that spread and become bushy, 8–12 in. (20–30 cm) tall, in the front of borders.
• Medium-tall cutting asters, which grow 12 to 24 in. (30–60 cm) tall and are generally quite strong-stemmed.
• Tall, midseason asters grow 20 to 32 in. (50–80 cm) tall and bloom from late July to early September.
• Late-flowering cutting asters reach a height of 12 to 24 in. (30–60 cm) and start to flower in late August.
• Single marguerite asters have one ring of petals and bloom from August to September, reaching a height of 28 to 32 in. (70–80 cm).

Within these groups, cultivars occur in all the colors listed above.

Canterbury Bells
Campanula medium

Campanula medium

May–July ○
H 20–28 in. (50–70 cm)

Showy, popular biennial, despite short blooming season.
Flower: Light blue, large bell-shaped single blossoms in free-flowering racemes.
Leaf: Ovate with irregularly scalloped margin, dull green.
Growth: A leaf rosette forms the first year, followed the second year by an erect, tapering head.
Origin: Southern Europe.
Site: Sun, warm; in well-drained, nutrient-rich, loose soils.
Care: Plant in late summer. Water in dry spells. Feed plentifully. No waterlogged soils!
Propagation: Sow from June to July. Plant in late August or September.
Use: Sunny borders, country gardens, cutting flower beds.
Good Partners: *Alcea rosea* hybrids, *Dianthus barbatus*—double-flowered roses.
Cultivars:
• 'Alba', white.
• 'Rosea', pink.

Marguerite Chrysanthemum, Shrub Marguerite, Paris Daisy
Chrysanthemum frutescens

'Jamaica Primrose'

June–October ○
H 16–40 in. (40–100 cm)

Commonly used as a tub plant, marguerite chrysanthemum also is attractive in beds.
Flower: Many small, white, daisy-like flowers—some cultivars also pink- or yellow-flowered.
Leaf: Depending on cultivar, finely laciniate to lobed, lush green to silvery gray.
Growth: Spreading and bushy, erect.
Origin: Canary Islands.
Site: Sun, warm. Soil well-drained and permeable, nutrient-rich. No waterlogged soils!
Care: Good feeding and regular water supply. Pruning the wilted flowers prolongs the blooming season. Can be overwintered indoors in a bright, cool place.
Propagation: By cuttings.
Use: In borders.
Good Partners: White cultivars with almost all annuals. Yellow cultivars good with *Heliotropium, Verbena bonariensis*.
Cultivars/Relatives:
• 'Silver Leaf', white, finely divided gray foliage.
• 'Schöne von Nizza', golden yellow, with lobed, dark-gray foliage.
• 'Rosali', pink, with dark-gray, lobed foliage.

Feverfew
Chrysanthemum parthenium

Cultivar 'Santana'

June–September ○ ✂
H 8–24 in. (20–60 cm)

Old cultivated plant, only cultivars of which are in use.
Flower: White or yellow, usually double, daisy-like flowers.
Leaf: Pinnatisect, dull green.
Growth: Erect, spreading and bushy, at times not altogether strong-stemmed.
Origin: Caucasus, Asia Minor, naturalized in almost all of Europe.
Site: Sun. Soil well-drained to moist, loose, nutrient-rich.
Care: Good nutrient and water supply. Deadhead faded flowers. If aphids attack, removal of heavily infested shoots usually suffices.
Propagation: By seed sown from late February to early March.
Use: In plantings of annual flowers and as a filler in perennial borders.
Good Partners: White cultivars with almost all annuals and bedding perennials. Yellow cultivars with *Cosmos sulphureus, Heliotropium, Salvia farinacea, Tagetes*.
Cultivars/Relatives:
• 'Schneeball', white, double, 12 in. (30 cm).
• 'Roya', white with yellow center, single, 20 in. (50 cm).
• 'Goldgelb', golden yellow, double, 10 in. (25 cm).

Spiderflower
Cleome spinosa

Common Cosmos
Cosmos bipinnatus

Cultivar 'Gloria'

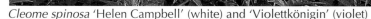
Cleome spinosa 'Helen Campbell' (white) and 'Violettkönigin' (violet)

July–October   ○ ✂
H 32–56 in. (80–140 cm)

Tall, enchanting summer flower that needs plenty of room in the garden.
Flower: Depending on cultivar, white, pink, cherry-red, or violet, with long, protruding stamens. Flowers in continually developing, many-blossomed racemes.
Leaf: Five- to seven-lobed, dark green.
Origin: South America.
Site: Sun, warm. Soil moderately dry to well-drained, permeable.
Care: Plant outdoors only after the ground has warmed up, in late May to June. Before that, cut back the plants to induce improved branching. Good nutrient supply.
Propagation: Sow seeds indoors from March on, plant in bed in late May.
Use: Annual flower beds and perennial borders, cutting flower beds.
Good Partners: *Cosmos bipinnatus, Heliotropium, Verbena bonariensis—Echinacea, Liatris*—pink and white roses.

Cultivar 'Kirschkönigin'

Cultivars/Relatives:
- 'Helen Campbell', white.
- 'Rosa Königin', pink.
- 'Kirschkönigin', crimson-pink.
- 'Fliederfarbe', light violet.
- 'Violettkönigin', violet.

June–October   ○ ✂
H 20–44 in. (50–110 cm)

Graceful summer flowers with fine, decorative foliage.
Flower: White, pink, or crimson saucer-shaped flowers with a yellow center.
Leaf: Light green, bipinnate.
Growth: Erect, spreading and bushy.
Origin: Mexico.
Site: Sun, warm. Soil well-drained, vigorous, nutrient-rich, with loose structure.
Care: Good nutrient and water supply.
Propagation: Sow seeds indoors in late March or April, plant outdoors from mid-May. Alternative: Sow directly in bed.
Use: Annual flower beds, as filler in perennial borders, cutting flower beds, and country gardens.
Good Partners: The white cultivars go with almost all annuals and bedding perennials; the pink and crimson cultivars are good with *Cleome spinosa, Verbena bonariensis* or with *Monarda* and *Phlox.*
Cultivars/Relatives:
- 'Unschuld', pure white, 40 in. (100 cm).
- 'Gloria', pink with crimson ring, 36 in. (90 cm).
- 'Karminkönig', crimson, 40 in. (100 cm).

Yellow Cosmos
Cosmos sulphureus

Cultivar 'Sunset'

July–October
H 16–28 in. (40–70 cm)

Very pretty, less well known summer flower.
Flower: Depending on cultivar, orange or strong yellow, saucer-shaped flowers.
Leaf: Fresh green, pinnate.
Growth: Spreading and bushy.
Origin: Mexico.
Site: Sun, warm. Soil well-drained, loose, nutrient-rich
Care: Good water and nutrient supply.
Propagation: As for *Cosmos bipinnatus* (see page 84).
Use: In perennial borders and annual flower beds. Looks good with blue, violet, and yellow colors.
Good Partners: *Calendula, Salvia farinacea, Tagetes, Tithonia, Verbena bonariensis—Delphinium, Helenium, Heliopsis, Rudbeckia.*
Cultivars/Relatives:
• 'Ladybird Yellow', yellow.
• 'Ladybird Orange', orange.

Sweet William
Dianthus barbatus

Cultivar of *Dianthus barbatus*

May–August
H 20–24 in. (50–60 cm)

Plant with a long history of cultivation.
Flower: Salmon-red, crimson, pink, white, also bicolored with white, closely packed in umbrella-shaped heads.
Leaf: Broad lanceolate, dark green.
Growth: Forms a leaf rosette the first year, erect, loose clumps the second year.
Origin: Southern Europe to China.
Site: Sun; soil moderately dry to well-drained, permeable and nutritious.
Care: Good nutrient supply (inorganic). Protect in winter by covering with boughs.
Propagation: Sow seeds from May to July; plant in ultimate location in September.
Use: In annual flower beds, in country gardens. Plant them in the middle of the bed, because they leave gaps after blooming.
Good Partners: *Alcea rosea* hybrids, *Campanula medium, Chrysanthemum parthenium.*
Cultivars/Relatives:
• 'Albus', pure white.
• 'Pink Beauty', pink.
• 'Heimatland', velvety red with white center.
• 'Atrosanguineus', velvety dark purple.

Common Sunflower, Cut-and-come-again
Helianthus annuus

Cultivar 'Estate'

July–October
H 16–100 in. (40–250 cm)

Well-known annual flower.
Flower: Yellow ray flowers around a large, black-brown center, singly on firm stems.
Leaf: Large, broad oval, rough, dull green.
Growth: Tall, erect, sometimes floppy.
Origin: North America; prairies.
Site: Sun, warm. Soil moderately dry to well-drained, nutrient-rich. No compacted soils!
Care: Good nutrient and water supply. Support tall, weak-stemmed cultivars.
Propagation: Sow seeds directly in bed after April.
Use: In background of borders. Good in front of fences, against which the plants can lean.
Good Partners: *Ageratum, Heliotropium, Tithonia—Delphinium, Heliopsis, Rudbeckia.*
Cultivars/Relatives:
• 'Holiday', golden yellow with dark center, 48–60 in. (120–150 cm), bushy.
• 'Hohes Sonnengold', golden yellow, double flowers, 72 in. (180 cm).
• 'Sunspot', golden yellow, single, 16 in. (40 cm).
• 'Intermedius Abendsonne', russet to dark purple, with dark center, 80 in. (200 cm).

ANNUALS

Strawflower, Everlasting, Immortelle
Helichrysum bracteatum

Cultivar 'Rosenschimmer'

July–September ○ ✂
H 12–40 in. (30–100 cm)

For dried bouquets.
Flower: White, yellow, orange, pink, velvety red, or red-brown flower heads.
Leaf: Lanceolate, matte green.
Growth: Erect, clump-forming.
Origin: Australia.
Site: Sun, warm. Soil moderately dry to well-drained, permeable, nutrient-poor.
Care: Feed only moderately; otherwise, the plants will flop over. Cut flowers shortly before center petals open, hang upside down to dry in a shady, airy place.
Propagation: Sow seeds indoors in March or April, plant outdoors in late May.
Use: In beds of cutting flowers.
Good Partners: Other flowers for drying.
Cultivars/Relatives:
• 'Album', white, 24 in. (60 cm).
• 'Luteum', yellow, 24 in. (60 cm).
• 'Kupferorange', orange-brown shades, 24 in. (60 cm).
• 'Hotbikini', fire-red, 12 in. (30 cm).
• *Limonium sinuatum,* annual statice, with blue, umbrella-shaped flower clusters or panicles. 'Rosenschimmer', pink, 24 in. (60 cm).
• 'Modra Dunkelblau', dark blue, 16–20 in. (40–50 cm).

Common Heliotrope, Cherry Pie
Heliotropium arborescens

Cultivar 'Marine'

June–September ○ ☠
H 12–24 in. (30–60 cm)

Delightful, fragrant plant for borders; its flowers are quickly spoiled by rain.
Flower: Violet-blue with vanilla scent. Numerous tiny, single flowers in umbrella-shaped heads.
Leaf: Ovate with deep-set veins, dark green with violet shimmer.
Growth: Erect, spreading and bushy.
Origin: Peru and Ecuador.
Site: Sun, warm. Soil well-drained, permeable, nutrient-rich. No wet sites! Does well in places sheltered from rain.
Care: Good nutrient and water supply.
Propagation: Sow seeds indoors from January to March, plant out in bed from mid-May.
Use: In annual flower beds and in perennial borders.
Good Partners: *Calendula, Helianthus, Tagetes, Tithonia, Verbena bonariensis—Coreopsis, Helenium, Heliopsis, Rudbeckia, Solidago.*
Cultivars/Relatives:
• 'Marine', violet-blue, 40–24 in. (50–60 cm).
• 'Mini Marine', violet-blue, 12 in. (30 cm).
Warning: All parts of this plant are poisonous.

Sultan Snapweed, Busy Lizzie, Patience Plant
Impatiens walleriana Hybrids

A novelty, 'Expo Picotée'

June–October ○ ◑
H 4–12 in. (10–30 cm)

Group plant, also for areas with light shade.
Flower: Depending on cultivar, white, pink, various shades of red, and violet. Some also bicolored with white. Solitary, plate-shaped flowers are single or double.
Leaf: Ovate, pointed, margin scalloped, grass-green.
Growth: Low, broad-lying.
Origin: Cultivated form.
Site: Sun to partial shade, cool. Soil well-drained to moist, well loosened, nutrient-rich. No hot sites!
Care: Good water and nutrient supply.
Propagation: Sow seeds indoors (February to March) at 68° to 75°F (20–24°C). Plant out in bed in late May.
Use: As group plant in annual flower beds or to fill gaps in perennial borders.
Good Partners: *Cosmos,* fuchsias, *Salvia uliginosa—Phlox, Physostegia.*
Cultivars/Relatives: Countless cultivars in a variety of colors.
• *Impatiens* New Guinea hybrids, 16 in. (40 cm) tall, all parts larger. Very compact-growing, with bronze-green to purple-brown or multicolored foliage. Cultivars in various colors. Propagation by cuttings, newer cultivars also by seed.

Sweet Pea
Lathyrus odoratus

Tree Mallow
Lavatera trimestris

Lobelia
Lobelia erinus

Cultivar of *Lathyrus odoratus*

Cultivar 'Silver Cup'

Multicolored 'Colour Cascade'

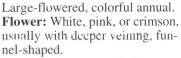

July–September	July–September	June–September
H 40–80 in. (100–200 cm)	H 20–32 in. (50–80 cm)	H 4–8 in. (10–20 cm)

Fragrant climber.
Flower: Depending on cultivar, pink, crimson, scarlet, white, lavender, and violet, with intense scent.
Leaf: Tripartite, dull light green, hairy.
Growth: Climbs by means of tendrils.
Origin: Southern Italy.
Site: Sun, warm. Soil well-drained, permeable, loose, nutrient-rich, lime-rich. No wet sites!
Care: Good nutrient supply, water in dry spells. Keep deadheading faded flowers.
Propagation: Sow seeds indoors from February on. Alternative: Sow directly outdoors in April.
Use: Along fences or on lattice-like climbing frames. Cutting flowers.
Good Partners: *Cosmos bipinnatus, Lavatera, Verbena bonariensis.*
Cultivars/Relatives:
• Mammoth type, with five to six blossoms on long, strong stalks. Many cultivars designated by the flower color, for example, 'Lavender'.
• Royal type with five to seven blossoms per stalk.

Large-flowered, colorful annual.
Flower: White, pink, or crimson, usually with deeper veining, funnel-shaped.
Leaf: Cordate, matte dark green, rough-haired.
Growth: Erect, spreading and bushy.
Origin: Mediterranean region.
Site: Sun, warm. Soil well-drained, loose, permeable, and not overly nutrient-rich. No wet sites!
Care: Plant 20 in. (50 cm) apart, or thin out to that distance. Moderate nutrient supply.
Propagation: Sow seed directly in bed in April. Alternative: Sow seeds indoors, but no earlier than mid-March; otherwise, the plants often flop over. Plant out in bed in mid-May.
Use: In annual flower beds and to fill gaps in perennial plantings.
Good Partners: *Cleome, Cosmos bipinnatus, Nicotiana, Salvia farinacea, Verbena bonariensis.*
Cultivars/Relatives:
• 'Mont Blanc', pure white, 20 in. (50 cm).
• 'Silver Cup', pink with dark red veining, 24 in. (60 cm).
• 'Ruby Regis', bright pink, 24–28 in. (60–70 cm).

Cultivars in intense colors flower long and abundantly.
Flower: Brilliant gentian blue, medium blue, or light blue, also white and pink, some with white eye.
Leaf: Obovate to lanceolate, dark green.
Growth: Low and broad-lying.
Origin: South Africa.
Site: Sun. Soil well-drained to moist, nutrient-rich, vigorous. No waterlogged soils!
Care: Good water and nutrient supply. Don't allow to dry out! Cut back by one-third toward end of blooming season to obtain second bloom.
Propagation: Sow seeds indoors from February to April. Plant out after late May.
Use: Edging and mat-forming plant. For troughs and flower boxes.
Good Partners: *Lobularia, Salvia farinacea, Tagetes.*
Cultivars/Relatives:
• 'Schneeball', pure white.
• 'Rosamunde', pink with white eye.
• 'Cambridge Blue', light blue.
• 'Blaue Perle', ultramarine, blooms very early.
• 'Kristallpalast', dark blue, with dark foliage.

Scarlet Lobelia
Lobelia fulgens

Lobelia fulgens

July–September ○ ✂
H 24–32 in. (60–80 cm)

Brilliantly colored summer flower.
Flower: Flaming scarlet. Asymmetrical solitary flowers in terminal racemes.
Leaf: Lanceolate, pointed, dark green.
Growth: Erect, with little branching.
Origin: Mexico.
Site: Sun, warm. Soil well-drained, nutritious, loose. No wet sites.
Care: Feed well, in dry spells water regularly. The plants can be overwintered indoors in a bright place.
Propagation: Sow indoors in February or March, plant out in bed from late May. After over-wintering, offshoots or "daughter rosettes" also can be separated from parent.
Use: In annual flower beds and perennial plantings.
Good Partners: *Cosmos sulphureus, Heliotropium, Salvia coccinea—Chrysanthemum maximum, Helenium, Hemerocallis*—scarlet and orange *Canna indica* hybrids, *Dahlia.*
Cultivars/Relatives:
• 'Queen Victoria' has scarlet flowers and deep red-brown foliage.

Sweet Alyssum
Lobularia maritima

'Snow Cristals'

June–October ○
H 2–6 in. (5–15 cm)

Splendid group plant.
Flower: White, pink, or purple-violet with honey-like scent. Free-flowering.
Leaf: Small, linear to lanceolate, medium green.
Growth: Shallow, more or less broad cushions.
Origin: Mediterranean region.
Site: Sun, warm. Soil well-drained to moderately dry and permeable.
Care: Deadheading flowers prolongs the blooming season.
Propagation: Sow indoors, but no earlier than March; don't keep young plants too wet. After May, plant out in bed.
Alternative: Sow directly in bed, thin out later.
Use: In the front of beds, good near patios because of scent. Good temporary filling in rock garden after other flowers have faded.
Good Partners: All annuals—*Phlox, Solidago.*
Cultivars/Relatives:
• 'Snow Crystals', pure white, large-flowered, grows very broad and well.
• 'Wonderland', bright pink, small and slow-growing.
• 'Orientalische Nächte', purple-violet, darkest cultivar.

Brampton Stock
Matthiola incana

Double form

May–August ○ ✂
H 12–40 in. (30–100 cm)

Scented cut flower.
Flower: Depending on cultivar, white, pink, crimson, velvety red, lavender, or pale yellow, scented and usually double, in terminal racemes.
Leaf: Lanceolate to spatulate, dull green to gray-green.
Growth: Erect, with little branching except for the bush stocks.
Origin: Southern Europe, Mediterranean region, Asia Minor.
Site: Sun, warm. Soil well-drained, vigorous, permeable, and lime-rich. No waterlogged or dry soils!
Care: Good water and nutrient supply. Deadhead spent flowers regularly.
Propagation: Sow seeds after early February; plant out in bed in late May.
Use: In borders and as cut flowers.
Good Partners: A mix of different stock cultivars looks prettiest.
Cultivars/Relatives: There are two types, columnar stocks and bush stocks.
• Columnar stocks are best suited for cutting.
• Bush stocks can also be used in borders.

Woodland Forget-me-not
Myosotis sylvatica

Myosotis sylvatica

April–June ○ ✂
H 6–12 in. (15–30 cm)

Endearing biennial that is self-sowing in appropriate sites.
Flower: Azure with yellowish or orange eye. The tiny flowers are borne in terminal, arched racemes.
Leaf: Linear to lanceolate, dull green and rough.
Growth: Spreading and bushy.
Origin: Europe to central Asia and north Africa.
Site: Sun. Soil well-drained to moist, nutrient-rich, loose, and humus-rich.
Care: Light winter protection with evergreen boughs or burlap is advisable. Water also in winter in dry weather and open ground. Good nutrient and water supply.
Propagation: Sow seeds in July, transplant to final site in September. Alternative: Sow in July, overwinter started plants in a bright, frost-free place, and plant them out in March.
Use: In beds that are cleaned out after the spring bloom and replanted.
Good Partners: *Bellis*—Narcissuses and tulips.
Cultivars/Relatives:
• 'Amethyst', bright blue, 6 in. (15 cm).
• 'Indigo Compacta', intense, bright blue, 12 in. (30 cm).

Tobacco Plant
Nicotiana sylvestris

Cultivar 'Nicki Deep Rose'

Nicotiana sylvestris

June–October ○ ☠
H 40–60 in. (100–150 cm)

Decorative summer flower.
Flower: White, tubular, in loose racemes.
Leaf: Large, broad ovate, vivid green.
Growth: Erect, in clumps.
Origin: South America.
Site: Sun, warm. Soil well-drained, loose, nutrient-rich.
Care: Water in dry spells.
Propagation: Sow indoors in March, plant out in late May.
Use: In borders.
Good Partners: *Cosmos, Verbena bonariensis*—*Aster novae-angliae, Delphinium.*
Cultivars/Relatives:
• *Nicotiana* x *sanderae*, only 12–20 in. (30–50 cm), with a broader range of colors:
• 'Nicki Lime', light yellow.
• 'Nicki Rose', crimson-pink.
Warning: All parts of these plants are poisonous.

Beard Tongue, Penstemon
Penstemon Hybrids

Hybrid from the Earlibird Series

June–October ○
H 20–36 in. (50–90 cm)

Perennial in mild regions.
Flower: White, rose, crimson, scarlet, and lilac bell-shaped flowers, often with light throats.
Leaf: Oblong to narrow ovate, rich green, shiny.
Growth: Erect, in clumps. Sometimes needs staking.
Origin: Southern United States, Mexico.
Site: Sun, warm. Soil well-drained, nutrient-rich.
Care: Water in dry spells. Stake tall cultivars for support.
Propagation: Sow indoors in February and plant in late May. Alternatively, by cuttings taken in fall. Overwinter young plants indoors in a bright, cool spot.
Use: In borders.
Good Partners: *Chrysanthemum frutescens, Salvia uliginosa*—*Aster novi-belgii, Chrysanthemum maximum, Veronica longifolia.*
Cultivars/Relatives:
• 'Scharlachkönigin', scarlet with white-spotted throat.
• 'Southgate Gem', red, 20 in. (50 cm).
• *Penstemon barbatus* hybrids very similar, somewhat inferior with narrower leaves:
• 'Alba', white, 16 in. (40 cm).
• 'Evelyn', delicate pink, 16 in. (40 cm).

Black-eyed Susan
Rudbeckia hirta

Scarlet Sage
Salvia coccinea

Mealycup Sage, Mealy Sage
Salvia farinacea

Cultivar 'Marmalade'

Cultivar 'Lady in Red'

Cultivar 'Victoria'

July–September ○ ✂
H 16–32 in. (40–80 cm)

Can withstand very mild winters in this country.
Flower: Yellow, tongue-shaped flowers surrounding a dark brown center, large, single heads at the ends of erect stalks.
Leaf: Lanceolate to narrow ovate, margins saw-toothed, matte green, and—like the stems—covered with coarse hair.
Growth: Erect, in clumps.
Origin: North America.
Site: Sun, warm. Soil moderately dry to moist and nutrient-rich.
Care: Good nutrient supply. Keep cutting off spent heads.
Propagation: Sow indoors from March to April, plant out in May.
Use: In borders, combines well with perennials.
Good Partners: *Ageratum, Cosmos bipinnatus* 'Unschuld', *Heliotropium, Salvia farinacea, Salvia uliginosa—Delphinium, Helenium—Calamagrostis.*
Cultivars/Relatives:
• 'Meine Freude', golden yellow, 32 in. (80 cm). Reliable standard cultivar.
• 'Goldilocks', golden yellow, semidouble, 24 in. (60 cm).
• 'Marmalade', bright orange-yellow, 24 in. (60 cm).

June–September ○
H 16–24 in. (40–60 cm)

Long-blooming annual with brilliant red blossoms.
Flower: Scarlet labiate flowers in a loose spike.
Leaf: Ovate, scalloped margin. Dark green and slightly shiny.
Growth: Erect, bushy.
Origin: Southern United States to South America.
Site: Sun, warm. Soil well-drained, permeable, and nutritious.
Care: Good nutrient and water supply.
Propagation: Sow indoors from late March to April, plant in bed in late May.
Use: In small groups in borders.
Good Partners: *Chrysanthemum frutescens, Cosmos sulphureus, Heliotropium, Salvia farinacea—Delphinium, Rudbeckia—Miscanthus.*
Cultivars/Relatives:
• 'Lady in Red', scarlet, early blooming, 20 in. (50 cm).
• *Salvia involucrata,* purple sage. Crimson, bushy, July–September, 32–44 in. (80–110 cm).
• *Salvia splendens,* scarlet sage. Brilliant scarlet, compact inflorescences that are hard to combine with other flowers, June–September, 8–20 in. (20–50 cm).

June–October ○
H 20–32 in. (50–80 cm)

Undemanding and extremely long-blooming summer flower.
Flower: Dark blue labiate flowers in dense spikes at the ends of the stems.
Leaf: Lanceolate, grass-green.
Growth: Erect, profusely branching clumps. Stems downy grayish white, hence "mealycup" sage.
Origin: Texas and New Mexico.
Site: Sunny. Soil fresh, loose, nutrient-rich.
Care: Good nutrient and water supply. It is worthwhile to over-winter attractive plants in a bright, cool place; they will start to bloom in May.
Propagation: Sow indoors in March to April, plant out in bed in May.
Use: Very versatile. In annual flower beds and as continually blooming filler plant in perennial borders. Also in plantings with roses.
Good Partners: Almost all annuals. Many bedding perennials, including *Helenium, Heliopsis, Rudbeckia—Roses.*
Cultivars/Relatives:
• 'Unschuld', silvery white.
• 'Victoria', dark blue, free-flowering.

Gentian Salvia, Blue Sage
Salvia patens

Salvia patens

July–September	○
H 24–32 in. (60–80 cm)	

A striking species of sage with gentian-blue flowers, though not particularly free-flowering.
Flower: Brilliant gentian-blue labiate flowers in loose, terminal spikes.
Leaf: Ovate, scalloped margins. Deep green, hairy.
Growth: In clumps, erect.
Origin: Mexico.
Site: Sun, warm. Soil well-drained to moderately dry, permeable, loose, and nutrient-rich.
Care: Good nutrient supply; water during prolonged dry spells.
Propagation: Sow indoors in late January to February, plant out in bed in May.
Use: Versatile when combined in borders with other annuals, perennials, and roses.
Good Partners: *Cosmos sulphureus, Sanvitalia procumbens, Tagetes, Tithonia—Helenium, Heliopsis, Rudbeckia*—also roses.

Swamp Sage
Salvia uliginosa

Salvia uliginosa

August–October	○ ◐
H 48–64 in. (120–160 cm)	

Little known, but very pretty summer flower. Perennial in milder regions.
Flower: Light-blue labiate flowers with white eye in terminal spikes.
Leaf: Oblong, margins deeply serrate, or saw-toothed, dark green.
Growth: Erect, tall clumps.
Origin: South America.
Site: Sun to partial shade. Soil well-drained to moist, nutrient-rich, loamy. Avoid soils that dry out easily!
Care: Good water and nutrient supply. Can be overwintered in a bright, cool place indoors.
Propagation: Take cuttings from September to October, overwinter in boxes in a bright, cool spot, and plant out from May on.
Use: In borders with perennials and annuals.
Good Partners:
Chrysanthemum parthenium, Impatiens, Penstemon, Rudbeckia—Chrysanthemum maximum, Phlox—Miscanthus.

Joseph Sage
Salvia viridis

'Pink Sundae'

July–August	○ ✂
H 16–28 in. (40–70 cm)	

Large, striking bracts adorn this sage species, which blooms for only a few weeks. Very good cutting flower.
Flower: Unpretentious, with showy violet-blue, crimson, pink, or creamy white bracts in terminal spikes.
Leaf: Ovate, vivid green.
Growth: Erect, bushy.
Origin: Southern Europe to western Asia.
Site: Sun. Soil well-drained to moderately dry, loose, and nutrient-rich.
Care: Water moderately. Deadhead spent flowers to prolong blooming season.
Propagation: Sow indoors in March, plant out after late May.
Use: Group plant in borders.
Good Partners: *Cleome, Cosmos bipinnatus, Salvia farinacea.*
Cultivars/Relatives:
• 'White Swan', creamy white usually, however, some plants with pink or violet bracts; 16–24 in. (40–60 cm).
• 'Pink Sundae', old-rose, 20–24 in. (50–60 cm).
• 'Oxford Blue', violet-blue, 24–28 in. (60–70 cm).

Marigolds
Tagetes

Tagetes erecta hybrid

June–October
H 6–8 in. (15–20 cm)

Marigolds owe their popularity to their immense quantities of blossoms, hardiness, and great vigor. The variety of their forms is almost unparalleled among the annual flowers. Newer cultivars lack the typical marigold scent.

Flower: Lemon-colored, golden yellow, orange, red-brown, or russet heads, often bicolored ones as well. Single, semidouble, or heavily doubled to ball-shaped.

Leaf: Pinnate with scalloped margin. Dark green, slightly shiny. Except for newer cultivars, highly pungent.

Growth: Depending on cultivar, low or tall, generally broad clumps.

Origin: Mexico and Central America.

Site: Sun. Soil moist to moderately dry, moderately nutrient-rich. Almost all garden soils are suitable, unless they have an extremely high clay content.

Patula hybrid 'Bolero'

Care: Moderate nutrient supply; water during extended dry spells. Protect marigolds from slugs, which consider the flowers a delicacy.

Propagation: Sow indoors from late March to April, plant out in bed from May on. Alternative: Sow directly in May. The plants will bloom much later, however.

Use: In groups or small areas in borders.
• Because of their gaudy colors, don't plant lemon-yellow and orange cultivars in large masses.
• Cultivars with ball-shaped flowers should be used with restraint; when planted in masses they look awkward.

Good Partners: *Calendula, Cosmos sulphureus, Heliotropium, Salvia farinacea, Tithonia—Helenium, Rudbeckia, Solidago.*

Cultivars/Relatives:
• *Tagetes erecta* hybrids (African or Aztec marigolds) reach a height of 12 to 48 in. (30–120 cm). They have large, mostly double, chrysanthemum- or carnation-shaped flowers. The plants are better for cutting than for bedding. The cultivars with flowers resembling chrysanthemums have globe-shaped blossoms made up of long, curved, tongue-like blooms. With the carnation-like flower forms, the outer tongue-shaped blooms are broader and often have wavy edges. The available assortment is quite large, and the color spectrum ranges from light yellow to deep orange.

Tagetes tenuifolia 'Gnom'

• *Tagetes patula* hybrids (French marigolds) grow 8 to 20 in. (20–50 cm) tall. These are the most common marigolds in our gardens. The tremendous assortment includes single, semidouble, and double cultivars. Along with yellow and orange forms, red-brown, russet, and bicolored cultivars enrich the selection of garden marigolds on the market.
• *Tagetes tenuifolia* (dwarf or striped marigold) and its cultivars, 8 to 12 in. (20–30 cm) tall, are quite delicate. With their relatively small, single, unassuming flowers, they are the easiest to combine with other plants. Their fine, fern-like foliage is also highly decorative. A few cultivars include:
• 'Lulu', lemon yellow.
• 'Carina', yellow-orange.
• 'Ursula', golden yellow with red-brown center.
• 'Ornament', intense red-brown.

Black-eyed Susan Vine, Clockvine
Thunbergia alata

Cultivar of *Thunbergia alata*

July–October
H 56–72 in. (140–180 cm)

Warmth-loving climbing plant.
Flower: Orange-yellow, plate-shaped with black center, lightly scented.
Leaf: Cordate with saw-toothed margin, vivid green.
Growth: Twining climber.
Origin: South Africa.
Site: Sun, warm, sheltered from wind as much as possible. Soil well-drained to moderately dry, permeable, nutrient-rich and lime-rich.
Care: Good nutrient supply. Put up a trellis, wires, or stakes as a climbing frame.
Propagation: Sow indoors in March, plant out in late May.
Use: On lattice-like climbing frames or cords in front of south walls, on climbing pyramids in beds.
Good Partners: *Heliotropium, Salvia patens, Sanvitalia procumbens, Tagetes.*
Cultivars/Relatives:
• 'Susi Weiss mit Auge', white.
• 'Susi Gelb mit Auge', yellow.
• 'Susi Orange mit Auge', deep orange-yellow.
All the cultivars listed have a dark spot in the center of the flower.

Mexican Sunflower, Tithonia
Tithonia rotundifolia

Tithonia rotundifolia 'Fackel'

August–September
H 48–72 in. (120–180 cm)

Annual flower that grows very tall and also is good in perennial plantings. Something special!
Flower: Orange, daisy-like flowers with yellow-orange centers at the ends of firm stalks.
Leaf: Large and cordate. Matte green, rough.
Growth: Forms erect, tall, bushy clumps.
Origin: Mexico.
Site: Sun. Soil well-drained, nutrient-rich, not too sandy.
Care: Good water and nutrient supply. Trimming plants while young encourages branching. Deadhead faded flowers regularly. In general, simple to cultivate, healthy, and easy to tend.
Propagation: Sow indoors in late March, plant out in bed in late May.
Use: As dominant plant in small groups with low annuals, also in perennial borders.
Good Partners: *Calendula, Heliotropium, Salvia patens, Tagetes, Verbena bonariensis—Delphinium, Helenium, Rudbeckia.*
Cultivars/Relatives:
• 'Fackel', bright orange-red, the best cultivar.

Nasturtium
Tropaeolum Hybrids

Tropaeolum hybrid

July–October
H 12–120 in. (30–300 cm)

Large-leaved annuals with brilliant flowers.
Flower: Yellow, orange, brick red, scarlet, also semidouble or double, shaped like large funnel.
Leaf: Large, round, often lobed. Vivid green to grass-green with lighter undersides, tart fragrance.
Growth: Depending on cultivar, in clumps, creeping, or climbing.
Origin: Cultivated form.
Site: Sun to partial shade, warm. Soil moderately dry to moist, permeable; humus-rich, with moderate nutrient content.
Care: If fed too well, too many leaves develop. Needs very little care, because the large leaves keep out weeds successfully.
Propagation: Sow directly in early May. Alternative: Sow indoors and plant in late May.
Use: Twining cultivars cover walls decoratively or grow on climbing frames and serve as partitions. Use creeping types as ground covers for large areas, and bushy types in beds of annual flowers.
Good Partners: *Calendula, Cosmos sulphureus, Heliotropium, Salvia farinacea, Tagetes.*

Veit Verbena
Verbena bonariensis

Verbena bonariensis

July–October ◯ ✂
H 36–48 in. (90–120 cm)

These slightly sprawling plants, if planted in loose groups, lay a delicate veil over entire beds.
Flower: Lilac-colored, in dense, umbrella-shaped umbels.
Leaf: Oblong, with notched margins. Rich dark green, slightly shiny.
Growth: Erect, with sprawling branches.
Origin: South America.
Site: Sun, warm. Soil well-drained to moderately dry, nutrient-rich. No wet sites or compacted soils!
Care: None.
Propagation: Sow indoors in February. Because the seeds germinate very unevenly, it is advisable to chill the seed. Several days after sowing, chill at 39–46°F (4–8°C) for one week. Set the young plants in the bed in late May.
Use: In groups in borders with annuals and perennials.
Good Partners: *Calendula, Cosmos, Lavatera, Tagetes, Tithonia—Aster dumosus, Helenium, Rudbeckia, Solidago.*

Verbena, Vervain
Verbena Hybrids

Hybrid *'Novalis Blau mit Auge'*

June–September ◯
H 8–12 in. (20–30 cm)

Richly colored group plants with many cultivars.
Flower: Almost all shades except yellow, orange, and pure blue, often with white eye, free-flowering.
Leaf: Oblong, markedly scalloped, matte green.
Growth: Low; in silhouette almost hemispherical.
Site: Sun, warm. Soil well-drained to moderately dry, permeable, nutrient-rich. No wet sites or heavy soils!
Care: Good inorganic nutrient supply. Water in dry spells.
Propagation: Sow in February, treat as cold-temperature germinator to improve germination rate.
Use: In groups in borders.
Good Partners: *Chrysanthemum frutescens, Cleome, Cosmos bipinnatus, Echinacea.*
Cultivars/Relatives: Several good hybrid groups, including Amore, Novalis, Sandy. The cultivar names contain the flower color.
• 'Amore Violett', violet.
• 'Novalis Leuchtscharlach', bright scarlet.
• Cultivars of the Compacta series grow more compact, 8 in. (20 cm).
• 'Kristall', pure white.
• 'Delight', pink.

Tuber Verbena
Verbena rigida

Cultivar 'Polaris'

June–September ◯
H 8–16 in. (20–40 cm)

Rewarding and weather-resistant group plant. Perennial in mild climate with light winter protection.
Flower: Small, lilac-colored single flowers in terminal clusters.
Leaf: Oblong to narrow ovate, margins irregularly scalloped. Dark green with wrinkly surface.
Growth: Bushy clumps with sprawling branches.
Origin: South America.
Site: Sun to light shade, loves warmth. Soil moderately dry to well-drained, permeable, and nutrient-rich.
Care: Feed moderately with inorganic fertilizer. Trimming while young stimulates branching.
Propagation: Sow indoors in February, plant in bed in late May.
Use: In small groups in borders with annuals and perennials.
Good Partners: *Cleome, Cosmos bipinnatus, Heliotropium, Verbena bonariensis—Echinacea, Liatris.*

Pansy, Heart's-ease
Viola wittrockiana Hybrids

Zinnia
Zinnia elegans

Garden pansies

Zinnias are rewarding cutting flowers.

Semidouble red cultivar

| March–May | ○ |
| H 6–10 in. (15–25 cm) | |

Robust, cheerful spring bloomers.
Flower: In almost all imaginable flower colors. One-colored cultivars as well as others with dark eye.
Leaf: Ovate, scalloped margin, grass-green.
Growth: Low, spreading.
Origin: Cultivated form.
Site: Sun to light shade. Soil well-drained to moist, loose, nutrient- and humus-rich.
Care: After planting in fall, cover with evergreen boughs to overwinter. Good nutrient supply.
Propagation: Sow indoors in July and set in permanent site in early fall. Alternative: Overwinter young plants in a box in a bright, cool spot and plant them out in early spring.
Use: Always in groups or in flat areas. For decorative beds, also on graves.
Good Partners: *Bellis, Cheiranthus cheiri, Myosotis*—narcissuses and tulips.
Cultivars/Relatives: Because there is an abundance of cultivars, with new ones added annually, you should base your choice on color.

| July–October | ○ ✂ |
| H 12–40 in. (30–100 cm) | |

These warmth-loving garden plants come in many forms and colors.
Flower: Depending on cultivar, pink, scarlet, crimson, orange, yellow, white. Single, semidouble, or double.
Leaf: Grass green, ovate, pointed.
Growth: Upright, in clumps.
Origin: Mexico.
Site: Sun, warm. Soil well-drained to moist, vigorous, and nutrient-rich.
Care: Good water and nutrient supply.
Propagation: Sow indoors in April and plant in bed in late May.
Use: In groups in borders. Coordinate the colors with those of the neighboring plants.
Good Partners: *Ageratum, Chrysanthemum frutescens, Cosmos bipinnatus* 'Unschuld', *Salvia farinacea, Verbena bonariensis.*
Cultivars/Relatives:
• Low cultivars for beds and pots: Cultivars in all zinnia colors, usually double, 12 in. (30 cm). Many hybrid groups, including the Countdown, Dasher, Dreamland, and Peter Pan series. The cultivars embrace the entire color range of zinnias, and the flower color is part of the cultivar name.
• Medium-tall cultivars for bedding and cutting: In a variety of colors, 16–20 in. (40–50 cm). These include the Ruffles hybrids.
• Tall cultivars for bedding and cutting: Dahlia-flowered and chrysanthemum-flowered forms in many colors. Slightly stiff growth, over 24 in. (60 cm). Excellent as cut flowers.
• *Zinnia angustifolia*, yellow-orange to orange-brown, single or double flowers with narrower leaves. A pretty cultivar: 'Classic', orange-yellow, single-flowered.

95

Fernleaf Yarrow
Achillea filipendulina

Cultivar 'Parker'

July–September ○ ✂
H 28–52 in. (70–130 cm)

Well-known, common garden plant.
Flower: Warm yellow. Umbrella-shaped umbels with long blooming season.
Leaf: Pinnate, gray-green, pungent.
Growth: In clumps, takes up increasingly more room because of short runners. Sometimes weak-stemmed.
Origin: Caucasus and Asia Minor. Mountain meadows.
Site: Sun, warm, heat-tolerant. Soil moderately dry to well-drained, permeable, nutrient-rich.
Care: Cut back to ground in late winter. Feed occasionally. Cut off faded flowers about 8 in. (20 cm) below the umbels to sustain the bloom. Stake if necessary.
Propagation: By division, by small plant segments, or by tip cuttings in May.
Use: In sunny borders, in steppe gardens.
Good Partners: *Anthemis, Echinops, Salvia nemorosa*—various grasses.
Cultivars/Relatives:
• 'Parker', golden yellow, shallow umbels, 52 in. (130 cm).
• 'Coronation Gold', bright golden yellow, compact, 28 in. (70 cm).

Yarrow, Milfoil
Achillea millefolium Hybrids

Hybrid 'Paprika'

June–August ○ ✂
H 12–32 in. (30–80 cm)

Hybrid forms into which native common yarrow was bred.
Flower: Pink to crimson or yellowish; depending on cultivar, often with white center; in umbrella-shaped umbels.
Leaf: Finely pinnate, gray-green.
Growth: In clumps, spreads by means of short runners.
Origin: Cultivated form.
Site: Full sun, warm. Soil moderately dry to well-drained, for all garden soils.
Care: Feed regularly, cut back in fall. Remove seedlings, as they yield pale flower colors.
Propagation: By division, by small plant segments, and by tip cuttings taken in May.
Use: In sunny beds, with blue, pink, or white partners. Avoid warm yellow, orange, and red tones close by, unless the cultivars themselves are yellow, coppery red, or brick-red.
Good Partners: *Artemisia, Campanula carpatica, Centranthus ruber, Salvia nemorosa.*
Cultivars/Relatives:
• 'Schwefelblute', sulfur-yellow, foliage gray, 24 in. (60 cm).
• 'Orangekönigin', coppery orange, 28 in. (70 cm).
• 'Sammetriese', velvety red, late blooming, 32 in. (80 cm).
• 'Kelway', bright crimson with white center, 24 in. (60 cm).

Sneezewort
Achillea ptarmica

Cultivar 'Schneeball'

June–August ○ ◐ ✂
H 24–36 in. (60–90 cm)

The lovely heads of sneezewort are excellent in bouquets.
Flower: Dazzling white tongue-shaped flowers and brownish-white tubular flowers. Heads in loose umbelliferous inflorescences.
Leaf: Narrow lanceolate, with fine-toothed margin, dull green.
Growth: Irregularly broad and bushy, produces runners.
Origin: Europe to western Asia. Wet meadows and riverbank bushes.
Site: Sun to light shade, air humid. Soil well-drained to moist, vigorous; loamy soils are best, also clay- or humus-rich soils.
Care: Feed regularly in spring. If growth is too rampant, cut away the edges of the clump with your spade.
Propagation: By division, rhizome cuttings, and tip cuttings. The species, also by seed.
Use: At edge of ponds.
Good Partners: *Alchemilla, Hemerocallis, Lythrum.*
Cultivars/Relatives:
• 'Schneeball', double, pure white, globe-shaped.
• 'Nana Compacta', white, semidouble, slow-growing, not rampant.

Azure Monkshood
Aconitum carmichaelii

Aconitum carmichaelii 'Arendsii'

English Monkshood, Aconite
Aconitum napellus

Aconitum x *cammarum* 'Bicolor'

Aconitum napellus 'Album'

September–October ◑ ✂ ☠
H 40–56 in. (100–140 cm)

The monkshood species, with their intensely blue flowers, are important garden plants. Because of the strong toxin, yellow-flowered wolfsbane *(Aconitum vulparia)* at one time was used in Germany to poison wolves.
Flower: Medium blue with faint pink shimmer. Large single flowers in elongated, loose panicles. First frosts do not harm the flowers.
Leaf: Deeply cut into five lobes, glossy, rich green.
Growth: In clumps.
Origin: Cultivated form.
Site: Out of sun to partial shade, with good water supply also sun, cool. Soil always sufficiently well-drained and nutrient-rich. No hot sites!
Care: Good nutrient supply from organic or inorganic fertilizers. Water adequately in dry spells. Cut back completely after bloom finishes.
Propagation: By division in late fall or early spring. Use gloves because the roots contain the toxin aconite in a strong concentration. The seeds of this species can be sown in fall; chill the seeds for a few weeks (cold-temperature germinator).

Use: As a blue fall-flowering plant in light shade and shifting sunlight, an extremely valuable treasure in your garden. In well-drained, largely sunny borders, these are also a pleasure as the gardening year draws to a close.
Good Partners: *Anemone japonica* hybrids, *Cimicifuga*—ferns—woody plants with fall color. In beds, *Aster ericoides*, *Aster novae-angliae*, *Aster novi-belgii*.
Cultivars/Relatives:
• *Aconitum carmichaelii* var. *wilsonii*, from central China, also very pretty, with loose panicles, 48–72 in. (120–180 cm).
• *Aconitum* x *cammarum* 'Bicolor', with white-and-blue flowers, July–August, 48 in. (120 cm).
Warning: Even small amounts of the toxin aconite, present in all this plant's parts, are fatal.

June–July ◑ ✂ ☠
H 36–60 in. (90–150 cm)

Popular country garden plant.
Flower: Dark blue, helmet-shaped flowers in dense panicles.
Leaf: Palmately divided, almost black-green.
Growth: Upright clumps, occasionally floppy.
Origin: Western to central Europe. In damp bushes and forests.
Site: Light shade to shade; with good water supply, also may be in sun, cool, air humid. Soil well-drained to moist, nutrient-rich and humus-rich, loamy soils are best. No sandy or gravelly soils!
Care: Good nutrient supply. Water in dry spells, to prevent infestation with aphids.
Propagation: As for azure monkshood.
Use: In light shade of trees and shrubs, in beds out of sun, with sufficiently well-drained soils also in sunny beds.
Good Partners: *Aruncus, Astilbe, Hemerocallis, Ligularia, Lysimachia.*
Cultivars/Relatives:
• 'Album', white flowers.

Stonecress
Aethionema Hybrid 'Warley Rose'

Agapanthus, African Lily
Agapanthus 'Headbourne' Hybrids

Bugleweed, Carpet Bugle
Ajuga reptans

Hybrid *'Warley Rose'*

Agapanthus 'Headbourne Hybrid'

Ajuga reptans

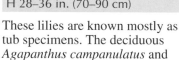

July–August ○ ✂
H 28–36 in. (70–90 cm)

May–June ○
H 6–8 in. (15–20 cm)

April–May ◐
H 6–8 in. (15–20 cm)

Little-known, but beautifully flowering rock garden plant, able to compete with moss phlox and candytuft.
Flower: Bright pink, flowers profuse, bloom long-lasting.
Leaf: Needle-shaped, blue-green.
Growth: Cushion-shaped sub-shrub.
Origin: The species comes from the Anatolian highlands.
Site: Full sun, warm. Soil permeable, sandy or gravelly.
Care: Remove heads after bloom finishes. Light winter protection is advisable: cover with evergreen boughs.
Propagation: By cuttings after the blooming season.
Use: On dry walls and in rock gardens.
Good Partners: *Cerastium, Dianthus gratianopolitanus, Iberis saxatilis,* blue and violet *Iris barbata-nana* hybrids, *Phlox subulata* hybrids—*Festuca ovina.*
Cultivars/Relatives:
• *Aethionema grandiflora,* masses of light-pink blooms, 12 in. (30 cm) tall. Self-sowing in congenial places without becoming troublesome, propagation by seeds.

These lilies are known mostly as tub specimens. The deciduous *Agapanthus campanulatus* and 'Headbourne' hybrids, however, are also perennial outdoors with light protection from winter wet and from heavy frosts. With its blue heads, a major vehicle for midsummer color.
Flower: Medium blue, almost hemispherical umbels with blooms lasting for weeks.
Leaf: Broad linear, dark green.
Growth: In clumps, with crown of leaves near ground and upright peduncles.
Origin: Cultivated form.
Site: Full sun, warm. Soil deep, permeable, but nutrient-rich, sufficiently moist in spring and summer. Absolutely no places that are wet in winter!
Care: Plant only in spring. During vegetative period, feed and water abundantly. Deadhead faded flowers. Use dry leaves and evergreen boughs as winter protection.
Propagation: By seeds or by division of older plants in spring.
Use: In sunny beds, good in front of a warm south wall.
Good Partners: *Kniphofia, Crocosmia* x *cocosmiiflora.* Also in the vicinity of roses.
Cultivars/Relatives:
• 'Albus', white-flowered.

Wild perennial in common use; native to Germany.
Flower: Steel blue, in dense candle shapes.
Leaf: Spatulate, slightly brownish green, evergreen.
Growth: Quickly grows by layering to form an expansive mat.
Origin: Europe, Asia Minor to Iran. In meadows and thin woods.
Site: Light shade to partial shade, with enough moisture, also sun; cool. Soil well-drained to moist, nutrient-rich, loamy.
Care: Short-lived if not fed regularly in spring. Water in dry spells. Cut back near slow-growing partners to keep them from being overgrown by bugleweed.
Propagation: By detaching layers.
Use: In small patches in shifting light of trees, not close to root area! In shade of walls, on pond banks.
Good Partners: *Alchemilla, Epimedium, Waldsteinia.*
Cultivars/Relatives:
• 'Atropurpurea', with red-brown foliage, for light shade.

Lady's-mantle
Alchemilla mollis

Alchemilla mollis can be combined with great versatility.

June–August   ○ ◑ ✄
H 12–20 in. (30–50 cm)

Few garden plants are as versatile and easy to use as the extremely attractive lady's-mantle, although this perennial's true value long went unrecognized. Only in the past few years has it finally found its way into our gardens.
Flower: Greenish yellow, with a honey-like scent. Many tiny single flowers in loose cymes, which form delicate veils over the decorative clumps of leaves.
Leaf: In silhouette, round, folded like a fan, and with sinuous margins, very decorative. Dull green with a tinge of olive-brown; early flush. If atmospheric humidity is high, drops of excreted water are found on the leaf margins.
Growth: Hemispherical, compact clumps.
Origin: Carpathians to Caucasus. In well-drained meadows.
Site: Full sun to partial shade; with sufficient moisture, also hot places, otherwise predominantly cool ones. Soil well-drained and nutrient-rich. Loamy soils are best; soils with high clay content are also possible. No nutrient-poor sandy soils! Susceptible to black sooty mold from trees:

Don't plant under oaks and lindens!
Care: Lady's-mantle is easy to tend, as the ground becomes completely covered by its leaf material, and virtually no weeds appear. Remove the old, dead leaves before the flush in March. Good organic or inorganic nutrient supply. Water in dry spells. Cut back or mow down after bloom finishes.
Propagation: By division at any time of year or by cutting away small pieces with spade. Also possible by seed.
Use: Highly versatile. In well-drained beds, at edge of pond, in light shade of woody plants, and even in the shade of a wall or in crevices in paving stones. The greenish yellow flowers harmonize with almost all other flower colors.
Good Partners: *Campanula, Chrysanthemum maximum, Delphinium, Geranium* x *magnificum, Hemerocallis, Paeonia, Polemonium, Solidago,* and many others.

Goldentuft, Rock Alyssum, Basket-of-gold
Alyssum saxatile

Alyssum saxatile

April–May   ○
H 10–16 in. (25–40 cm)

Favorite rock garden plant.
Flower: Rich yellow with pleasant honey-like scent.
Leaf: Spatulate, dull green or gray-green.
Growth: Cushion-shaped subshrub, tends to flop over when old.
Origin: Central Europe to Asia Minor. In cracks in rocks and on stony subsoil.
Site: Full sun, warm, also hot and dry. Soil moderately dry to well-drained, highly permeable.
Care: Among the long-lived and easy-upkeep rock garden plants. Light pruning after the blooming season keeps the plants compact; no other procedures necessary. Cut older, mature plants back hard, to about 2 to 4 in. (5–10 cm).
Propagation: By seeds or by cuttings in summer. Transplanting and division of older plants is difficult.
Use: In rock gardens, on edges, and in crevices of dry walls. In the front of borders with full sun.
Good Partners: *Aubrieta, Iberis*—tulips.
Cultivars/Relatives:
• 'Compactus', compact growth, 8–12 in. (20–30 cm).

Pearly Everlasting
Anaphalis triplinervis

Japanese Anemone
Anemone japonica Hybrids

Anaphalis triplinervis

Japanese anemones produce fruits with soft white hair—here, *'Ouvertüre'*

July–September　　　　　○
H 8–20 in. (20–50 cm)

August–October　　　
H 24–56 in. (60–140 cm)

Easy-to-keep perennial with few soil requirements; makes a good dried flower.
Flower: Silvery white, pearl-like rounded, clusters of flowers in an umbelliferous raceme at the ends of erect shoots.
Leaf: Lanceolate, three-nerved, gray, and woolly.
Growth: Erect shoots with many leaves, clumps about as wide as they are tall.
Origin: Himalayas. In stony mountain meadows.
Site: Full sun, warm to hot. Soil moderately dry to well-drained, permeable.
Care: Cut back to ground in fall.
Propagation: By division, except during blooming season.
Use: In small areas in dry beds and in rock gardens.
Good Partners: *Aster amellus, Campanula glomerata, Nepeta,* and other drought-tolerant perennials.
Cultivars/Relatives:
• *Anaphalis margaritacea,* from North America and northeastern Asia, produces runners and grows to about 12 to 24 in. (30–60 cm). Occasionally needs support, leaves narrower and upper sides less gray, good in sandy soils.

Of the roughly 60 different anemones, several particularly lovely species have found their way into our gardens.
Flower: Depending on the cultivar, pink or white, single or semidouble large saucer-shaped flowers in loose, free-flowering panicles. Attractive fruits in white, downy bunches, which contrast nicely with the dark-brown fall foliage.
Leaf: Large, tripartite with irregularly saw-toothed to lobed margins, dull green.
Growth: Produces short runners and gradually takes up more and more space. Can reach width of over 40 in. (approximately 1 m).
Origin: Extremely old cultivated plants from eastern Asia.
Site: In shifting sunlight and light shade of woody plants, in cool to moderately warm places. Soil well-drained to moist, rich in nutrients and humus. <u>No soils that dry out easily!</u>
Care: Water amply in dry spells. Good organic fertilization by covering with leaf mold or well-aged manure. During severe frosts cover young plants especially those without protective snow cover. Cut back in early spring. With spade, cut off edges of overly broad plants from time to time.
Propagation: By division and rhizome cuttings.
Use: In light shade of tall trees and in shade of walls. <u>Do not plant in direct vicinity of tree roots!</u>
Good Partners: *Aconitum carmichaelii, Cimicifuga ramosa—Carex morrowii* 'Variegata', ferns.
Cultivars/Relatives:
• 'Wirbelwind', white, semidouble; stake, as it is less sturdy; 32–40 in. (80–100 cm).
• 'Königin Charlotte', delicate pink, semidouble, late blooming, 36 in. (60 cm).
• 'Prinz Heinrich', bright pink, semidouble, 24 in. (60 cm).
• *Anemone hupehensis* 'Septembercharme', delicate pink, single-flowered, 32 in. (80 cm).
• 'Praecox', bright pink, single flowers, 32 in. (80 cm).
• *Anemone tomentosa* 'Robustissima', light pink, single-flowered, very early blooming, extremely robust and strong-stemmed, 40 in. (100 cm).

Golden Marguerite
Anthemis tinctoria

Cultivar 'Wargrave'

June–September ○
H 16–40 in. (40–100 cm)

The plant's Latin or scientific name (translated as dyer's chamomile) is derived from the use of the yellow coloring matter in its flowers as a dye for wool.
Flower: Golden yellow daisy-like flowers in masses.
Leaf: Pinnate, upper side dull green and underside gray-green, aromatic.
Growth: In clumps, loosely hemispherical, usually not strong-stemmed.
Origin: Europe to western Asia. In dry, permeable sandy soils, on ledges of rock, and in dry grass.
Site: Full sun, warm. Soil dry to moderately dry, highly permeable. No heavy soils!
Care: Cut back hard after bloom, to prolong the plants' life span. Even so, you need to replace the plants every three or four years.
Propagation: By cuttings in summer. Reproduces by self-sowing without coaxing.
Use: In front of south walls, on dry slopes, on crests of walls, and in roof gardens.
Good Partners: *Calamintha, Nepeta, Salvia nemorosa, Stachys byzantina.*
Cultivars/Relatives:
• 'Wargrave', creamy yellow, large-flowered, 40 in. (100 cm).
• 'Beauty of Grallagh', yolk-yellow, 24–32 in. (60–80 cm).
• 'Grallagh Gold', yellow-orange, 28 in. (70 cm).

Columbine
Aquilegia Hybrids

'Crimson Star'

'Blue Star'

May–June ◑ ✂ ☠
H 16–28 in. (40–70 cm)

Usually short-lived perennials with pretty flower form.
Flower: In many different colors, often bicolored, occasionally also double. Nodding, spurred, bell-shaped flowers, in threes.
Leaf: Leaflet compound, bluish green, yellowing soon after blooming season.
Growth: Upright, in loose clumps, sometimes floppy.
Site: Light shade to part shade, cool to warm. Soil well-drained and humous-rich. No hot sites!
Care: Water in dry spells. Leave some self-sown seedlings, to avoid having to replace columbines after a few years.
Propagation: By seeds. Reproduces by self-sowing without coaxing.
Use: In borders with partial shade, in light shade of walls and woody plants. Always plant in

Aquilegia vulgaris

smallish groups, so that the gaps left after columbines finish blooming are concealed by other plants.
Good Partners: *Anemone, Astilbe, Brunnera, Geum* hybrids, *Hosta*—ferns.
Cultivars/Relatives:
• 'Nivea', with pure-white flowers.
• 'Olympica', blue-and-white flowers.
• 'Biedermeier', blue, double.
• *Aquilegia vulgaris,* common columbine, with blue, but also pink or white flowers. Readily self-sowing.
• *Aquilegia caerulea* hybrids, 16–24 in. (40–60 cm) tall, 'Kristall', pure white. Also the following:
• 'Blue Star', light blue-and-white.
• 'Crimson Star', red-and-white.
• 'Olympia Rot-Gold', red-and-yellow.
• *Aquilegia chrysantha,* bright yellow, 28 in. (70 cm).
Warning: Columbine contains toxic compounds.

Wall Rockcress, Wallcress
Arabis caucasica

Cultivar 'Schneeball'

April–May ○ ✂
H 6–12 in. (15–30 cm)

One of the most rewarding and easiest to keep perennials for rock gardens.
Flower: Small, white blooms in free-flowering racemes.
Leaf: Spatulate, gray-green, in rosettes.
Growth: Creeps slowly by means of runners, mat-forming.
Origin: Mediterranean region to Caucasus. On sunny rocky slopes.
Site: Full sun, warm. Soil moderately dry to well-drained, permeable. No heavy soils, or it will rot.
Care: Remove faded flowers. Cut back if growth is too vigorous. No other care needed.
Propagation: Easily possible by detaching individual leaf rosettes. Also by cuttings.
Use: In rock gardens and on fringes of sunny beds. Pretty in free spaces in flagged walks.
Good Partners: *Alyssum, Aubrieta, Iris barbata* hybrids.
Cultivars/Relatives:
• 'Schneehaube', compact-growing, only 6 in. (15 cm) tall.
• 'Plena', double flowers.
• *Arabis procurrens* forms evergreen carpets.

Thrift, Armeria, Sea Pink
Armeria maritima

Cultivar 'Frühlingszauber'

May–June ○
H 8–12 in. (20–30 cm)

Despite the name this is not a "pink."
Flower: Depending on cultivar, crimson, pink, or white.
Leaf: Grass like, dark green.
Growth: Dense, arched cushions of leaves with numerous upright pedicels.
Origin: Europe to Russia. Sandy seacoasts, salt meadows, sparse grassy areas.
Site: Full sun. Soil moderately dry to well-drained, permeable. No heavy soils, or plants will rot.
Care: Cut off flowers when bloom finishes to prevent self-sowing. In winters without snow, cover lightly with boughs. If the cushions start to become bare at the center after a few years, lift the plants and divide them.
Propagation: By division.
Use: In small groups, never two-dimensionally. In rock gardens, in heath areas, in crevices between paving stones, and in stone troughs.
Good Partners: *Campanula carpatica, Cerastium, Thymus.*
Cultivars/Relatives:
• 'Alba', white.
• 'Frühlingszauber', pink.
• 'Düsseldorfer Stolz', crimson.

Goatsbeard
Aruncus dioicus

Aruncus dioicus

June–July ◑
H 60–80 in. (150–200 cm)

An altogether stately and impressive perennial.
Flower: White to cream-yellow. Large, branching panicles with a mass of tiny flowers.
Leaf: Large, pinnate, leaflets pointed and serrated, vivid green. Yellow fall coloration.
Growth: Imposing clumps.
Origin: Moderate latitudes of the northern hemisphere. In forest ravines, near shady springs, and along the course of streams.
Site: Light shade to part shade, also sun if soil is evenly moist and cool; soil well-drained to moist, rich in nutrients and humus, loamy.
Care: Water in dry spells. Cut back in fall. Undemanding and long-lived.
Propagation: By seed. Division of older plants difficult, as rootstock is woody. Self-sowing.
Use: In light shade of woody plants and walls. With sufficient water supply, also in borders.
Good Partners: *Campanula lactiflora, Campanula latifolia. Aconitum napellus, Geranium, Rodgersia.* In sunny, cool borders with *Delphinium elatum* hybrids.

Aster Species and Hybrids ASTER

A potpourri of asters—the violet flowered Italian aster 'Welttriede' and the white-flowered heath aster 'Brimstone'.

Within the enormous aster genus, which includes some 600 species, there are a number of exceptionally pretty garden plants. They are characterized by their star-shaped, often bicolored heads.

Spring-, summer-, and fall-flowering species are available for garden use. Almost all are sun-loving plants. In particular, those that bloom in September and October make the heart of every amateur gardener leap for joy, because they help the garden achieve one last display of splendor as the year ends. It is hard to imagine a decorative garden without the free-flowering and thoroughly attractive asters.

Although the large-flowered late bloomers have long been held in high esteem, the small-flowered "veil" asters (*Aster ericoides* and other species) and the species intended for use with woody plants (*Aster divaricatus*, for example) were not sufficiently appreciated for many years. Even today, these plants still do not hold the position they deserve in our gardens. In the garden, asters can be infested with nematodes and with aster wilt, caused by *Verticillium* fungus. The most seriously endangered are the cultivars of *Aster dumosus* and *Aster novi-belgii*. Old and malnourished plants are especially susceptible. As a preventive measure, feed these asters well. In addition, dig them up every three to five years, divide them into many pieces, and replant them elsewhere. Premature aging can be delayed

by adding a layer of compost about 1 inch (3 cm) deep in early spring.

If you choose the best possible site and the plants still are attacked by wilt, you need to remove those specimens and throw them in the garbage. Under no circumstances should you add them to the compost pile, because the fungus can continue to spread there. Moreover, no asters should be planted in the infested areas for the next few years. That will help prevent a renewed infection.

Alpine Aster, Mountain Daisy
Aster alpinus

Cultivar 'Albus'

May–June ○
H 8–12 in. (20–30 cm)

Short-lived, but free-flowering perennial for rock gardens.
Flower: Violet-yellow, resembles daisy, solitary on erect, leafy stalks.
Leaf: Spatulate, dull green, rough-haired.
Growth: Forms compact cushions of leaves, above which the pedicels rise.
Origin: Mountains of the northern hemisphere. In sunny, rock-covered areas of the alpine stage.
Site: Full sun. Soil well-drained, highly permeable.
Care: Water in dry spells. Cut back flower stalks after bloom. Often very short-lived, so divide after three or four years and replant.
Propagation: By division after the bloom. Also by seed for the species and many common cultivars.
Use: In rock gardens, on wall cornices.
Good Partners: *Dianthus gratianopolitanus, Gypsophila repens, Iberis sempervirens.*
Cultivars/Relatives:
• 'Albus', white-and-yellow.
• 'Happy End', lavender-blue to pink.
• 'Dunkle Schöne', dark violet-and-yellow.

Italian Aster, Italian Starwort
Aster amellus

Cultivar 'Lady Hindlip'

July–September ○ ✂
H 16–24 in. (40–60 cm)

Wild perennial with a great many lovely cultivars.
Flower: Lilac, violet-blue, or pink, with yellow center, daisy-like.
Leaf: Broad lanceolate, dull green, rough-haired.
Growth: Erect clumps.
Origin: Europe to Asia Minor and western Asia. Along dry, sunny edges of woods, in lime-rich ground with sparse grass, and in steppe grass.
Site: Full sun, warm, also hot and dry places. Soil moderately dry to well-drained, permeable, lime-rich.
Care: Plant only in spring; with fall planting, failures are common. Feed moderately. In rich soils they are short-lived and need to be divided after three years. Cut back in fall, right after bloom.
Propagation: By cuttings, by division in spring.
Use: Sunny, predominantly dry borders.
Good Partners: *Achillea filipendulina, Anaphalis—Calamagrostis* x *acutiflora.*
Cultivars/Relatives:
• 'Lady Hindlip', pink.
• 'Dr. Otto Petschek', lavender-blue.
• 'Sonora', bright violet.
• 'Veilchenkönigin', dark violet, late blooming.
• *Aster pyrenaeus* 'Lutetia', lavender-pink, 20 in. (50 cm).
• *Aster* x *frikartii* 'Wunder von Stäfa', delicate blue with yellow center, bloom lasts for weeks, 24–32 in. (60–80 cm).

Bushy Aster, Cushion Aster
Aster dumosus Hybrids

Hybrid 'Prof. Anton Kippenberg'

Hybrid 'Silberteppich'

September–October ○
H 6–20 in. (15–50 cm)

Perennials that look good all year long.
Flower: Violet to lilac, pink, crimson, white, yellow center.
Leaf: Lanceolate, dark green.
Growth: Creeping, mat-forming.
Origin: Cultivated form.
Site: Full sun, cool; with abundant water supply also tolerates warmth. Soil well-drained to moist, loamy and humus-rich.
Care: Water well in dry spells to prevent mildew. Cut back plants after blooming, to prevent self-sowing.
Propagation: By division.
Use: In the front of borders. Never at the base of warm house walls.
Good Partners: Fall-flowering perennials.
Cultivars/Relatives:
• 'Schneekissen', white, 12 in. (30 cm).
• 'Heinz Richard', bright pink, 8 in. (20 cm).
• 'Kassel', crimson, 16 in. (40 cm).
• 'Prof. Anton Kippenberg', blue, 16 in. (40 cm).
• 'Silberblaukissen', silver-blue to lavender-blue, 16 in. (40 cm).

Heath Aster, North American Aster
Aster ericoides

Aster ericoides 'Erlkönig'

September–October
H 32–48 in. (80–120 cm)

Small-flowered, but free-flowering fall aster.
Flower: Countless white, pale pink, or pale violet heads in freely branching, veil-like panicles.
Leaf: Narrow linear to almost needle-shaped, dark green.
Growth: In loose clumps.
Origin: North America; prairies.
Site: Sun, warm. Soil moderately dry to well-drained. No waterlogged soils!
Care: Feed in spring. Cut back completely after blooming.
Propagation: By division in spring and by basal cuttings.
Use: In sunny borders. Good near woody plants with fall colors. As dominant plants in plantings with low companions.
Good Partners: *Aster dumosus* hybrids, *Aster novae-angliae*, *Chrysanthemum indicum* hybrids, also gray-leaved perennials like *Nepeta—Panicum virgatum*.
Cultivars/Relatives:
• 'Schneetanne', white, 48 in. (120 cm).
• 'Ringdove', pink-and-lilac, 32 in. (80 cm).
• 'Erlkönig', pale violet, 48 in. (120 cm).
• *Aster cordifolius* 'Ideal', lavender-blue, 40 in. (100 cm), with cordate leaves.
• *Aster pringlei* 'Monte Cassino', the well-known September offering of florists, bears white flowers well into November, 48 in. (120 cm).

Smooth Aster
Aster laevis

Aster laevis

September–October
H 52–64 in. (130–160 cm)

Marvelously beautiful, but little-known fall aster.
Flower: Delicate medium-blue with a faint tinge of lilac. In free-flowering, elegantly drooping panicles.
Leaf: Broad lanceolate to narrow ovate, green.
Growth: In clumps, spreads slowly by means of short runners without crowding the neighbors.
Origin: North America. In thin, usually dry woods.
Site: Full sun, predominantly warm. For all well-drained garden soils. Tolerates brief spells of dryness. No exclusively sandy or clay soils.
Care: Feed in spring. Cut down after bloom.
Propagation: By division in spring; by basal cuttings.
Use: In sunny borders.
Good Partners: *Aster dumosus* hybrids, *Aster novae-angliae*, *Chrysanthemum indicum* hybrids, *Helianthus decapetalus*, *Rudbeckia fulgida* var. *sullivantii* 'Goldsturm', *Solidago caesia—Panicum virgatum*.

New England Aster
Aster novae-angliae

Cultivar 'Rosa Sieger'

September–October
H 40–64 in. (100–160 cm)

More robust than the New York asters.
Flower: Crimson, purple-red, pink, violet, white, lavender-blue, daisy-like.
Leaf: Broad linear, dull green, hairy and rough.
Growth: Stiffly erect clumps, produces no runners.
Origin: Eastern and central North America. Along sunny edges of woods and in meadows.
Site: Full sun, warm places, also briefly dry places. Soil well-drained, nutrient-rich. No heavy soils; the clumps will flop over!
Care: Balanced feeding with emphasis on potassium. Water in dry spells. Cut back after bloom.
Propagation: By division.
Use: In sunny borders.
Good Partners: *Aconitum carmichaelii*, *Aster ericoides*, *Chrysanthemum serotinum—Panicum virginatum*, woody plants with fall colors.
Cultivars/Relatives:
• 'Herbstschnee', white, 56 in. (140 cm).
• 'Rudelsburg', pink, 48 in. (120 cm).
• 'Rubinschatz', bright ruby-red, 60 in. (150 cm).
• 'Andenken an Paul Gerber', crimson, 56 in. (140 cm).

107

New York Aster
Aster novi-belgii

Continually blooming—New York aster 'Rubinkuppel'

September–October ○ ✄
H 32–56 in. (80–140 cm)

There is a wide range of cultivars of these plants, probably the most important of the fall asters. Their flowers stay open even in rainy weather and in the evening.
Flower: Depending on cultivar, blue, violet, lilac, white, pink, or crimson. In loose, dome-shaped, free-flowering panicles.
Leaf: Lanceolate, dark green, smooth.
Growth: Erect clumps, creeping by means of short runners, sometimes not altogether stable.
Origin: Eastern North America. In damp meadowland and riverside meadows.
Site: Sun, cool. Soil well-drained to moist, nutrient-rich, humus, loamy. No hot sites or sandy soils!
Care: Feed well, but don't overdo nitrogen. Water thoroughly in dry spells. That is also the best way to prevent mildew infestation, which primarily threatens the red-flowered cultivars. Stake floppy cultivars. Cut back right after bloom finishes, to keep plants from setting seed.
Propagation: By division, by small plant segments, or by basal cuttings taken in spring.
Use: In sunny borders.

Cultivar 'Sailor Boy'

Good Partners: *Aster dumosus* hybrids, the blue cultivars also good with *Helianthus atrorubens* and late blooming *Helenium* cultivars—*Miscanthus sinensis*.
Cultivars/Relatives:
• 'Bonningdale White', white, double, 40 in. (100 cm).
• 'Patricia Ballard', crimson-pink, double, 48 in. (120 cm).
• 'Royal Ruby', ruby-red, double, only 24 in. (60 cm).
• 'Dauerblau', soft medium-blue, long flowering, 48 in. (120 cm), an unusual cultivar.
• 'Sailor Boy', dark blue with a tinge of violet, semidouble, 36 in. (90 cm).
• 'Schöne von Dietlikon', dark violet-blue with yellow center, 36 in. (90 cm). Splendid, venerable garden plant.
• 'Fuldatal', bright purple-violet, semidouble, 40 in. (100 cm).

Narrow-leaved Aster
Aster sedifolius

Aster sedifolius 'Nanus'

September–October ○
H 12 in. (30 cm)

Pretty fall aster, whose cultivar 'Nanus', unlike the taller-growing species, is quite strong-stemmed.
Flower: Lavender-blue with yellow center, countless tiny heads.
Leaf: Narrow linear, almost needle-shaped, light matte green.
Growth: In clumps, very compact, almost hemispherical unlike the species does not flop over.
Origin: Southern Europe to the Caucasus and western Africa. In dry places, often on south slopes.
Site: Full sun, warm. Soil well-drained to moderately dry, permeable, nutrient-poor.
Care: Feed moderately. Water only in prolonged dry spells. Cut back in spring, because the whitish fruit structures look good in winter.
Propagation: By division.
Use: In dry borders, in steppe gardens, and on south slopes.
Good Partners: *Achillea filipendulina, Aster amellus, Scabiosa caucasica—Achnatherum calamagrostis, Calamagrostis* x *acutiflora*.

Astilbe ASTILBE

With their colors and forms, astilbes give life to garden areas with light shade.

June–September
H 8–48 in. (20–120 cm)

Among the plant genera, the astilbes are virtually unrivaled in their ability to look decorative in light shade for a relatively long time, with strikingly beautiful flowers. By choosing species and cultivars skillfully, you can obtain successive, varied displays of the feather-like panicles from June to September.

Flower: Pink, salmon-pink, crimson, red, red-violet, lilac, cream-colored, or white. Many single flowers in panicles. Reddish flush in many cultivars.

Leaf: Multipinnate, irregularly saw-toothed, dark green, matte sheen. Reddish flush in many cultivars.

Growth: In clumps, erect to spreading.

Origin: East Asia. Woods in mountains and ravines, foot of mountains.

Site: Light shade to partial shade, cool, air humid. No places with dry air, because plants are susceptible to heat! Soil well-drained to moist; nutrient-rich, loamy humus soil is best.

Care: Water thoroughly in dry spells and sprinkle with water frequently. Apply organic fertilizer regularly. Cut back pedicels in spring. Add compost frequently, to fill in around and pad the emerging root swellings.

Propagation: By division in winter or spring.

Use: In shifting light under tall trees or in shadow of walls. Strong pressure from tree roots is not tolerated.

Good Partners: *Aconitum, Astrantia, Campanula lactiflora, Campanula latifolia, Cimicifuga, Epimedium, Hosta, Rodgersia,*

Astilbe thunbergii 'Moerheimii'

Tiarella—shade-tolerant grasses and ferns.

109

Astilbe, False Spirea
Astilbe Species and Hybrids

Arendsii hybrid 'Erica'

The major species and cultivar groups are these:

<u>*Astilbe arendsii* hybrids</u>, garden astilbes: The most important astilbes for garden use, with variable flower colors and forms, July–September, in clumps, 24–48 in. (60–120 cm).

• 'Brautschleier', white, July, 28 in. (70 cm). Best white cultivar.
• 'Grete Püngel', light pink, July, 28 in. (70 cm). Flushes late, with bronze-green foliage.
• 'Cathleya', crimson-pink, July–September, 40 in. (100 cm). Considered the best astilbe cultivar.
• 'Amethyst', violet-pink, July, 36 in. (90 cm). Prettiest cultivar in this hue.
• 'Feuer', vivid ruby-red, late blooming, July–August, 32 in. (80 cm).
• 'Fanal', dark red, July, 24 in. (60 cm), with pleasant bronze-colored foliage.

<u>*Astilbe chinensis,*</u> mat-forming astilbes: valuable, late blooming perennials that spread by means of runners, but never become troublesome. Good as ground covers.

• var. *pumila,* dwarf astilbe, lilac-pink, August–September, 8 in. (20 cm). Highly adaptable, for sun to partial shade. Forms flat carpets. Less susceptible to drought than the other astilbes.
• var. *taquetii* 'Superba', purple-pink, July–August. With narrow cone-shaped, stiffly erect heads, 44 in. (110 cm) tall. Tolerates some dryness and also can stand in the sun, with enough soil moisture.

Japonica hybrid 'Europe'

Astilbe chinensis var. *pumila*

• 'Finale', light pink, August–September, 24 in. (60 cm).
• 'Serenade', pink, September, 16 in. (40 cm).
<u>*Astilbe japonica* hybrids,</u> Japanese astilbes: early blooming, small clump-forming plants with cone-shaped panicles, June–July, 16–24 in. (40–60 cm).
• 'Deutschland', milky white, 20 in. (50 cm).
• 'Red Sentinel', deep crimson, late blooming, 20 in. (50 cm), foliage bronze-green.
• 'Mainz', bright lilac-pink, 20 in. (50 cm).
<u>*Astilbe thunbergii* hybrids,</u> woodland astilbes: with loosely drooping branches of panicles, July–August, very vigorous, 32–48 in. (80–120 cm).
• 'Van der Wielen', milky white, 48 in. (120 cm).
• 'Straussenfeder', salmon-pink, 32 in. (80 cm).

Pink Masterwort
Astrantia major

Astrantia major

June–August
H 20–28 in. (50–70 cm)

This pretty, wild perennial is indigenous to European countries.
Flower: Silvery white with faint pink tinge, button-shaped heads.
Leaf: Palmately divided, saw-toothed, glossy dark green.
Growth: Clump-forming, gradually spreading and lush.
Origin: Central and eastern Europe. In mountain meadows, canyon forests, and elder thickets.
Site: Light shade to partial shade, with good water supply also sun, cool. Soil well-drained to moist, nutrient-rich, loamy humus. <u>No sandy soils or hot sites</u>!
Care: Feed in spring. You can mow down the plants after the bloom. That prevents self-sowing, however, which in many places can be desirable.
Propagation: By division after the bloom; for the species, by seed.
Use: In thin undergrowth or at the edge of a grove. For meadowy plantings in a natural garden on moist subsoil. Also in borders with light shade or part shade.
Good Partners: Early blooming white or pink *Astilbe* hybrids, *Geranium pratense, Hosta, Polemonium foliosissimum*— *Dryopteris filix-mas.*

Purple Rockcress, False Rockcress
Aubrieta Hybrids

Aubrieta hybrid

April–May	○
H 2–6 in. (5–15 cm)	

Purple rockcresses are well-known, popular garden flowers, without which a rock garden would be incomplete.
Flower: Lilac-blue, violet, violet-blue, velvety red, or pink. Broad sheets of long-blooming flowers.
Leaf: Small, elliptical to lanceolate, evergreen, gray-green.
Growth: Low cushions that expand by means of shoots that take root.
Site: Full sun, warm. Soil dry to well-drained, permeable, but nutritious and lime-rich. No heavy soils!
Care: Feed carefully in spring. If purple rockcresses are fed too heavily and too late, they will freeze in the winter. Water only in prolonged dry spells. After the bloom, cut back hard—to a shoot length of about 4–6 in. (10–15 cm)—so that the cushions that are getting bare in the center can regenerate. Remove seedlings, which usually have only pale lilac blooms. Cover with boughs in late fall to prevent frost damage.
Propagation: By small plant segments in late fall, by division in spring.

Use: In rock gardens, on dry walls, in gaps in flagged paths. The long-lived lilac-blue and violet-blue cultivars are more versatile. Do not combine the shorter-lived pink and crimson forms with yellow-, orange-, or scarlet-flowered neighbors.
Good Partners: *Arabis caucasica, Iberis sempervirens, Iris barbata-nana* hybrids, *Phlox subulata* hybrids, blue cultivars also good with *Alyssum saxatile, Euphorbia myrsinites, Euphorbia polychroma.*
Cultivars/Relatives:
- 'Rosenteppich', dark pink.
- 'Vesuv', crimson.
- 'Red Carpet', velvety red.
- 'Tauricula', medium blue.
- 'Schloss Echberg', blue-violet.
- 'Dr. Mules', dark blue-violet.

Heartleaf Bergenia
Bergenia cordifolia

Hybrid *'Silberlicht'*

April–May	
H 12–16 in. (30–40 cm)	

With their large, fleshy leaves, heartleaf bergenias often have a slightly exotic effect.
Flower: Crimson, in dense cymes.
Leaf: Round to cordate, tough and leathery, glossy dark green. Good for cutting.
Growth: Rhizomatous plant, gradually spreads over flat surfaces.
Origin: Mongolia to Siberia. Larch and pine forests.
Site: Light shade to partial shade, occasional shade, with good water supply also sun. Flowers threatened by late frost. Soil moderately dry to well-drained, in all garden soils.
Care: Tenacious, easy-to-tend perennials; all they need is to have their foliage tidied in spring. Shorten overly long shoots.
Propagation: By root cuttings and by division.
Use: In root area of woody plants. Also in shade of walls.
Good Partners: *Astilbe, Geranium, Vinca—Carex.*
Cultivars/Relatives:
- *Bergenia* hybrids, numerous cultivars with white, pink, and crimson flowers, occasionally also purple-red leaves.

Siberian Bugloss
Brunnera macrophylla

Brunnera macrophylla
'Blaukuppel'

March–May ◐◑
H 12–20 in. (30–50 cm)

Problem-free, long-lived perennial, also suitable for beginners.
Flower: Pure, bright blue, slightly scented, small flowers resembling forget-me-nots in loose panicles. Bloom lasts for weeks.
Leaf: Cordate, up to 8 in. (20 cm) across, long-stemmed, rough, very attractive, vivid green.
Growth: Clump-shaped, spreads gradually and colonizes large areas.
Origin: Caucasus. In mountain meadows and mountain forests.
Site: Light shade; with moist soil, also sun, sheltered from wind. Soil well-drained to moist, loamy, also clay. No hot sites or light, sandy soils!
Care: If too many self-sown seedlings appear, cut off the seed-bearing pods in May, after the bloom.
Propagation: By seed, by division, or by root cuttings in fall. Propagates itself by self-sowing without coaxing.
Use: As ground cover under woody plants and at the sunny edge of a grove.
Good Partners: *Aquilegia, Dicentra, Doronicum, Paeonia, Trollius* hybrids—narcissuses.

European Bugloss
Buglossoides purpurocaerulea

Buglossoides purpurocaerulea

May–June ◐◑
H 8–12 in. (20–30 cm)

Hardy plant that makes a good ground cover.
Flower: Bright gentian-blue. The tiny blossoms are borne in small groups in a terminal corymb.
Leaf: Lanceolate, small, gray-green, hairy.
Growth: Spreads by means of long, tendril-like layers and forms dense mats. Hangs down loosely over wall crests.
Origin: Europe to Asia Minor. Deciduous forests and thin bushes.
Site: Sun to light shade, heat-tolerant. In shade, blooms poorly and is much less dense. Soil moderately dry to well-drained.
Care: Easy to tend. Often has trouble taking root. Plant in spring, then water regularly. Prune in fall.
Propagation: By layers and division, by cuttings.
Use: Ground cover in light shade under woody plants. Also on wall crests.
Good Partners: Doesn't like company, so use alone or with a robust competitor like *Geranium macrorrhizum* or *G. sanguinum*.

Marsh Marigold Cowslip
Caltha palustris

Caltha palustris

April–May ◐◑☠
H 8–12 in. (20–30 cm)

Common, well-known marsh plant.
Flower: Glossy yellow, medium-sized, saucer-shaped flowers.
Leaf: Almost round to cordate, dark green, quite shiny.
Growth: Forms broad clumps near the ground.
Origin: Moderate latitudes of the northern hemisphere. Marshy meadows, banks of streams and rivers, riverside woods.
Site: Full sun to light shade. Soil well-drained to wet; loam or clay. Also in shallow water up to 4 in. (10 cm) deep. No soils that dry out quickly!
Care: Tidy the clumps in late fall. Feed occasionally. In damp meadows of a natural garden, mow down after June; it will reappear.
Propagation: By division after the blooming season, or by seed after the seed is harvested.
Use: At edge of ponds, in damp beds, and in natural gardens.
Good Partners: *Iris pseudacorus* and *sibirica, Polemonium —Fritillaria meleagris.*
Cultivars/Relatives:
• 'Alba', with milky white flowers and yellow stamens.
Warning: All parts are toxic.

Campanula BELLFLOWERS

Campanula persicifolia and the white cultivar 'Grandiflora Alba'

The *Campanula* genus includes about 300 species, most of which are perennials that originated largely in Europe and the Near East. Their habitats include mountains, meadows, and woodlands. Bellflowers bloom in various shades of blue or in white, more rarely in pink. These plants owe their name to the shape of the flower: the five-pointed bell is typical, but many species also have funnel- or star-shaped flowers.

Although the solitary blossoms of the bellflowers are similar in shape and color, the plants are extremely dissimilar in terms of their growth and requirements.

While the short species are used primarily in rock gardens and on dry walls, the taller-growing ones are good in partial shade in a natural garden, as well as in sunny borders. In addition, they go exceptionally well with old garden rose cultivars. Because of the pale blue color they bring to gardens, bellflowers are of inestimable value.

Tips for Bellflower Lovers
• All bellflowers have in common the fact that slugs consider their foliage a great delicacy. Slug damage, particularly in the small species, often results in the death of the entire plant. Consequently, these charming flowering plants have to be protected from injury by slugs.
• *Campanula* seed grains are quite diminutive. When you sow them, leave them uncovered or use only a very thin layer of fine soil. Then most of the bellflowers listed here will germinate easily. Only a few species, including *Campanula latifolia*, are cold-temperature germinators. *Campanula portenschlagiana* germinates irregularly. It takes patience to wait for the first seedlings to appear. For this reason, it is better to propagate *C. portenschlagiana*, as well as other low-growing forms, by division or by small plant segments. For many species and cultivars, that can be done with great ease by detaching runners.

Carpathian Harebell, Tussock Bellflower
Campanula carpatica

Campanula carpatica

June–August ◯ ◖
H 8–12 in. (20–30 cm)

A highly recommended continuous bloomer.
Flower: Violet to blue. Broad bell- to saucer-shaped.
Leaf: Cordate-ovate, about 1 in. (3 cm) across, vivid green.
Growth: Low, clump-shaped, doesn't spread by means of runners.
Origin: Carpathians. On limestone rocks.
Site: Sun, warm. Soil permeable. No waterlogged soils!
Care: Protect from slug damage. Water only in dry spells. Feed moderately; overfeeding makes plants flop over. Cut back after main bloom!
Propagation: By seed or by small plant segments. Division difficult with old plants. In congenial spots, species is self-sowing.
Use: In the front of borders with full sun, in rock gardens.
Good Partners: *Geranium dalmaticum, Helianthemum* hybrids, *Iris barbata* hybrids.
Cultivars/Relatives:
• 'Weisse Clips', white, see 'Blue Clips'.
• 'Blue Clips', light blue, breeds true from seed.
• 'Karpatenkrone', light blue, lustrous.
• 'Kobaltglocke', dark violet.

Fairy's Thimble
Campanula cochleariifolia

Campanula cochleariifolia

June–August ◯
H 4–6 in. (10–15 cm)

Small-flowered, cushion-forming perennial.
Flower: Blue, bell-shaped, solitary or in twos or threes on short, erect stalks, free-flowering.
Leaf: Small; basal leaves oval, stem leaves oblong, with coarsely saw-toothed margins, vivid green.
Growth: Small, but very vigorous perennial that spreads almost like grass, by means of underground runners.
Origin: Mountains of Europe. On rocks, in scree material, or on sunny slopes on lime-rich subsoil, from the valleys to altitudes of almost 2 miles (3000 m).
Site: Full sun, warm. Soil well-drained, permeable, lime-rich, also nutrient-poor. No heavy loam or clay soils where water accumulates!
Care: Water occasionally in dry spells. Feeding unnecessary. Protect from slug damage. If the vigorous plant threatens to overwhelm its neighbors, trim around its edges with a spade.
Propagation: By cutting off runners, by division of younger plants.
Use: In rock gardens, in rock and wall crevices, and in dry walls.
Good Partners: *Cerastium, Saponaria, Thymus.*
Cultivars/Relatives:
• 'Alba', white, otherwise like the species.

Clustered Bellflower, Dane's-blood Bellflower
Campanula glomerata

Species, along with white cultivar 'Schneekrone'

June–August ◯ ◖ ☠
H 6–24 in. (15–60 cm)

Attractive, unproblematic bellflower.
Flower: Dark violet, funnel-shaped, up to 10 or 20 in dense cluster.
Leaf: Oblong cordate, matte dark green, hairy.
Growth: Rosettes with stiffly erect, densely leaved stems. Forms many runners.
Origin: Europe to Near East. In meadows and thin woods.
Site: Sun, warm. Soil moderately dry to well-drained, also nutrient-poor. No waterlogged soils!
Care: Water only in dry spells. Cut back completely after bloom finishes.
Propagation: By seed or by division.
Use: In natural gardens, in flowery meadows with a variety of species, in beds. Cutting flowers.
Good Partners: *Aster amellus, Centranthus, Nepeta* x *faassenii, Oenothera missouriensis.*
Cultivars/Relatives:
• 'Schneekrone', pure white, 20 in. (50 cm), can be propagated by seed.
• 'Acaulis', dark violet, 6 in. (15 cm).
• 'Superba', darker than the species, taller and more compact.

Milky Bellflower
Campanula lactiflora

Great Bellflower
Campanula latifolia

Cultivar 'Loddon Anne'

Campanula latifolia var. *macrantha* and the white form 'Alba'

June–August ◯ ◑
H 32–60 in. (80–150 cm)

Tall-growing bellflower.
Flower: Milky blue with a tinge of delicate pink. Star-shaped flowers in panicles.
Leaf: Ovate to lanceolate, fresh green.
Growth: In clumps, with erect to sloping stems, sometimes needs support.
Origin: Caucasus. In damp woods, clearings, and mountain meadows.
Site: In light shade under largish woody plants, cool, air humid; with adequate water supply also sun. Sheltered from wind. Soil well-drained to moist; nutrient-rich humus, loamy. No sandy soils!
Care: Feed and water well. Protect from slug damage. Support tall-growing cultivars. Cut down in fall.
Propagation: By seed after the seed harvest. Also self-sowing.
Use: See *Campanula latifolia.*
Good Partners: *Aconitum, Aruncus, Astilbe, Lysimachia.*
Cultivars/Relatives:
• 'Alba', white.
• 'Loddon Anne', lilac-pink, 36 in. (90 cm).
• 'Prichard', violet, 20 in. (50 cm).

June–July ◑
H 32–40 in. (80–100 cm)

Wild perennial with attractive heads.
Flower: Blue-violet, large, elongated bell-shaped, in loose racemes.
Leaf: Basal leaves large, cordate-ovate; stem leaves smaller, oblong-ovate, pointed. Matte green and rough with hairs.
Growth: Large clumps, erect, does not produce runners.
Origin: Europe to the Near East and Siberia. In mountain and canyon forests, quite often near springs.
Site: Light shade to partial shade, cool. Soil well-drained to moist, nutritious, humus-rich.
Care: Watering essential during dry spells. Apply organic fertilizer, preferably well-aged cow manure. Protect from slug damage.
Propagation: By seed, ideally right after seed harvest. If the seeds germinate poorly, chill for four weeks. Taproots make division impossible. The species is self-sowing in suitable sites.

Use: In light shade under trees, in shadow of walls; with sufficiently well-drained soil, in beds out of sun; in natural gardens. Outstanding as link between lawn plantings and woody plants.
Good Partners: *Aruncus, Cimicifuga, Hosta*—woodland grasses and ferns.
Cultivars/Relatives:
• *Campanula latifolia* var. *macrantha,* larger-flowered and more vigorous than the species, hence more commonly used in gardens. Its flowers are darker; it tolerates drought better.
• *Campanula latifolia* var. *macrantha* 'Alba', purest white, very beautiful.

Peach-leaved Bellflower
Campanula persicifolia

Campanula persicifolia

June–August   ◯◐
H 20–40 in. (50–100 cm)

Vigorous species.
Flower: Delicate blue with white styles, more than 1 in. (3 cm) across, in loose racemes.
Leaf: Narrow oblong, glossy dark green.
Growth: Leafy flower shoots rising from ground-level rosette. Produces short runners.
Origin: Europe. In thin woods, forest clearings, and bushes.
Site: Light shade; with enough soil moisture also full sun. Best in loamy soils. No heavily sandy or clay soils!
Care: Water in sunny borders. After the bloom, cut stems back to the leaf crowns to prevent self-sowing. Near woody plants, remove fallen leaves to keep the plants from being smothered.
Propagation: By division. In favorable sites, self-sowing.
Use: In light stands of woody plants and in largely sunny beds.
Good Partners: *Alchemilla, Chrysanthemum maximum, Geranium psilostemon.*
Cultivars/Relatives:
• 'Grandiflora Alba', white, almost 40 in. (1 m) tall.

Dalmatian Bellflower
Campanula portenschlagiana

Campanula portenschlagiana

June–July/   ◯◐
August–September
H 16–24 in. (40–60 cm)

Undemanding bellflower for rock gardens.
Flower: Light violet, broad-tipped, almost star-shaped when fully open. Bloom lasts for weeks.
Leaf: Cordate, wrinkled, toothed, vivid green.
Growth: Cushion-shaped.
Origin: Dalmatia. On rock slopes.
Site: Sun, also out of sun, warm. Soil moderately dry to well-drained, moderately nutrient-rich; best is sandy loam. No clay soils!
Care: Water occasionally. Protect from slug damage.
Propagation: By cuttings or by division in spring.
Use: In dry walls and rock gardens.
Good Partners: *Dianthus, Geranium dalmaticum, Stachys byzantina—Festuca ovina.*
Cultivars/Relatives:
• 'Birch Hybrid', somewhat darker and larger flowers than the species, more vigorous.
• *Campanula poscharskyana,* Serbian bellflower, lavender-blue, star-shaped, 4–8 in. (10–20 cm). Often looks slightly tousled, produces up to 32 in. (80 cm) shoots that lie on the ground. Spreads vigorously by rank growth and self-sowing, so do not combine with less-vigorous neighbors. In rock gardens, quite pretty hanging down from wall crests. Many cultivars in blue, lilac, white, and pink.

Bitter-cress
Cardamine trifolia

Cardamine trifolia

May–June   ◐●
H 8–12 in. (20–30 cm)

Ground cover for small areas.
Flower: White, small, in loose cymes.
Leaf: Tripartite, flush vivid green, in summer rich green, in winter streaked with bronze.
Growth: Forms low mats of leaves by means of short runners.
Origin: Mountains of central and southern Europe. In well-drained to damp mountain forests.
Site: Light shade to shade, cool. Soil well-drained to moist humus. No sites in direct vicinity of woody plants or rampant perennials!
Care: Water in dry spells. Sensitive to heavy load of leaves, so remove some (not all) fallen leaves near woody plants.
Propagation: Easily, by division and by leaf cuttings taken at any time except blooming season.
Use: Let grow wild in shady natural garden, at the edge of woody plantings, also in shadow of walls.
Good Partners: *Dicentra eximia, Epimedium, Saxifraga* x *urbium—Carex morrowii,* ferns.

Globe Centaurea
Centaurea macrocephala

Centaurea macrocephala

July–August
H 40–44 in. (100–110 cm)

Genus with a number of easily cared for garden perennials.
Flower: Yellow. Artichoke-like, fist-sized buds covered with brownish scales.
Leaf: Ovate to oblong, large, matte green with a tinge of ocher, rough.
Growth: In clumps, tall bushes.
Origin: Armenia and the Caucasus. In mountain mead ows.
Site: Full sun, warm. Soil moderately dry to well-drained, nutrient-rich, loose. No wet sites!
Care: Cut back completely after bloom finishes, as the plants turn brown then. Older plants almost impossible to transplant.
Propagation: By seed in spring.
Use: In sunny, dry borders and on slopes, as solitary plant, in gravel bed, in gardens among large slabs of stone.
Good Partners: *Echinops, Eryngium, Inula, Nepeta* x *faassenii, Scabiosa caucasica— Achnatherum calamagrostis.*

Mountain Bluet, Knapweed; Perennial Cornflower
Centaurea montana

'Grandiflora'

May–July
H 16–20 in. (40–50 cm)

Species with beautifully shaped flowers.
Flower: Blue, cornflower like, borne singly on stiff stalks.
Leaf: Broad lanceolate, dark gray-green.
Growth: Erect clumps that spread by means of creeping rootstock. Sometimes floppy.
Origin: Europe to Asia Minor. In forest clearings and at sunny edges of woods in mountainous regions.
Site: Partial shade; with adequate water supply also sun; moderately warm. Soil moderately dry to well drained. No waterlogged or compacted soils!
Care: Feed occasionally and moderately; otherwise, becomes floppy. After bloom finishes, cut back pedicles or mow down.
Propagation: By division in spring and by root cuttings.
Use: On east and west sides of woody plants, in borders with partial shade, or in well-drained, sunny beds. In rock gardens and woods-like natural gardens.
Good Partners: *Anemone sylvestris, Digitalis grandiflora, Geum coccineum, Lamium, Lysimachia.*
Cultivars/Relatives:
• 'Alba', white.
• 'Grandiflora', blue-violet, with larger flowers.

Red Valerian, Jupiter's-beard
Centranthus ruber

Centranthus ruber

June–July/
August–September
H 20–28 in. (50–70 cm)

Easily satisfied, easy-to-tend perennial for sunny sites.
Flower: Crimson-pink, free-flowering, in cymes on erect, branching stems.
Leaf: Oblong ovate, blue-green or gray-green.
Growth: Clumps with arched, upward-thrusting stems.
Origin: Mediterranean area and Portugal. Warm, stony places, walls, and rock slopes.
Site: Full sun, warm, also hot. Soil moderately dry to well-drained, permeable.
Care: Cutting back after primary bloom promotes second bloom. Seedlings easy to remove.
Propagation: By seed. Frequently self-sowing on a large scale.
Use: On dry slopes, in rock gardens, and in dry walls. Let grow wild in steppe gardens. In roof gardens, shaped brick walls, and crevices in paving.
Good Partners: *Aster amellus, Centaurea dealbata, Echinops, Nepeta, Salvia nemorosa— Achnatherum calamagrostis.*
Cultivars/Relatives:
• 'Albiflorus', white.
• 'Coccineus', crimson.

PERENNIALS

Snow-in-summer
Cerastium tomentosum var.
columnae

Cerastium tomentosum var.
columnae

May–June
H 4–6 in. (10–15 cm) ○

Attractive, silver-gray, cushion-forming perennial.
Flower: White, small, star-shaped, in loose cymes.
Leaf: Small, oblong, silver-gray, with downy hair.
Growth: Low cushion- to mat-forming perennial.
Origin: Southern Italy. In poor soil, in rock crevices.
Site: Full sun, warm, also hot places. Soil dry to well-drained, permeable, loamy-sandy or stony.
Care: The more barren and hotter the site, the less care is needed. Tidy the clumps in early spring. Cut back hard if cushions get too large.
Propagation: By division or by seed.
Use: In rock gardens, in dry walls and crevices in stone, in containers, and in roof gardens. Pretty in gaps in stone steps and flagged walks.
Good Partners: All perennials for rock gardens. Goes well with *Campanula portenschlagiana—Festuca cinerea.*
Cultivars/Relatives:
• *Cerastium biebersteinii,* taurus cerastium or taurus chickweed, white. Less gray, felt-like hair; grows rampantly. Only for largish areas.

Leadwort, Blue Ceratostigma, False Plumbago
Ceratostigma plumbaginoides

Ceratostigma plumbaginoides

September–October ○ ◐
H 8–12 in. (20–30 cm)

Ground cover with stunning autumn colors.
Flower: Pure azure, small, in clusters at shoot ends.
Leaf: Obovate, late-flushing, upper surface rich green, undersides gray-green, in fall bronze to orange-red.
Growth: Grassy, spreads by means of runners, grows slowly at first.
Origin: Western China. At sunny edges of woods.
Site: Full sun to partial shade, warm, also hot and dry places. Soil moderately dry, permeable. No wet sites, no clay or heavy loam!
Care: Before planting, loosen soil well. Don't injure flat-spreading roots by hoeing. In harsh weather, cover with boughs.
Propagation: By cuttings in early summer or by division.
Use: In small areas, on the south side of woody plants. On slopes, in rock gardens, on wall edges, and in crevices between flagstones.
Good Partners: *Solidago caesia, Stachys byzantina.* Pretty at the foot of junipers and of pines that stand alone.

Rose Turtlehead
Chelone obliqua

Chelone obliqua

July–September ○ ◐
H 20–32 in. (50–80 cm)

Little-known perennial for damp places in the garden.
Flower: Light pink to dark pink, helmet-shaped, in dense candle-like spikes.
Leaf: Broad lanceolate, margins toothed, unstemmed, shiny dark green.
Growth: In clumps, rigidly erect, formal.
Origin: Eastern North America. At damp edges of woods and in meadows.
Site: Sun to out of sun, cool, air humid. Soil well-drained to moist, nutrient-rich; heavy loams are best.
Care: Water abundantly in dry spells. Cut back in fall.
Propagation: By division and by seed.
Use: In damp borders, at edges of ponds.
Good Partners: *Filipendula purpurea, Polygonum amplexicaule, Veronica virginica—Molinia arundinacea.*
Cultivars/Relatives:
• 'Alba', white.
• *Chelone lyonii,* crimson, with stemmed leaves, 20–28 in. (50–70 cm).

118

Chrysanthemum CHRYSANTHEMUMS

Chrysanthemum indicum hybrid 'Bronze Elegance' (in front) and *Aster lateriflorus* var. *horizontalis* (in back)

Chrysanthemums are one of the oldest cultivated plants known to mankind. They were grown in China more than 2,000 years ago. The chrysanthemum has long been the floral emblem of the Japanese imperial family, and it continues to decorate the throne and coat of arms of Japan.

The *Chrysanthemum* genus contains close to 200 different annual, perennial, or subshrubby species. Although the subshrubs are not apt to be hardy in this country, many perennials and annual flowers belonging to this genus are among our best-known garden plants.

Breeding of individual species has resulted in large retail assortments with countless forms. The cut chrysanthemums seen in florists' shops are, for the most part, cultivated under glass. These cultivars are not winter-hardy. The fall chrysanthemums alone include more than 5,000 different cultivars. The flowers of late-blooming fall chrysanthemum cultivars bring the gardening year to an end and signal the approach of winter.

In accordance with their diverse origins, fall chrysanthemums are usually arranged in these groups: *Chrysanthemum indicum* hybrids, *Chrysanthemum koreanum* hybrids, and *Chrysanthemum rubellum* hybrids. Because the dividing lines between the individual groups are not clear-cut and this classification has little significance in actual day-to-day gardening, the groups are not mentioned in the descriptions of the cultivars in this book. Instead, they are listed according to their blooming season and flower form.

However much we appreciate the fall chrysanthemums, we should not ignore the other species and cultivars. Chrysanthemums in bloom can enrich your garden from early summer to late fall. Additionally, all the species named here provide good cut flowers for your vases.

Pyrethrum, Painted Daisy
Chrysanthemum coccineum

Shasta Daisy
Chrysanthemum maximum

Cultivar 'Laurin'

Chrysanthemum maximum 'Wirral Supreme'

May–July
H 20–32 in. (50–80 cm)

Formerly known as *Pyrethrum*.
Flower: Daisy-like flowers with yellow center, single or double.
Leaf: Finely laciniate, dull green.
Growth: In clumps, often needs staking.
Origin: Caucasus, Armenia, and Iran. In mountain meadows.
Site: Full sun, warm. Soil moderately dry to well-drained, readily permeable, moderately nutrient-rich. <u>In heavy soils, short-lived</u>.
Care: Feed in spring, cut back after bloom. Stake weak stems. The plants are hard to transplant.
Propagation: By division and by small plant segments.
Use: In sunny borders, in beds of cutting flowers.
Good Partners: *Achillea millefolium* hybrids, *Campanula glomerata, Salvia nemorosa, Scabiosa caucasica.*
Cultivars/Relatives:
• 'Robinson's Rosa', various pink shades, single, can be propagated by seed.
• 'Robinson's Rot', red, single, can be propagated by seed.
• 'Regent', wine-red, single.
• 'Alfred', cherry-red, double.

June–September
H 20–36 in. (50–90 cm)

Perennials with large, white, daisy-like flowers that bloom a second time if cut back at the end of the first bloom.
Flower: White, and depending on the cultivar single, semidouble, or double; single-flowered cultivars have yellow center. Large, daisy-like flowers on tall stems.
Leaf: Lanceolate, shiny dark green.
Growth: Broad and clump-shaped, sometimes weak-stemmed.
Origin: Pyrenees. In mountain meadows.
Site: Full sun, moderately warm to cool. Soil well-drained, nutrient-rich. <u>No light sandy soils or heavy clay soils, no sites that are wet in winter!</u>
Care: Water in dry spells. Feed adequately. Cut back completely after first blooming season, then water and feed well to encourage an abundant second bloom. Short-lived unless clumps are divided every three to four years.
Propagation: Easily possible by division in spring, also by small plant segments in late summer.
Use: In small groups that can be combined with many other perennials in borders.

Good Partners: *Alchemilla, Campanula persicifolia, Delphinium, Geranium* x *magnificum, Lychnis chalcedonica, Phlox paniculata, Physostegia.*
Cultivars/Relatives:
<u>Single flowers:</u>
• 'Beethoven', large-flowered, free-flowering, very good cultivar, 32 in. (80 cm).
• 'Gruppenstolz', inferior cultivar, can be used in small areas, 20 in. (50 cm).
<u>Semidouble flowers:</u>
• 'Julischnee', late blooming, 32 in. (80 cm).
<u>Double flowers:</u>
• 'Christine Hagemann', large-flowered, excellent cutting flower, 28 in. (70 cm).
• 'Schwabengruss', snow-white, 32 in. (80 cm).
• 'Wirral Supreme', early blooming, very good cultivar for cutting flowers, 32 in. (80 cm).
• *Chrysanthemum leucanthemum (=Leucanthemum vulgare)* 'Maistern', white, May–June, large-flowered cultivar of the German indigenous meadow daisy, 20–32 in. (50–80 cm).

Winter Asters
Chrysanthemum indicum Hybrids

Chrysanthemum indicum hybrid 'Anastasia'

July–September   H 16–40 in. (40–100 cm)

Huge assortment with a great many forms.
Flower: In all colors except blue; single, semidouble, double, ball-shaped, or pompon.
Leaf: Deeply notched, dull green to gray-green, strongly pungent.
Growth: In clumps, spreads by means of short runners, sometimes needs staking.
Site: Sun, warm. Soil moderately dry to well-drained, permeable, well supplied with nutrients
Care: Plant in spring. Feed well. Stake heavy heads. Use boughs for light winter protection.
Propagation: By division and by basal cuttings.
Use: In beds in front of walls, near woody plants with fall color.
Good Partners: Grasses.
Cultivars/Relatives:
Blooms August–September:
Single flowers:
• 'L'Innocence', delicate pink to almost white, 28 in. (70 cm).; 'Clara Curtis', pink, 24 in. (60 cm).
Semidouble:
• 'Citrus', lemon-yellow, 32 in. (80 cm).; 'Gold Marianne', yellow, 32 in. (80 cm).
Double:
• 'Orchid Helen', pink, 20 in. (50 cm).; 'Altgold', bronze-gold, 20 in. (50 cm), reliable cultivar.

• 'Anastasia', violet-pink, globe-shaped flowers, 20 in. (50 cm).
Blooms September–October:
Single flowers:
• 'Fellbacher Wein', red, 24 in. (60 cm).; 'Arcadia', salmon, 36 in. (90 cm).
Semidouble:
• 'Edelweiss', milk-white, 28 in. (70 cm).; 'Rosennymphe', pink, 32 in. (80 cm).
Double:
• 'Ordensstern', bronze-orange, very long-blooming, 32 in. (80 cm).; 'Red Velvet', dark velvety red, 28 in. (70 cm).
Pompon:
• 'White Bouquet,' white, 20 in. (50 cm).; 'Bienchen', yellow, 28 in. (70 cm).
Blooms October–November:
Single flowers:
• 'Ceddie Mason', red, 32 in. (80 cm).; 'Rotfuchs', red-brown, 28 in. (70 cm).
Semidouble:
• 'Schneewolke', white, 24 in. (60 cm).; 'Vreneli', orange, 36 in. (90 cm).
Double:
• 'Novembersonne', golden yellow, 32 in. (80 cm).; 'Nebelrose', pink, fall color red, 36 in. (90 cm).; 'Schwyz', brick-red, 24 in. (60 cm).
Pompon:
• 'Herbströschen', lilac-pink, 32 in. (80 cm).

Giant Daisy
Chrysanthemum serotinum

Cultivar 'Herbststern'

September–October   H 52–64 in. (130–160 cm)

Large perennial, valuable because of late blooming season, but too little used.
Flower: White with greenish yellow center, large daisy-like flowers in many-flowered cymes.
Leaf: Lanceolate with deeply toothed margins, rich green.
Growth: In clumps, erect, strong-stemmed.
Origin: Southeastern Europe. In pastures and damp meadows.
Site: Sun to partial shade. Soil well-drained to moist (short dry spells are tolerated); loamy or loamy-humus, nutrient-rich.
Care: Good nutrient supply. Water in prolonged dry spells. Cut back after bloom finishes in fall. Otherwise, needs little care.
Propagation: Easily possible by division.
Use: Together with other fall-blooming plants in borders, also near ponds, very pretty with woody plants that have fall colors.
Good Partners: *Aconitum carmichaelii, Aster novi-belgii, Delphinium, Vernonia crinita — Miscanthus.*
Cultivars/Relatives:
• 'Herbststern', pure white with yellow center, free-flowering.

121

PERENNIALS

Cohosh Bugbane, Black Snakeroot, Black Cohosh
Cimicifuga racemosa

Cimicifuga racemosa

July–August
H 60–80 in. (150–200 cm)

Impressive, long-lived perennials that take several years to develop their full beauty.
Flower: White, with astringent scent, many tiny flowers clustered in dense, cylindrical racemes that look like bottle brushes and can reach 24 in. (60 cm) in length. The heads, borne on long stems, rise well above the leaf clumps. They are often arched and elegantly drooping.
Leaf: Pinnate, leaflets oblong ovate and coarsely saw-toothed, dark green.
Growth: In clumps, not always completely stable.
Origin: Eastern North America, in deciduous and mixed forests.
Site: Light shade or shifting sunlight, cool, air humid, protected from wind. Soil well-drained to moist, loose, humus. No hot sites or soils that dry out easily!
Care: Apply weak solution of organic fertilizer periodically. Water thoroughly during dry spells.
Propagation: By division in spring.
Use: In light shade of tall trees or on the north side of walls. These plants need to stand undisturbed, if possible; don't put

them near extremely vigorous neighbors.
Good Partners: *Aconitum napellus, Astilbe, Campanula lactiflora, Hosta*—also pretty in front of evergreen woody plants.
Cultivars/Relatives:
• var. *cordifolia,* creamy yellow, in branching racemes, from August on. Somewhat smaller than Cohosh bugbane.
• *Cimicifuga ramosa,* September bugbane, also creamy white. Blooms for weeks, from September to October, can grow more than 80 in. (2 m) tall. Quite lovely with woody plants that have fall color, *Aconitum carmichaelii* and *Anemone japonica* hybrids.
• 'Atropurpurea', with purple-brown foliage.
• *Cimicifuga simplex,* Kamchatka bugbane, white, starts to bloom in late October. At no more than 60 in. tall (150 cm), markedly smaller than Cohosh bugbane.
• 'Armleuchter', pure white, profusely branching candle-shaped blooms.

Jouin Clematis
Clematis x jouiniana

Cultivar 'Praecox'

July–September
H 8–12 in. (20–30 cm)

Along with the well-known climbing woody plants, the clematis genus also includes virtually unknown perennials.
Flower: White-and-blue, scented, medium-sized ray flowers in dense cymes. Feathery, tufted fruits.
Leaf: Tripartite, dark green, stays green a long time.
Growth: Abundantly and densely leaved shoots, often more than 40 in. (1 m) long, rest on the ground. They cover the ground completely, and can also droop or climb.
Site: Sun to partial shade, warm, also briefly dry places. Soil moderately dry to well-drained humus, lime-rich.
Care: Cut back in spring; simply leave the cut-off shoots on the ground, where they will quickly rot.
Propagation: By cuttings in early summer.
Use: As ground cover in front of individual shrubs, or at the edge of thin groups of woody plants. Very pretty hanging down from wall cornices. Also makes a good climber, if you tie up the shoots.
Good Partners: *Aster divaricatus, Ceratostigma, Geranium sanguineum.*

Tickseed, Bigflower Coreopsis
Coreopsis grandiflora

Cultivar 'Schnittgold'

June–September ○ ✂
H 24–36 in. (60–90 cm)

Usually short-lived perennial.
Flower: Yellow head up to 2 in. (5 cm) across, solitary on long stems.
Leaf: Highly variable, pinnate or lanceolate, rich green.
Growth: In clumps, in some cases drooping over.
Origin: Eastern North America. In dry, sandy places on prairies.
Site: Sun, warm. Soil moderately dry to well-drained, moderately nutrient-rich. The heavier and more nutrient-rich the soils, the more weak-stemmed are the plants.
Care: Cutting back completely immediately after blooming increases frost-hardiness. As the species is short-lived, it needs to be divided often and planted elsewhere.
Propagation: By division and by basal cuttings.
Use: In borders, in beds of cutting flowers.
Good Partners: *Achillea filipendulina, Aster amellus,* red-flowered *Helenium, Salvia, Scabiosa caucasica.*
Cultivars/Relatives:
• 'Badengold', golden yellow, with flowers up to 4 in. (10 cm) across.

Threadleaf Coreopsis
Coreopsis verticillata

Cultivar 'Zagreb'

June–September ○
H 12–28 in. (30–70 cm)

Flowers freely all summer long.
Flower: Golden yellow, star-shaped heads almost 2 in. (4 cm) across.
Leaf: Tripartite to pinnate, with needle-like, light green segments.
Growth: Rigidly erect, forms dense bushes by means of many small runners, but never becomes troublesome; long-lived.
Origin: Eastern North America. Thin woods.
Site: Sun. Soil well-drained, moderately nutrient-rich; all but sandy soils.
Care: Feed in spring. Water occasionally in dry spells. Cut back right after bloom. Needs little care.
Propagation: By division.
Use: In sunny borders.
Good Partners: *Delphinium, Solidago, Veronica— Calamagrostis* x *acutiflora.*
Cultivars/Relatives:
• 'Moonbeam', light, cold yellow, rather difficult to use, only 12 in. (30 cm) tall.
• 'Zagreb', golden yellow, 12 in. (30 cm)
• 'Grandiflora', golden yellow, like the species, but even more free-flowering. The most common cultivated form.

Crambe
Crambe cordifolia

Crambe cordifolia

June–July ○ ✂
H 56–80 in. (140–200 cm)

Long-lived, impressive perennial that takes about three years to develop its full growth and beauty.
Flower: White, strongly scented, countless tiny flowers in huge, profusely branching panicles.
Leaf: Quite large, cordate, violet during flush, later shiny black-green.
Growth: Forms commanding clumps, which at times are weak-stemmed and flop over.
Origin: Caucasus. Steppes and gravelly plains.
Site: Full sun, warm. Soil moderately dry to well-drained, with good nutrient supply. No wet sites; it will rot!
Care: Feed well, largely with inorganic fertilizer. Stake pedicles.
Cut off faded pedicles to keep energy from being directed toward setting fruit.
Propagation: By rhizome cuttings. Also by seed (tedious).
Use: Solitary perennial in prominent locations. Goes well with roses.
Good Partners: *Iris barbata-elatior* hybrids, *Kniphofia* hybrids, *Nepeta, Stachys byzantina, Yucca—Helictotrichon—* roses.

DELPHINIUMS, LARKSPURS
Delphinium Hybrids

Delphinium belladonna hybrids 'Völkerfrieden' (blue) and 'Kleine Nachtmusik' (violet) with rose 'Bantry Bay'

Delphiniums, with their clear-blue turrets of flowers, are indispensable for the color they bring to the garden.

Flower: In many different blue tones or white, with Pacific hybrids also in pink. Dense, large, candle-shaped, usually sparse-branched racemes. After the first bloom, cut back completely—almost level with the ground—to obtain a second bloom in fall.

Leaf: Deeply lobed to palmately divided, vivid green.

Growth: Large, upright clumps. Sometimes unstable.

Origin: Cultivated form.

Site: Sun to out of sun. Slopes with slight northerly incline are good. Soil well-drained, nutrient-rich, deep, loamy. No hot places or light, sandy soils! Don't plant near fast-growing perennials or woody plants!

Care: Feed amply when flush occurs, about 4 oz. (100 g) of compound fertilizer per square yard (1 m²) every year; also protect from slug damage. Water in dry spells. Delphiniums are prone to mildew, depending on the cultivar; they are endangered particularly by warm places—for example, in front of walls and when too crowded. Stake weak-stemmed cultivars, especially Pacific hybrids. Cut back for a second time in late fall.

Propagation: By division or by basal cuttings.

Use: As dominant plants in borders and in many possible combinations with other perennials.

Good Partners: For the first bloom: *Alchemilla, Chrysanthemum maximum, Hemerocallis, Heliopsis, Lychnis chalcedonica*—lilies—roses. For the second bloom: *Aster novae-angliae, Aster novi-belgii, Chrysanthemum serotinum, Heliopsis helianthoides* var. *scabra*—*Calamagrostis, Miscanthus*—roses.

Warning: The entire plant is poisonous!

124

Garland Larkspur
Delphinium belladonna Hybrids

Hybrid 'Piccolo'

June–July/
August–September
H 32–48 in. (80–120 cm)

Small, graceful garden delphiniums, characterized by their loose, many-branched, strong-stemmed inflorescences, which make them seem less stern than the other hybrid groups. The plants bloom early and put forth again nicely after being cut back, some as early as late August.

Cultivars/Relatives:
• 'Casablanca', pure white, 52 in. (130 cm).
• 'Capri', light blue with white eye, 40 in. (100 cm).
• 'Piccolo', pure azure, 32 in. (80 cm).
• 'Völkerfriede', azure, 44 in. (110 cm).
• 'Kleine Nachtmusik', dark violet, 32 in. (80 cm).

Candle Larkspur, Bee Larkspur
Delphinium elatum Hybrids

Hybrid 'Ouvertüre'

June–July/
August–September
H 48–80 in. (120–200 cm)

The most frequently used garden delphinium, with tall, dense, candle-shaped inflorescences.

Cultivars/Relatives:
• 'Abgesang', azure with white eye, blooms late, 72 in. (180 cm).
• 'Berghimmel', clear, light blue with white eye, blooms in midseason, 68 in. (170 cm).
• 'Fernzünder', dazzling medium-blue with white eye, blooms in midseason, 60 in. (150 cm).
• 'Jubelruf', light blue with white eye, 72 in. (180 cm).
• 'Lanzenträger', medium blue with white eye, blooms in midseason, strong-stemmed, 80 in. (200 cm).
• 'Ouvertüre', medium blue with pink veil and dark eye, early-blooming, 64 in. (160 cm).
• 'Perlmutterbaum', light blue with pink, dark eye, blooms in midseason, 72 in. (180 cm).
• 'Polarnacht', dark gentian-blue with white eye, blooms in midseason, 64 in. (160 cm).
• 'Schildknappe', dark blue-violet with white eye, blooms in midseason, 68 in. (170 cm).
• 'Sommernachtstraum', gentian-blue, early, 64 in. (160 cm).
• 'Zauberflöte', blue with pink, white eye, late, 72 in. (180 cm).

Delphinium
Delphinium Pacific Hybrids

Hybrid 'Percival'

June–July/
August–September
H 60–72 in. (150–180 cm)

The densely filled spikes of the cultivars in this hybrid group seem somewhat ponderous, hence less elegant than the other delphinium hybrids. If they are not divided and replanted, they will last no longer than three or four years in your garden.

The Pacific hybrids make better cut flowers than any of the other delphiniums. Attractive plant groups can be made by combining the pastel cultivars with old, heavily doubled rose cultivars.

Care: The plants have to be staked.
Propagation: By seed, by division, and by basal cuttings.
Cultivars/Relatives:
• 'Gallahad', pure white, 60 in. (150 cm).
• 'Rosa Sensation', pastel pink, 72 in. (160 cm).
• 'Blue Bird', medium blue with white eye, 60 in. (150 cm).
• 'Summer Skies', azure with white eye, 68 in. (170 cm).
• 'Black Knight', black-violet with dark eye, 64 in. (160 cm).

PERENNIALS

Maiden Pink
Dianthus deltoides

Dianthus deltoides

June–September ◯
H 4–8 in. (10–20 cm)

In addition to the annual sweet Williams, this genus includes many lovely cushion-forming perennials for rock gardens.
Flower: Crimson, blood-red, pink, white, often with dark eye.
Leaf: Linear, dull green, turning brown after bloom.
Growth: Creeps in loose, grass-like way. Older cushions become bare.
Origin: Europe to Asia. Heathland, edges of woods, and clear-cut areas.
Site: Full sun, warm. Soil moderately dry to well-drained, permeable, nutrient-poor, acid; otherwise plant is short-lived.
Care: Cut back after bloom to prevent denuding. Replace plants often, as they are short-lived.
Propagation: By seed, also for the cultivars.
Use: In small areas in heath and rock gardens, in furrows and in crevices between flagstones.
Good Partners: *Campanula, Thymus—Festuca, Molinia.* No rapidly growing neighbors!
Cultivars/Relatives:
• 'Albus', white with red ring.
• 'Vampir', crimson.
• 'Heideglut', wine-red.
• 'Brillant', velvety red.

126

Cheddar Pink
Dianthus gratianopolitanus

Cultivar 'Stäfa'

May–July ◯
H 2–8 in. (5–20 cm)

Cushion-forming *Dianthus*.
Flower: White, pink, crimson, velvety red, some bicolored or double, scented. Plate-shaped, often fringed.
Leaf: Grass-like; depending on cultivar gray-green to silver-gray.
Growth: Cushion-forming.
Origin: Europe. Rocks and thin pine forests.
Site: Full sun, warm, also hot. Soil moderately dry, highly permeable, moderately nutrient-rich. No heavy, moist soils, or the plant will rot.
Care: Cut back pedicles after bloom finishes. Feed lightly to prevent cushions from fading.
Propagation: By division.
Use: In rock gardens, in dry walls and flagged walks.
Good Partners: *Campanula, Cerastium, Gypsophila.*
Cultivars/Relatives:
• 'Blaureif', pink, 6 in. (15 cm).
• 'La Bourbille', pink, 2 in. (5 cm).
• 'Badenia', blood-red.
• 'Rotkäppchen', velvety red, 6 in. (15 cm).
• *Dianthus plumarius,* grass or cottage pink, larger, strong-scented, feather-like flowers, 6–14 in. (15–35 cm).
• 'Ine', white with red, double.
• 'Heidi', blood-red, double.

Fringed or Plumed Bleeding Heart
Dicentra eximia

Dicentra eximia

May–June ◐
H 8–12 in. (20–30 cm)

Relative of common bleeding heart.
Flower: Pastel crimson, small, heart-shaped, in a loose raceme.
Leaf: Filiform pinnate, blue-green to pike-blue.
Growth: Forms dense mats by means of short runners.
Origin: Eastern North America. Fresh, thin woods.
Site: Light shade, cool, air humid. Soil well-drained, loose, humus.
Care: Water in dry spells.
Propagation: By detaching runners and by basal cuttings.
Use: In shade plantings.
Good Partners: *Epimedium, Lamium, Pulmonaria, Saxifraga* x *urbium. Tiarella—Carex.*
Cultivars/Relatives:
• 'Alba', white, showier.
• 'Bountiful', dark pink, larger flower.
• *Dicentra formosa,* western bleeding heart, from North America, very similar. The dark-red flowers rise higher above the green foliage and appear three weeks later.
• 'Luxuriant', blooms for months on end, 16 in. (40 cm).

Common Bleeding Heart
Dicentra spectabilis

Dicentra spectabilis

May–June
H 8–12 in. (20–30 cm) ◑ ✂

Old, traditional perennial for country gardens.
Flower: Bicolored pink and white. The flowers resemble a heart from which a white tear issues. In elegant, drooping racemes.
Leaf: Pinnate, dull blue-green. Dies back soon after bloom.
Growth: Loose clumps, not always strong-stemmed.
Origin: China and Korea. In thin woods.
Site: Light shade to partial shade; with moist enough soil, also sun; cool, air humid. Soil well-drained to moist, loose.
Care: Specimens planted in overly sunny sites need to be covered for protection from late frosts, because they often begin to bud too early.
Propagation: By basal cuttings.
Use: In borders and country gardens. Because they die back early and leave gaps, don't plant in foreground, plant toward back. Use only a few solitary specimens, widely scattered.
Good Partners: *Myosotis—Brunnera*—late blooming white narcissuses, pink and white tulips.
Cultivars/Relatives:
• 'Alba', less well-known form with enchanting, pure white flowers. More competitive and versatile, can also be combined with yellow colors.

Common Foxglove
Digitalis purpurea

Digitalis purpurea 'Gloxiniaeflora'

June–July
H 40–56 in. (100–140 cm) ● ◑ ☠

This highly decorative plant is quite short-lived, often only biennial. Like all other *Digitalis* species, extremely poisonous!
Flower: Pastel pink to purple-red, with darker spots inside the corolla tube, bell-shaped to thimble-shaped, in erect inflorescences.
Leaf: Ovate and pointed, large, dull green, coarse and hairy-surfaced.
Growth: Leaf rosette with long, rigidly upright pedicles.
Origin: Europe. Common plant in cleared areas and at thin, warm edges of woods.
Site: Partial shade, warm. Soil moderately dry to well-drained, acid, humus-rich, loamy. Never under deciduous woody plants, as fall leaves are not tolerated.
Care: Cut back after blooming to prolong life span of plants and to prevent self-sowing.
Propagation: By seed. In favorable locations, it is self-sowing.
Use: In partially shady borders, in close-to-nature garden areas resembling the edge of woodlands.
Good Partners: *Geranium macrorrhizum, Geranium* x *magnificum, Geranium wlassovianum, Monarda* hybrids.

Cultivars/Relatives:
• 'Gelbe Lanze', milky light yellow, 48 in. (120 cm)
• 'Gloxiniaeflora', color mixture with largish, light purple-and-white-spotted flowers.
• *Digitalis* x *mertonensis,* Merton foxglove, salmon-pink, large-flowered, 32–40 in. (80–100 cm)
• *Digitalis grandiflora,* yellow foxglove, resembles red foxglove, but with yellow flowers, June–July, long-lived. In loose clumps, 24–40 in. (60–100 cm). Occurs in central Europe to western Asia in warm, thin stands of woody plants, on slopes, and on scree.
Warning: The plants are highly poisonous!

Leopard's-bane
Doronicum orientale

Purple Coneflower
Echinacea purpurea

Globe Thistle
Echinops bannaticus

Doronicum orientale

Echinacea purpurea

Echinops bannaticus 'Taplow Blue'

April–May
H 16–24 in. (40–60 cm)

This perennial is in widespread use because of its early blooming season. It also is a good cutting flower.
Flower: Bright yellow, large, daisy-like flowers at the ends of erect stems.
Leaf: Round to cordate, conspicuously scallopped, vivid green.
Growth: In clumps.
Origin: Southeastern Europe to Asia Minor. In loose formations of woody plants.
Site: Light shade to partial shade, with adequate water supply also sun, cool. Humus soil, well-drained, loose, loamy.
Care: Protect from slug damage. Feed occasionally. Water during dry spells. Cut off flowers to extend blooming season.
Propagation: By division, except during blooming season.
Use: In borders, in light shade of walls, and in dappled shade of woody plants.
Good Partners: *Brunnera—Muscari,* narcissuses, tulips.
Cultivars/Relatives:
• 'Frühlingspracht', double.
• 'Riedels Goldkranz', with two rows of ray flowers.
• *Doronicum plantagineum* 'Excelsum', 24–32 in. (60–80 cm). Dies back after bloom.

July–September
H 28–40 in. (70–100 cm)

Popular with butterflies.
Flower: Matte crimson, ray flowers around an orange-brown center. Large, solitary, daisy-like flowers on rigid stems.
Leaf: Pointed and ovate, dark green, covered—as are all other parts—with rough hair.
Growth: Clumps with stiff flower shoots, not always stable.
Origin: North America. On prairies and in waste land.
Site: Full sun, warm. Soil well-drained, nutritious, loamy.
Care: Spring is best planting time. Protect from slug damage. Cut back after bloom. Remove seedlings, as they usually bloom in other colors. Short-lived, has to be replaced every three to four years.
Propagation: Sowing seeds usually disappointing; division of fleshy roots difficult.
Use: In borders.
Good Partners: Fall-blooming *Aster, Liatris, Monarda* hybrids, pink or white *Phlox.*
Cultivars/Relatives:
• 'Abendsonne', crimson.
• 'Magnus', intense red, can be propagated by seed.
• 'Rubinstern', purple-red.

July–September
H 32–48 in. (80–120 cm)

Attractive perennial with striking, unusual flower heads.
Flower: Lustrous blue, globe-shaped, at ends of erect stems. Honey-producing plant.
Leaf: Deeply lobed with spiny margins, surface dull green, underside white and downy.
Growth: In loose clumps, not always stable.
Origin: Southeastern Europe. In meadow steppes.
Site: Sun, warm, also hot, sheltered from wind. Soil dry to well-drained, permeable, lime-rich. No moist, heavy soils; otherwise, plants rot and become floppy.
Care: Stake if necessary. Cut back hard after blooming; otherwise, too many seedlings come up and the globe thistles run riot.
Propagation: By seed and by root cuttings.
Use: Plant only in small numbers to prevent thicket-like growth. In borders.
Good Partners: Striking color contrast with red-leaved ornamental woody plants, along with white perennials like *Gypsophila paniculata*. Without the red-leaved shrubs, very pretty with yellow perennials like *Achillea filipendulina*.

Long-spur Epimedium, Bishop's-hat
Epimedium grandiflorum

Cultivar 'Lilofee'

| April–May | ◑ |
| H 6–10 in. (15–25 cm) | |

For a long time, long-spur epimediums were known only as ground covers and for their pretty leaves. Now, however, there are new forms with frothy, elegant blooms.
Flower: White or pink, long-spurred, in groups of four to 15 on wiry stems.
Leaf: Three-fold, the segments asymmetrical with thorny, saw-toothed margins, bronze during flush, later vivid green.
Growth: Forms broad clumps, has creeping rootstock.
Origin: Manchuria and Japan. In rhododendron bushes in the alpine zone.
Site: Light shade to partial shade, air humid, cool. Soil well-drained to moist, permeable, sandy or loamy humus.
Propagation: By division.
Use: In undergrowth of thin stands of woody plants. Group plant.
Good Partners: *Hosta, Saxifraga, Tiarella*—grasses.
Cultivars/Relatives:
• 'Rose Queen', bright pink.
• 'Lilofee', violet.
• *Epimedium* x *rubrum,* red epimedium, small, bicolored, red-and-yellow flowers, April–May. Leaf has reddish tinge, good ground cover, 10–14 in. (25–35 cm).

Persian Epimedium
Epimedium pinnatum ssp. *colchicum*

Epimedium pinnatum ssp. *colchicum*

| April–May | ◑ ● |
| H 8–12 in. (20–30 cm) | |

Good ground cover with strikingly pretty fall colors.
Flower: Clear yellow, in loose racemes.
Leaf: Three- to five-fold, the individual leaflets are pointed and cordate, green in winter; in mild winters they are also evergreen. Shiny green, in late fall many hues with metallic gleam.
Growth: By means of runners, gradually forms large mats.
Origin: Western Caucasus. In damp mountain forests.
Site: Light shade to shade. Soil moderately dry to moist, nutrient and humus-rich, loamy.
Care: Cut off old leaves in spring. In winters with little snow, the leaves are nipped by frost, but in spring the plants put forth again.
Propagation: By division.
Use: As ground cover in undergrowth of woody plants.
Good Partners: *Galium, Hosta, Waldsteinia*—grasses.
Cultivars/Relatives:
• *Epimedium* x *perralchicum* 'Frohnleiten', bright yellow, compact, moderately frost-hardy.
• *Epimedium* x *warleyense,* with unusual copper-orange flower. Leaves streaked with reddish color during initial spring growth and in fall, green in winter. Vigorous, but loose growth. Both species are more group plants than ground covers.

Snowy Epimedium
Epimedium x *youngianum*

Epimedium x *versicolor* 'Sulphureum'

| April–May | ◑ |
| H 8–10 in. (20–25 cm) | |

Small group of cushion-shaped epimediums.
Flower: White, pink, or lilac, bell-shaped, hanging, in groups at stalk ends.
Leaf: Pinnate with three to six asymmetrical leaflets, bronze during initial spring growth, later turning green.
Growth: Low, cushion-forming, slow-growing.
Site: Light shade to partial shade, cool, air humid. Soil loose, sandy humus.
Care: Spray in dry spells.
Propagation: By division.
Use: In undergrowth of thin shrubs and trees, together with low partners.
Good Partners: Common species of *Hosta, Primula,* and *Saxifraga*—common *Carex* species, slow-growing ferns.
Cultivars/Relatives:
• 'Niveum', white cultivar that stays small, 6 in. (15 cm).
• 'Lilacinum', pink-lilac, looks quite dark during initial spring leaf growth.
• *Epimedium* x *versicolor* 'Sulphureum', yellow epimedium, sulfur-yellow, April–May. Leaves evergreen in some cases, good ground cover, 12–14 in. (30–35 cm).

Fleabane
Erigeron Hybrids

Hybrid 'Sommerneuschnee'

June–July/September
H 20–32 in. (50–80 cm)

Not only do fleabanes resemble asters, they also are closely related to them. The parent forms of the hybrids come from the prairies of North America.
Flower: Violet, lilac, crimson, or white ligulate flowers around an orange-yellow center. Aster-like heads; the ligulate flowers are finer than those of asters. Free-flowering. After being cut back, they bloom a second time in September.
Leaf: Lanceolate, dull green.
Growth: In clumps with rigid, but often unstable stems.
Origin: Cultivated form.
Site: Sun, warm. Soil well-drained to moist, permeable. Does not grow well in heavy soils.
Care: Cut back to ground immediately after initial bloom in early summer to encourage reblooming in fall. After the first bloom, feed once more: the better-nourished the plants, the more abundant the second bloom. Stake unstable cultivars with dry, branched twigs. Older plants bloom less well, so divide and transplant frequently.
Propagation: By division.
Use: In perennial gardens, together with other summer and fall perennials, as cutting flowers; cut opened flowers rather than buds for display.
Good Partners: *Chrysanthemum maximum, Coreopsis, Delphinium, Gypsophila paniculata, Monarda* hybrids, *Rudbeckia fulgida* 'Goldsturm'.
Cultivars/Relatives:
Violet shades:
• 'Dunkelste Aller', dark blue-violet.
• 'Schwarzes Meer', deep violet.
Blue-violet shades:
• 'Mrs. E. H. Beale', pale lilac, long blooming.
• 'Adria', light blue-violet, semidouble, good second bloom.
• 'Strahlenmeer', light blue-violet, loose growing.
Pink and crimson shades:
• 'Rosa Triumph', bright pink, lighter as blooming ceases, semidouble.
• 'Rotes Meer', crimson.
White colors:
• 'Sommerneuschnee', white, whitish pink as blooming ceases, very pretty, traditional cultivar.

Hybrid 'Mrs. E. H. Beale'

Alpine Eryngo
Eryngium alpinum

Eryngium x *zabelii* 'Violetta'

June–July
H 24–32 in. (60–80 cm)

Thistle-like umbellate flower. Dried flower.
Flower: Steel-blue, elongated flower heads with light violet, lacerated bracts at the ends of rigid stems. Attractive fruits in winter.
Leaf: Large, lobed, coarsely leathery and prickly, gray-green.
Growth: In clumps, loosely branching with few shoots.
Origin: Alps, northern Balkans. On grassy hillsides.
Site: Sun, warm, also hot. Soil dry to moderately dry, permeable, sandy-gravelly or slightly loamy, lime-rich. In wet sites the fleshy taproots rot.
Care: Cut back in spring. Stake unstable cultivars. Short-lived.
Propagation: By seed and by root cuttings.
Use: In terraced beds and in gravelly gardens.
Good Partners: *Achillea, Artemisia, Lavandula, Linum, Salvia, Veronica spicata.*
Cultivars/Relatives:
• 'Blue Star', deep blue.
• 'Opal', silvery lilac.
• 'Amethyst', silvery violet.
• *Eryngium* x *zabelii* 'Violetta', unusual, deep violet flower heads, short-lived, 24–32 in. (60–80 cm).

Hollow-stemmed Joe-Pye Weed
Eupatorium fistulosum

Cultivar 'Atropurpureum'

August–October ◯ ◗
H 60–80 in. (150–200 cm)

Decorative, free-flowering perennial of great size. Well liked by butterflies.
Flower: Gray-pink to purple-crimson, muted colors, astringent scent. Huge, dome-shaped flowers 10 to 20 in. (25–40 cm) across.
Leaf: Lanceolate, whorled, dark green with red midrib, bright yellow in fall.
Growth: Grows in clumps with rigidly erect, bright purple-red stems.
Origin: North America. In damp meadows.
Site: Sun to light shade, warm. Soil well-drained to moist, also briefly dry, nutrient-rich, heavy.
Care: Cut shoots back to ground in winter or early spring. Astonishingly wind-resistant, needs no staking.
Propagation: By division.
Use: As a solitary perennial at the edge of a pond and at the back of smaller perennials.
Good Partners: Pretty with other late bloomers, including *Aconitum carmichaelii* or *Chrysanthemum serotinum*.
Cultivars/Relatives:
• 'Album', white.

SPURGE
Euphorbia

Cushion spurge *(Euphorbia polychroma)* and blue-flowered *Mertensia virginica*

More than 1,000 species of the *Euphorbia* genus are known. Not only do they include unusually colored perennials that have been introduced into gardens as highly prized plants, but also a great many annual and biennial or subshrubby wild species from mixed forests, meadows, and fields that have yet to be discovered for use in natural gardens. Several exotic, mostly shrubby *Euphorbia*, cultivated as house plants, are well-known. The poinsettia is one such familiar example. There are also cactuslike forms, thickly covered with thorns.

The actual flowers of *Euphorbia* are usually some shade of green, extremely tiny, and inconspicuous. The flower-like plant parts that appear in such splendid colors are bracts, which are intended to substitute for the flowers in enticing insects.

All the members of this genus are highly poisonous to humans and animals. All plant parts—whether green or withered—are dangerous. When working with these perennials, you must wear gloves to avoid contact with the toxic white juice that wells out of the plant when it is injured. Absolutely do not put the gloves to your face or smell the inflorescences; eye damage and facial swelling can result. In our test gardens we have worked with these attractive plants for decades. If you take the proper precautions, nothing will happen, and there is no need to deprive yourself of these handsome plants.

Himalayian Euphorbia
Euphorbia griffithii

Cultivar 'Fireglow'

May–June ○ ◐ ☠
H 20–32 in. (50–80 cm)

Exotic perennial for garden use.
Flower: Fiery orange-red bracts on terminal umbels. Long-blooming; colors develop best in sun.
Leaf: Lanceolate, dull green, in fall yellowish orange.
Growth: Grows in clumps, with rigidly erect shoots. Gradually forms larger stands by means of runners.
Origin: Himalayas, western China. On fringes of woods and on rocky hillsides.
Site: Sun to light shade, warm. Soil dry to well-drained, permeable, nutrient-rich. No moist soils or plants rot during winter. No overly shady growing locations; too many runners form there.
Care: Wear gloves! Cut off dried shoots in late fall, and reduce overly large stands with your spade. In the first planting year, cover with branches from November to December as winter protection, as plant is only moderately frost-hardy.
Propagation: By division and by seed.
Use: In sunny beds, also at edge of woody plants, where it will proliferate.
Good Partners: *Artemisia, Geranium* x *magnificum, Nepeta, Salvia, Stachys byzantina.*
Warning: All plant parts are extremely poisonous!

Myrtle Euphorbia
Euphorbia myrsinites

Euphorbia myrsinites

April–May ○ ☠
H 6–10 in. (15–25 cm)

Uniquely shaped perennial plant with ornamental foliage.
Flower: Green-yellow bracts.
Leaf: Triangular, fleshy, blue-green, arranged in spirals around the thick shoots. Evergreen.
Growth: Cushion-shaped, drooping when old. The thick shoots become bare.
Origin: Southern Europe. On dry, hot rocky slopes.
Site: Sun, warm, also hot. Soil dry to well-drained, permeable, lime-rich. No heavy or moist soils, or plant will rot.
Care: Wear gloves! After the bloom, cut back leafless, overly long shoots to short pieces. This causes new leaf rosettes to form at the base; they will bloom the next spring. The plant is frost-hardy.
Propagation: By seed and by cuttings. First put cuttings in water for a few minutes, so that the sap runs out and the notch does not become sticky.
Use: In rock gardens, on wall crests, in wall crevices, in pebbled areas.
Good Partners: *Iberis sempervirens, Phlox subulata* hybrids—*Iris pumila*, wild tulips.
Warning: All plant parts are highly poisonous!

Cushion Spurge, Cushion Euphorbia
Euphorbia polychroma

Euphorbia polychroma

April–May ○ ◐ ☠
H 12–20 in. (30–50 cm)

Indigenous perennial plant from the edges of woodlands.
Flower: Bright green-gold bracts. Blooms for weeks.
Leaf: Ovate, velvety green, soft-haired. In fall, yellow, orange, and brick-red.
Growth: In clumps, with red shoots.
Origin: Central to southeastern Europe. Dry bushes, sunny fringes of woods.
Site: Sun to partial shade, warm. Soil moderately dry to well-drained, permeable, sandy-gravelly, loamy, lime-rich. Also normal, not overly moist garden soils.
Care: Wear gloves! Cut back in late fall.
Propagation: By division and by seed.
Use: In rock gardens, springtime gardens, crevices in paving.
Good Partners: *Alyssum, Aubrieta, Iberis—Muscari.*
Cultivars/Relatives:
• *Euphorbia amygdaloides*, April May flowers yellow-green, leaf dark green, often with reddish streaks, coarse, green in winter, clumplike, 12–24 in. (30–60 cm). Indigenous woodland plant for damp locations. Poisonous!
Warning: All plant parts are extremely poisonous!

Kamchatka Meadowsweet
Filipendula kamtschatica

Filipendula kamtschatica is an imposing giant perennial

July–August ◯◑
H 60–120 in. (150–300 cm)

The meadowsweet species are mostly impressive, tall-growing perennials that are not always stable. They produce large, terminal, pleasantly scented panicles and decoratively lobed or pinnate leaves. The name "meadowsweet" derives from the sweetish odor of the leaves and stalks, which emanates primarily after the plants are mowed down or when they are fading.

Kamchatka meadowsweet is an exceptionally large perennial for those who like enormous garden plants.
Flower: Creamy white, tiny flowers in a large umbel-like panicle.
Leaf: Very large, three- to five-lobed, dark green, in fall yellowish.
Growth: Tall, broad, vigorous perennial, usually stable.
Origin: Kamchatka Peninsula and northern Japan. In marshy woods.
Site: Sun to light shade; also heavier shade, though plant will no longer be stable. Cool, air humid, sheltered from wind. Soil moist to wet, also inundated, nutrient-rich, heavy, loam or clay.

Care: Cut back dead shoots in late fall. Stake if necessary. No other care needed.
Propagation: By division.
Use: At edges of ponds, in damp hollows, and in other places that do not dry out.
Good Partners: *Hemerocallis, Hosta, Iris pseudacorus, Lysichiton* species, *Lysimachia, Lytrum—Carex pendula.*
Cultivars/Relatives:
• *Filipendula rubra* 'Venusta' and 'Venusta Magnifica', prairie meadowsweet or queen-of-the-prairie, glowing pink, pleasantly sweet-scented, large, feather-like inflorescences. Blooming season July–August, spreads gradually.

Siberian Meadowsweet
Filipendula palmata

Filipendula palmata

June–July ◯◑
H 12–40 in. (30–100 cm)

Ornamental perennial for damp parts of the garden.
Flower: Light pink, delicately scented, in feathery, umbel-like panicles.
Leaf: Pinnate with large, lobed terminal leaflets, dark green, underside whitish green.
Growth: In clumps with rigidly upright pedicles.
Origin: Siberia to Kamchatka. In areas where rain and fog are plentiful.
Site: Sun to light shade, cool. Soil well-drained to moist, nutrient-rich, loam or clay. No hot, dry sites!
Care: Deadhead faded flowers.
Propagation: By division.
Use: In damp locations with periodic shade, at edges of ponds and on banks.
Good Partners: *Aconitum, Iris sibirica, Tradescantia andersoniana* hybrids.
Cultivars/Relatives:
• 'Nana', very intense, almost shrill pink, pleasant scent, free-flowering. Only 12–20 in. (30–50 cm).
• *Filipendula purpurea*, Japanese meadowsweet, purple to crimson, June–August, scented, 24–40 in. (60–100 cm).
• 'Elegans', crimson.

Sweet Woodruff
Galium odoratum

Galium odoratum

April–May
H 6–8 in. (15–20 cm)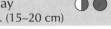

Indigenous wild perennial, survives for decades in shade.
Flower: Delicate white star-shaped flowers, sweet-smelling, in umbel-like inflorescences.
Leaf: Whorled, light green. Initial spring growth occurs quite early and in some cases withstands the winter. When dried, smell is pleasantly sweetish and aromatic.
Growth: Countless thin, tall shoots from shallow-rooting underground runners, gradually forming large mats.
Origin: Europe. In deciduous mixed forests.
Site: Partial to full shade, cool. Soil well-drained to occasionally moist, loose, humus, loam. Good in fallen leaves from taller trees. No compacted soils!
Care: Can be planted at any time of year. Leave alone!
Propagation: By division.
Use: As versatile ground cover, also in direct vicinity of tree roots.
Good Partners: *Astrantia, Hepatica, Lathyrus, Polygonatum, Pulmonaria—Anemone.*
Warning: In large quantities, woodruff is mildly poisonous!

Stemless Gentian, Trumpet Gentian
Gentiana acaulis

Gentiana dinarica

April–June
H 1–3 in. (3–8 cm)

Gentians are extraordinarily popular in rock gardens, but the most spectacular breeds, with their almost unearthly blue hues, are fussy and best left to specialists. The plant sold as "stemless gentian" is usually not the pure species, but a mixture of related types that is easier to cultivate.
Flower: Gentian-blue, bell-shaped, short-stemmed.
Leaf: Lanceolate, small, bright green, evergreen.
Growth: Low, loose, grassy cushions; produces short runners.
Origin: Alps and mountains of southern Europe. Meadows and poor grassy areas.
Site: Sun, cool. Soil well-drained, peat-humus, loamy, not too heavy.
Care: Sensitive to drying out, so mist if necessary. Apply only slow-acting fertilizer, ideally well-aged cow manure. Cover with branches in winters with scant snow.
Propagation: By seed after the seed ripens, or by division.
Use: In rock gardens don't plant together with highly competitive perennials.
Good Partners: Slow-growing perennials for rock gardens.
Cultivars/Relatives:
• *Gentiana dinarica,* deep blue, less susceptible to drought, 2–3 in. (5–8 cm).

Willow Gentian
Gentiana asclepiadea

Gentiana asclepiadea

July–October
H 8–24 in. (20–60 cm)

This gentian species is easier to grow.
Flower: Dark blue, cup-shaped, solitary or in threes in the leaf axils.
Leaf: Ovate-lanceolate, dark green, in fall vivid yellow.
Growth: Has many shoots, erect to drooping. Forms largish stands.
Origin: Central Europe to Near East. In vegetation of tall perennials, in mixed forests in mountains, and in moor meadows and damp meadows.
Site: Out of sun to light shade, cool. Soil well-drained to moist, nutrient-rich, loamy.
Care: Adaptable species. To replace dew, spray with water occasionally on dry days in late summer or fall, mornings or evenings. Cut off fruits only in winter or spring, so that the plants can self-sow.
Propagation: By seed and by division. Older and larger stands cannot be transplanted or divided.
Use: Fringes of bushes, light shade of buildings, and north sides of rock gardens.
Good Partners: *Saxifraga—*grasses and ferns.

Geranium CRANESBILL, GERANIUM

The leaves of *Geranium macrorrhizum* 'Spessart' turn an intense orange-red color in fall.

For a long time, the cranesbill species were only for in-the-know plant fanciers. That has changed drastically in the past few years. Now *Geranium* is right in fashion. People are discovering and appreciating the high quality of these flowering and ornamental foliage perennials, and new cultivars and color variations are constantly appearing. They are extremely versatile in garden use. Use them in undergrowth and along the edge of woody plants, as ground covers, in meadows, in rock gardens, in stone containers, and as partners for many kinds of perennials in borders.

Typical of the genus are the round, palmate or cocksfoot-shaped, more or less heavily divided leaves. The saucer-shaped flowers, made up of five petals, are borne in great numbers above the leaf tufts; some come in garish colors, others are more modest. All are in so-called "cool" colors: blue, lilac, violet, pink, and purple-red shades.

Care:

You can prevent mildew by cutting back completely after blooming ceases or when the plants begin to wither; this also helps to achieve strong new growth. Then new leaf tufts will form during the remainder of the year, and some of them will survive the winter. Large species with clump-like growth can also be cut or mowed down easily once the bloom is over. They will also produce new growth, and often even a second bloom.

Propagation:

All the species and cultivars can be divided during the vegetative period, from May to August. Rooted pieces can be separated into individual shoots the thickness of a finger. They will take root well, provided that they are planted immediately after division and are watered frequently; otherwise, they will quickly start to wilt. In spring (March–April), unrooted pieces can also be removed. A few species can be propagated by root cuttings.

135

Dalmatian Geranium
Geranium dalmaticum

Geranium dalmaticum

July–August
H 4–6 in. (10–15 cm)

Summer bloomer for rock gardens.
Flower: Glowing pink, nearly one half to an inch (1–2 cm), saucer-shaped.
Leaf: Roundish, deeply incised, small. Shiny green, sometimes has coppery red streaks during increasingly dry conditions, and in fall. Aromatic scent. Withstands mild winters.
Growth: Dense, low cushions up to 20 in. (50 cm) across.
Origin: Dalmatia and Albania. On rocky hillsides.
Site: Sun, warm. Soil well-drained to moderately dry, permeable, sandy-loamy or gravelly-loamy.
Care: Don't cut back after bloom. With potted root-ball, can be easily transplanted at any time.
Propagation: See page 135.
Use: In rock gardens, on walls, in wall crevices and niches, also in paving crevices about 1 in. (2 cm) wide. In containers and roof gardens. Likes to be in front of heat-storing rocks.
Good Partners: Other perennial plants for rock gardens, including *Campanula, Dianthus, Nepeta* x *faassenii*.

Cultivars/Relatives:
• 'Album', white, stays small, about 4 in. (10 cm) tall.
• 'Bressingham Park', shocking pink.
• *Geranium* x *cantabrigiense* 'Biokovo', bright pink, larger in all parts, very robust, 10 in. (25 cm).
• 'Karmina', pretty crimson, lush growth, 10 in. (25 cm). Very good cultivar with aromatic foliage.
• *Geranium cinereum* 'Ballerina', rock cranesbill, lilac-pink, strikingly veined, June–September, 6 in. (15 cm).
• *Geranium cinereum* ssp. *subcaulescens* 'Purpureum', purple-red, June–August, 6 in. (15 cm).
• 'Splendens', crimson-pink, June–August, 6 in. (15 cm).

Endres Cranesbill, Pyrenees Cranesbill
Geranium endressii

Geranium endressii

June–September
H 12–20 in. (30–50 cm)

Vigorous species, especially suitable for areas bordering woody plants.
Flower: Pink, broad funnel-shaped, blooms for weeks. Primary bloom late June to early July, then reblooming.
Leaf: Deeply notched, dark green, with large surface.
Growth: Covers large areas of ground and often climbs into shrubs by means of constantly growing shoots. When large, tends to flop over.
Origin: Pyrenees. At damp edges of bushes.
Site: Sun to partial shade, cool to warm. Soil well-drained to moist, loamy, nutrient-rich.
Care: Cut back after first bloom to keep clumps from becoming floppy. Can also be mowed down.
Propagation: See page 135.
Use: In largish groups or as ground cover near woody plants.
Good Partners: Other *Geranium* species, such as *Geranium magnificum* or *Geranium sylvaticum*—relatively tall grasses.
Cultivars/Relatives:
• 'Wageningen', pink, dense growth, new cultivar.

Himalayan Cranesbill
Geranium himalayense

Bigroot Cranesbill
Geranium macrorrhizum

Geranium himalayense 'Gravetye'

May–June ◐
H 12–24 in. (30–60 cm)

Attractive species with magnificent blue flowers and decorative leaves.
Flower: Pastel blue in various shades, large saucer-shaped blooms.
Leaf: Palmately notched, elegant filigree pattern, vivid green; in fall in poor soils turns yellowish or verges toward orange.
Growth: In clumps to flat-growing; covers ground by means of runners.
Origin: Himalayas. In mountain meadows and at edges of woods.
Site: Out of sun to light shade, cool and moist. Soil well-drained, sandy-loamy or loamy. No hot, dry sites or compacted soils!
Care: See page 135.
Propagation: See page 135.
Use: Best under loose shrubs. Also as ground cover, although some of the other *Geranium* species are better suited for that purpose.
Good Partners: Fantastic with frequently blooming pink, white, or yellow park roses.
Cultivars/Relatives:
• 'Gravetye', dazzling light blue, slightly purple in the center.
• 'Johnson's Blue', lovely lilac-blue, especially lustrous, free-

and long-flowering. Somewhat taller, growing to 16–24 in. (40–60 cm), dies back early. Cut off inflorescences to encourage second bloom.
• *Geranium nodosum*, knotty cranesbill, a long-term bloomer with tiny, lilac flowers, May–September. Leaf shiny light green. Produces runners and is self-sowing, colonizes large areas in undergrowth of woody plants and in natural gardens; also suitable for heavy soils.
• *Geranium wlassovianum*, Manchurian cranesbill, velvety blue-violet with large flowers, July–September. Flowers are less abundant, but longer-lasting. Matte dark green leaves with lovely fall colors. Cut for sunny edge of woody plants.

Geranium macrorrhizum 'Album'

May–July ○ ◐
H 8–12 in. (20–30 cm)

Long-lived and not problematic.
Flower: Whitish pink to crimson, plate-shaped, sometimes reblooming.
Leaf: Has deep palmate divisions, large, vivid green, sticky, with aromatic scent. Turns brick-red in fall.
Growth: Creeping ground cover with thick rhizomes.
Origin: Southern Alps to Balkans. High-altitude forests, in bushes and between rocks.
Site: Sun to partial shade, best in light shade of woody plants, warm. Soil moderately dry to well-drained.
Care: Cutting back in spring is optional; old leaves are quickly overgrown by new ones.
Propagation: See page 135. Self-sowing.
Use: As long-lived ground cover beneath shrubs and trees.
Good Partners: Other *Geranium* species—*Carex pendula,* ferns. Otherwise, best alone.
Cultivars/Relatives:
• 'Spessart', white with pink. Vigorous, with fall colors. Recommended.
• 'Ingwersen', pale pink, free-flowering.
• 'Czakor', purple-red, growth more clump-like.

Magnificent Cranesbill
Geranium x *magnificum*

Geranium x *magnificum*

June–July ◯ ◐
H 16–24 in. (40–60 cm)

Known for more than 100 years, *Geranium* x *magnificum* kindles an unparalleled blaze of color during the primary blooming season.
Flower: Lustrous blue-violet, large saucer-shaped flowers, free-flowering. Sets no seed, as it is sterile.
Leaf: Lobed and notched many times over, large, dull green, with shaggy hair. In fall vivid orange-yellow or brick-red.
Growth: Vigorously growing clumps, covers flat areas by means of short runners. Large plants often become floppy.
Origin: Cultivated form.
Site: Sun to light shade, warm. Soil moderately dry to moist, for all garden soils.
Care: Not problematic, long-lived. Simply trim overly large expanses with your spade.
Propagation: See page 135.
Use: In front of and between thin woody plants, or together with other perennials.
Good Partners: *Alchemilla, Chrysanthemum maximum, Lysimachia punctata,* pink-red or crimson *Paeonia.* With white, yellow, or pink shrub roses and park roses.

Meadow Cranesbill
Geranium pratense

Cultivar 'Mrs. Kendall Clark'

June–July ◯
H 20–48 in. (50–120 cm)

Indigenous wild perennial plant for garden areas with well-drained soil.
Flower: Light blue-violet saucer-shaped flowers, long-blooming.
Leaf: Deeply notched in fan shape, green.
Growth: In clumps, tall-growing, not always stable.
Origin: Europe to central Asia and Siberia. In meadows, damp hollows, and damp ditches.
Site: Sun to light shade, cool and damp. Soil well-drained to moist, nutrient-rich, heavy, loam or clay.
Care: Water during dry spells! If you want to prevent self-sowing, you need to cut back the seed-bearing structures right after the bloom; otherwise, the seeds will be ejected far into the surrounding area.
Propagation: By seed; readily self-sowing.
Use: Let grow wild in natural gardens. Goes well with other moisture-loving perennials.
Good Partners: *Filipendula, Iris sibirica, Lysimachia, Lythrum*—grasses.
Cultivars/Relatives:
• 'Mrs. Kendall Clark', faded gray-blue with a hint of pale pink, free-flowering, 20–24 in. (50–60 cm)
• *Geranium clarkei* 'Kashmir White', white with red veining.

Hairy Cranesbill
Geranium psilostemon

Geranium psilostemon

June–July ◯ ◐
H 24–48 in. (60–120 cm)

Spectacular bloomer.
Flower: Bright crimson or magenta with black eye and dark veining, large saucer-shaped flowers.
Leaf: Palmately divided, 8–10 in. (20–25 cm) across at the base, stalk leaves markedly smaller, green. Turns yellow in fall.
Growth: Tall clumps, not always stable.
Origin: Turkish-Armenian highlands. In damp birch stands or vegetation of tall perennials, up to altitudes of more than 1 mile (2,000 m).
Site: Full sun to light shade, cool, air humid, sheltered. Soil evenly moist, rich in nutrients and humus, slightly acid. No hot sites!
Care: Usually some support is needed. After the bloom, always cut back to the ground to avoid weakening the plants, which will shoot up once more. Cover carefully in cold winters. Demanding.
Propagation: See page 135.
Use: The striking color is hard to combine. Good with white- or light pink-flowered perennials.
Good Partners: *Astilbe* hybrids, *Astrantia major.*

Gray Cranesbill
Geranium renardii

Geranium renardii

June–July
H 8–10 in. (20–25 cm)

Free-flowering ground cover with decorative foliage.
Flower: Matte whitish pink with violet veining. Flowers freely.
Leaf: Divided, velvety gray-green to gray, with conspicuously wrinkled veining.
Growth: Forms broad cushions to mats; keeps leaves well into fall.
Origin: Caucasus. On sunny, rocky hillsides and at edges of bushes.
Site: Sun to light shade, warm, also hot. Soil permeable, moderately dry to well-drained. No wet, heavy soils!
Care: Cutting back in spring is optional.
Propagation: See page 135.
Use: Good ground cover under shrubs and thin stands of woody plants.
Good Partners: Other *Geranium* species—*Carex pendula,* ferns. Otherwise, best alone.

Blood-red Geranium
Geranium sanguineum

Geranium sanguineum

May–August
H 4–20 in. (10–50 cm)

Perennial with intense flower colors.
Flower: Brilliant crimson saucer-shaped flowers, free-flowering and long-blooming.
Leaf: Deeply incised, small, dark green, with red fall color.
Growth: Broad-growing with wiry, thin shoots.
Origin: Europe to Asia Minor. Sunny, thin areas at edge of woods, dry bushes.
Site: Sun to partial shade, warm, also hot. Soil dry to well-drained, sandy-loamy or gravelly, preferably lime-rich.
Care: Cut back from time to time.
Propagation: See page 135. Self-sowing.
Use: Along edges of bushes and in front of woody plants.
Good Partners: *Buglossoides, Campanula persicifolia, Stachys officinalis, Veronica*—grasses. With boxwood, pines, and juniper.
Cultivars/Relatives:
• 'Album', white, with yellow fall color.
• 'Compactum', like the species, but with compact, cushion-shaped growth, 4–6 in. (10–15 cm), for extensive use in roof gardens, in alpine gardens, or in containers.

Forest-loving Cranesbill
Geranium sylvaticum

Cultivar 'Mayflower'

June–July
H 12–24 in. (30–60 cm)

Rewarding species for flowery meadows.
Flower: Bluish or reddish violet with white center, changeable color, free-flowering.
Leaf: Palmately lobed, deeply notched.
Growth: In clumps, tall-growing, occasionally becomes floppy.
Origin: Europe to western Asia. Places with moist soil: mixed forests, mountain meadows, vegetation of tall perennials, and fringes of bushes.
Site: Light shade to partial shade, cool and moist. Soil well-drained to moist, nutrient-rich, vigorous, loam or also clay.
Care: See page 135.
Propagation: See page 135.
Use: For flowering meadows and large-area plantings in light shade. Let run wild in natural garden.
Good Partners: The various cultivars mixed with each other. *Filipendula, Ligularia, Lysimachia clethroides—Molinia.*
Cultivars/Relatives:
• 'Album', buds pink, flowers pure white.
• 'Birch Lilac', lilac-blue.
• 'Mayflower', clear blue-violet with whitish center.

Scarlet Avens
Geum coccineum

Cultivar 'Werner Arends'

May–August
H 8–16 in. (20–40 cm)

Blooms for weeks in brilliant colors.
Flower: Intense orange-red, long-stemmed, saucer-shaped flowers.
Leaf: Roundish, irregularly pinnate. Evergreen.
Growth: Cushion-shaped to flat, creeps over the ground.
Origin: Southeastern Europe. In damp mountain meadows and at edges of bushes.
Site: Light shade or with brief periods of sun, also warm. Soil well-drained to moist; nutrient-rich, humus-rich or sandy-loamy.
Care: Remove faded flowers to prolong bloom.
Propagation: By division.
Use: In groups among thin stands of woody plants.
Good Partners: *Brunnera, Campanula,* or *Omphalodes.*
Cultivars/Relatives:
• 'Borisii', pretty orange-red.
• 'Feuermeer', flaming orange-red.
• 'Werner Arends', orange-red and semidouble.
• *Geum* hybrids: splendidly colorful cultivars, 16–20 in. (40–50 cm), short-lived. Protect from winter damp.
• 'Bernstein', golden yellow, semidouble.
• 'Goldball', golden yellow, double.
• 'Georgenberg', orange-yellow, from late April, 8–10 in. (20–25 cm).
• 'Feuerball', scarlet, semidouble.
• 'Rubin', crimson, semidouble.

Baby's-breath, Chalk Plant
Gypsophila paniculata

Gypsophila paniculata

June–August ✂
H 32–48 in. (80–120 cm)

Drought-loving perennial.
Flower: White, star-shaped, in loose, many-branched panicles.
Leaf: Linear-lanceolate, gray.
Growth: Globe-shaped and bushy, with brittle peduncles.
Origin: Southeastern Europe, western and central Asia. In steppes.
Site: Full sun, warm to hot. Soil dry to well-drained, by all means permeable, loamy-sandy or sandy-gravelly loam, lime-rich. <u>No locations that are always wet in winter!</u>
Care: Cut back after bloom.
Propagation: Because of the far-reaching taproots, only young specimens can be transplanted; division also not possible. Propagate the species by seed, the cultivars by cuttings.
Use: As frothy filler between other perennials that thrive under dry conditions.
Good Partners: *Achillea, Echinops, Eryngium, Salvia, Nepeta, Veronica spicata,* and others—steppe grasses such as *Stipa* species.
Cultivars/Relatives:
• 'Bristol Fairy', white, double.
• 'Flamingo', whitish pink, double, up to 48 in. (120 cm).

Creeping Gypsophila, Creeping Baby's-breath
Gypsophila repens

Cultivar 'Letchworth'

May–June ○
H 4–10 in. (10–25 cm)

Rock garden plant.
Flower: Whitish pink in loose, forked, many-branched inflorescences.
Leaf: Linear-lanceolate, gray-green to gray.
Growth: Dense cushions, hanging over edges of walls.
Origin: Central and southern Europe. In sandy and gravelly areas: on stony hillsides.
Site: Sun, warm. Soil dry to well-drained, permeable, loamy-sandy or loamy-gravelly, lime-rich. Rots in heavy soils.
Care: None.
Propagation: By division and by cuttings.
Use: In rock gardens, on wall crests, in wall and paving crevices; and in containers.
Good Partners: *Campanula, Nepeta.*
Cultivars/Relatives:
• 'Rosea', pale pink.
• 'Rosa Schonheit', pink.
• 'Letchworth', rose-red, in large cushions.
• *Gypsophila* hybrids.
• 'Rosenschleier', pale pink, double, long-blooming, 12 in. (30 cm).
• 'Pink Star', dark pink, double, 12–16 in. (30–40 cm).

Helenium Hybrids SNEEZEWEED

Helenium hybrid 'Zimbelstern'

Helenium cultivar 'Waltraud'

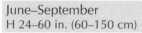
June–September
H 24–60 in. (60–150 cm)

The sneezeweed cultivars are among the flowers that decorate gardens in midsummer. With their warm, velvety colors, they reflect the August sun. These perennials are strong, free-flowering, extremely long-lived, and easy to tend. They are also highly suitable for beginning gardeners. Moreover, you can make delightful, colorful bouquets with them, along with other late-summer perennials like *Heliopsis, Monarda,* and *Phlox.* In vases they last a long time, and sometimes even the youngest buds will still open.

Flower: Shades ranging from yellow, orange, and red to russet, with a black, later yellowish brown, globe-shaped center. Medium-sized heads in plentiful, many-blossomed, umbel-like clusters.

Leaf: Lanceolate, vivid green.

Growth: Stout clumps, when old tall and broad.

Origin: Cultivated form.

Site: Full sun, warm. Soil well-drained to moist, nutrient-rich, loamy. No dry sites! In heavy soils, shoots are thin and plant is unstable.

Care: Watering essential in dry spells! Cut out faded shoots at once to prolong the bloom. Stake tall cultivars if necessary.

Propagation: By division.

Use: In sunny beds. Combine with smaller plants, so that they have elbow room. Position cultivars by their blooming season, then flowering will continue from July to September.

Good Partners: With blue *Aster* cultivars, *Delphinium, Heliopsis,* white or violet *Monarda* hybrids, *Phlox,* and *Rudbeckia.* Also with summer flowers like *Cosmos sulphureus, Salvia, Tagetes,* and *Verbena.*

Cultivars/Relatives:

Early bloomers (from July on):
• 'Blütentisch', rich yellow with brown center, 32–40 in. (80–100 cm).
• 'Moerheim Beauty', brick-red, 28–32 in. (70–80 cm), very good cultivar, but sometimes becomes floppy.
• 'Crimson Beauty', mahogany, 20–24 in. (50–60 cm), old English cultivar.

Midseason bloomers (late July/early August):
• 'Canaria', pure yellow, 40–48 in. (100–120 cm).
• 'Flammenrad', golden yellow, striped with red, 48–60 in. (120–150 cm).

• 'Waltraud', golden brown with yellow, compact, 32–40 in. (80–100 cm). One of the best old cultivars.
• 'Kupfersprudel', velvety copper-red, 44 in. (110 cm), very pretty old cultivar.
• 'Goldlackzwerg', yellowish red-brown, stays small, 28–32 in. (70–80 cm).
• 'Margot', red-brown with yellow edge, 32–48 in. (80–120 cm), a modern cultivar.

Late bloomers (August):
• 'Königstiger', yellow with red edge, 48–56 in. (120–140 cm). Very good, vigorous cultivar.
• 'Baudirektor Linné', brick-red to red-brown, 48–60 in. (120–150 cm), outstanding cultivar.

Very late bloomers (September):
• 'Sonnenwunder', light yellow, 60 in. (150 cm), one of the largest cultivars.
• 'Septembergold', dazzling yellow, 44 in. (110 cm), blooms at same time as fall asters.
• 'Septemberfuchs', brick-red, 48 in. (120 cm).

Sunrose, Frostweed
Helianthemum Hybrids

Hybrid 'Heufield Brilliant'

May–September
H 6–8 in. (15–20 cm)

Many-flowered subshrubs that resemble perennials.
Flower: In many shades, including yellow, orange, red, brown, pink, and white; single or double. Saucer-shaped flowers open in the morning and fall off in the afternoon.
Leaf: Linear to ovate, dark green or gray-green. Usually evergreen.
Growth: Broad cushions with thin shoots. Floppy when old.
Origin: Cultivated form.
Site: Full sun, warm or hot. Soil moderately dry, permeable, stony-loamy, lime-rich.
Care: Cut back after blooming to induce strong new growth. Cover the less hardy, gray-leaved cultivars in winter to protect from frost.
Propagation: By cuttings.
Use: In rock gardens, on wall crests, in paving crevices, in stone containers.
Good Partners: *Campanula, Linum, Sedum, Veronica.*
Cultivars/Relatives:
• 'Eisbär', white.
• 'Lawrenson's Pink', pink.
• 'Sterntaler', yellow, robust.
• 'Rubin', dark red.

Red-stemmed Sunflower
Helianthus atrorubens 'Monarch'

Helianthus atrorubens 'Monarch'

July–October
H 72–80 in. (180–200 cm)

Splendid, but short-lived perennial sunflower.
Flower: Golden yellow, 3 in. (8 cm) heads in lavish profusion.
Leaf: Ovate, dark green, coarse.
Growth: Huge, towering perennial with dark-red shoots, not always stable.
Origin: Eastern North America. In sunny, dry pine forests.
Site: Full sun, warm, sheltered from wind. Soil moderately dry to well-drained, nutrient-rich, sandy-loamy. Not stable in heavy, moist soils.
Care: Prune faded blossoms to stimulate new flower production. Stake in windy locations. In fall, cover with boughs; overwinter new divisions in frost-free spot.
Propagation: By division.
Use: In large bedding areas, and as solitary perennial near house.
Good Partners: Fall asters, *Chrysanthemum, Cosmos sulphureus, Verbena*—tall grasses.

Thinleaf Sunflower
Helianthus decapetalus

Cultivar 'Capenoch Star'

July–September
H 48–60 in. (120–150 cm)

A summer perennial that blooms inexhaustibly.
Flower: Yellow heads, relatively small for sunflowers.
Leaf: Oblong-ovate, matte green, rough-haired.
Growth: In dense clumps with erect shoots, long-lived.
Origin: Eastern North America. In meadows.
Site: Full sun, warm. Soil well-drained to moist, permeable, nutrient-rich, loamy.
Care: Prune faded shoots to induce repeated blooming. Protect from slug damage. Divide and move every five to eight years.
Propagation: By division.
Use: In sunny beds.
Good Partners: *Cosmos sulphureus* 'Sunset', *Salvia, Tagetes, Verbena bonariensis. Aster, Delphinium, Helenium,* and *Heliopsis.*
Cultivars/Relatives:
• 'Capenoch Star', light yellow, single, free-flowering, best cultivar.
• 'Meteor', golden yellow, semi-double.
• 'Soleil d'Or', golden yellow, double, with ball-shaped flowers.

Rough Heliopsis
Heliopsis helianthoides var. *scabra*

Cultivar 'Goldgrünherz'

Cultivar 'Venus'

Heliopsis helianthoides var. *scabra* 'Hohlspiegel'

July–September
H 32–60 in. (80–150 cm)

The commercial assortment of heliopsises lacks the broad range of colors that other groups have; all the available breeds are yellow-flowered and differ in the shade of yellow and the abundance of their blossoms. The entire spectrum of single, semidouble, and double flowers is represented, from sunflower-like singles to globe-shaped golden balls. The lustrous yellow of these tireless bloomers is indispensable to every amateur gardener. Once established they are lush summer-flowering perennials that last for decades in the same location. Like the related *Helenium* hybrids, they are so easy to tend that they present no problems to a beginning gardener.

Flower: Yellow, sometimes gold-orange or green-yellow, sunflower-like, single to double.
Leaf: Pointed and ovate, dark green, somewhat rough.
Growth: Broad, bushy clumps; the large-growing, double-flowered cultivars occasionally unstable. Needs several years to produce masses of flowers.
Origin: North America. In tallgrass prairies and damp hollows.

Site: Sun, warm, sheltered from wind. Soil well-drained, permeable, nutrient-rich, loamy. No soils that dry out easily!
Care: Prune faded shoots regularly; with good weather the blooming season can be extended to early October. After all blooming finishes, cut back to ground.
Propagation: By cuttings and by division.
Use: Bedding perennial that lasts for years in one place. Put together with other late-blooming perennials.
Good Partners: *Ageratum, Salvia, Tagetes,* and *Verbena bonariensis*—pretty with lilac- and blue-flowered *Aster novae-angliae* and *Aster novi-belgii,* dark violet *Delphinium* in its second bloom, yellow or the even lovelier red-brown *Helenium* hybrids, *Rudbeckia—Buddleja davidii* in blue or violet, summer-blooming *Clematis* x *durandii.*
Cultivars/Relatives:
• 'Sonnenzwerg', yellow, semidouble, one of the shortest cultivars, 24–32 in. (60–80 cm).
• 'Karat', rich yellow, single. Excellent as cut flower.
• 'Goldgrünherz', yellow with greenish center, double, 32–40 in. (80–100 cm). One of the classic cultivars.
• 'Hohlspiegel', golden yellow, semidouble, 48–52 in. (120–130 cm), old cultivar.
• 'Goldgefieder', golden yellow, double. Rewarding, highly recommended cultivar, 48–52 in. (120–130 cm).
• 'Venus', lustrous golden yellow, single, gorgeous as cut flower.
• 'Sonnenschild', yellow-orange, ball-shaped and double, old cultivar.
• 'Spitzentänzerin', orange-yellow, semidouble, the best cultivar.

Hellebore, Christmas Rose
Helleborus Hybrids

Helleborus hybrid 'Atrorubens'

Helleborus foetidus

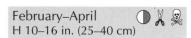

February–April
H 10–16 in. (25–40 cm)

Hellebores are increasingly popular in gardens. These attractive spring bloomers display their white, rose-pink, or purple flowers after the snow has melted.
Flower: Yellowish green to purple-red with metallic gleam, sometimes spotted or violet-veined, varying in color and markings. They form large, drooping saucers that turn green during seed formation. The seedlings often display surprisingly variable colors.
Leaf: Divided like a fan-shape, leathery, dark green. The leaves bud quite early and overwinter, still green, as dense, handsome leaf crowns.
Growth: Dense clumps from rhizomes that creep underground; they last for decades in the same location.
Origin: Cultivated form.

Site: Partial shade to shade, cool to moderately warm locations. Soil well-drained, humus, loam, lime-rich.
Care: After the bloom, cut off overwintered leaves that have become unsightly. The first blossoms may be damaged by spring frosts. Let grow undisturbed.
Propagation: By seed immediately after seeds are ripe. The colors of the seedlings usually differ from those of the parents. If you want uniform colors, it is advisable to divide the clumps in summer.
Use: In undergrowth beneath shrubs that flower in early spring.
Good Partners: Shrubs: *Corylopsis, Corylus avellana, Hamamelis, Viburnum bodnantense.* Very pretty with spring-flowering perennials like *Epimedium, Hepatica,* and *Pulmonaria* or bulbs like *Corydalis, Galanthus,* and *Leucojum.*
Cultivars/Relatives:
• 'Sirius', light yellow, 10 in. (25 cm).
• 'Taurus', white to pink, dotted, 10 in. (25 cm).
• 'Atrorubens', purple-red, blooms as early as February.
• 'Burgunder Blut', dark purple, 12 in. (30 cm).

• *Helleborus foetidus,* bearsfoot hellebore, blooms in yellow-green from February to April in branched inflorescences. Leaf digitally incised, dark green, leathery, evergreen. 12–24 in. (30–60 cm), indigenous perennial for edges of woods and bushes in loamy soils, for locations with mild winters.
• *Helleborus niger,* Christmas rose or black hellebore, white flowers appearing from December on. Gradually forms large clumps, long-lived. For warm, sheltered sites in absolutely permeable, well-aerated lime-rich sandy-loamy soils. Susceptible to fungus in damp locations or in wet summers.
• 'Praecox', All Saints' Day rose, whitish pink, October–December, 12 in. (30 cm).
Warning: The entire plant is poisonous.

Hybrid Day Lilies
Hemerocallis Hybrids

Hybrid 'Chicago Two Bits'

Hybrid 'Goldarama'

May–August ◯ ◐
H 16–44 in. (40–110 cm)

As early as the sixteenth century, two day lily species were imported to Europe from East Asia. Their native habitats were riverside woods and damp mountain meadows. In the past few decades, owing to splendidly successful efforts at hybridization by American and European *Hemerocallis* specialists, thousands of brilliantly colored day lilies have sprung from the modest shades of those original forms with their light yellow and rust-red blossoms.

Flower: Star-shaped, lily-like. The individual blossoms open for a single day, hence their name. New flower buds are produced continuously, which ensures that the plants will bloom for weeks. Yellow comes in hues ranging from light yellow, lemon-yellow, golden yellow, and melon-yellow to deep yellow. Orange ranges from golden, copper, and brown through apricot to dazzling orange-red, from cinnabar and velvety red to russet. Especially select shades of red are purple-red, mahogany, and blackish red. Pink surprises us with light tints—lilac, peach, and salmon. Breeders are close to a pure white, but it still has a greenish or yellowish hue. Lavender, bicolored, or even striped blossoms have an unusual effect. The flower form is dependent upon the cultivar; it may be open wide or shaped like a bell, funnel, star, or saucer, or have smooth or frilly edges. Many cultivars have a pleasant scent.

Hybrid 'Lanning Roper'

Leaf: Grassy and narrow. The leaves sprout early, in March, but are not affected by cold. Pleasing, yellow fall color.
Growth: In broad clumps.
Site: Sun to partial shade; with increasing shade the plant blooms less abundantly. Soil moderately dry to well-drained, also moist, best in nutrient-rich loamy soils.
Care: Easy to tend; just remove spent stalks and, later, fall leaves. Very easy to transplant.
Propagation: By division.
Use: Can be used everywhere. In beds, at edges of woody plants in sun or light shade, at edge of pond.
Good Partners: Other bedding perennials.
Cultivars/Relatives: Today there exist almost 10,000 cultivars, and every year dozens, sometimes hundreds, more are added. Many cultivars disappear again after a short time, as they are displaced by better ones. For

Hemerocallis hybrid

this reason, no specific information on cultivars is given here. The assortment is grouped as follows:
Miniature-flowered cultivars: Mostly early blooming, from late May on. Flowers 2–3 in. (5–7.5 cm) across. The lengthy blooming season of most cultivars captivates everyone. Plant miniature *Hemerocallis* away from the large-flowered cultivars, because they have a different, daintier character.
Small-flowered cultivars: Bloom from early June on, usually until late July, or even later. Flowers about 3–4 in. (8–11 cm) across. Many of the cultivars reveal a throat of a different color—usually greenish. 20–36 in. (50–90 cm) tall.
Large-flowered cultivars: Bloom from June to August–September, flowers measure 5–7 in. (12–18 cm) across. Included are some extremely valuable and free-flowering cultivars. Height 16–40 in. (40–100 cm).

145

PERENNIALS

Hepatica, Romanian Liverleaf
Hepatica transsylvanica

Hepatica transsylvanica

March–April
H 4–8 in. (10–20 cm)

Spring bloomer with anemone-like blossoms.
Flower: Pure blue, saucer-shaped, free-flowering.
Leaf: Three- to five-lobed, fresh green, glossy. Appears early and stays green a long time.
Growth: Cushion-shaped, gradually forms mats by means of runners.
Origin: Southeastern Europe woods.
Site: Partial shade to shade, also warm. Soil moderately dry to well-drained; humus, loam.
Care: Let grow undisturbed.
Propagation: By division.
Use: In spring gardens under shrubs. Also, let run wild in a stand of woody plants. Tolerates root pressure from woody plants.
Good Partners: Shrubs like *Corylus avellana—Helleborus, Lathyrus vernus—Anemone nemorosa.*
Cultivars/Relatives:
• 'Buis', light blue, large-flowered.
• *Hepatica nobilis*, three-lobed hepatica, blue, March–April. Indigenous. Leaves three-lobed, dies back early, 4 in. (10 cm) tall. For loose, humus- and lime-rich soils. Grows loosely scattered, not mat-forming.

Dame's Rocket, Sweet Rocket, Dame's Violet
Hesperis matronalis

Hesperis matronalis

May–June
H 24–40 in. (60–100 cm)

A shade-tolerant, naturalized wild perennial.
Flower: Whitish pink to deep violet, variable in seedlings, has pervasive, intensive scent in evenings. Flowers in dense racemes.
Leaf: Triangular-cordate, green.
Growth: Erect, many-branched, sometimes unstable.
Origin: Southern Europe to central Asia, naturalized in central Europe. In thin woods.
Site: Light shade to shade, warm, sheltered from wind. Soil well-drained, permeable, nutrient- and lime-rich. Rots in wet sites.
Care: To prolong blooming season, remove all faded stems at once. Dame's rocket is short-lived; it usually lasts no more than two years.
Propagation: By seed; self-sowing.
Use: In shady borders; or let grow wild in natural garden.
Good Partners: *Campanula lactiflora, Geranium, Primula japonica, Thalictrum.* Shade grasses and ferns.

Coral-bells, Alum Root
Heuchera Hybrids

Heuchera hybrid 'Lady Romney'

May–July
H 16–28 in. (40–70 cm)

Pretty perennial with graceful bell-shaped blossoms.
Flower: Pink, red, crimson, and white. Tiny, bell-like flowers in narrow panicles.
Leaf: Cordate, dull green, in some cases with light-colored markings.
Growth: Cushion-shaped.
Site: Sun to light shade, cool, air humid. Soil well-drained to moist, permeable; stony humus or stony loam.
Care: Water in dry spells. Cover in locations with threat of frost.
Propagation: By division and by cuttings.
Use: In rock gardens out of sun, in the front of borders, as edging. In small areas under thin shrubs.
Good Partners: *Campanula, Saxifraga arendsii* hybrids, perennials for rock gardens.
Cultivars/Relatives:
• 'Schneewittchen', white.
• 'Gracillima', salmon-pink, old cultivar for country gardens.
• 'Red Spangles', scarlet.
• *Heuchera micrantha* 'Palace Purple', white, inconspicuous, small flowers. Gorgeous purple foliage.

HOSTA, PLANTAIN LILY
Hosta

Hosta hybrid 'Snowdown' among *Geranium himalayense*

June–August
H 2–48 in. (5–120 cm)

For a long time, hostas were considered old-fashioned perennials from our great-grandparents' front yards. However, the results of new breeding have altered this image completely. Now top prices are paid for the modern, highly decorative American and German cultivars, and the breeding of spectacular crosses is in full swing. Classic and new *Hosta* forms that rank among the finest ornamental foliage plants in existence are available to gardeners. No other perennial has such surprising diversity of form, yet is so undemanding. Slugs may become a problem, because they greatly enjoy being in the humid air under the large leaves. Now and then the flush is endangered by late frosts.

Flower: White, violet-blue, lilac, or purple-violet, with light to heavy, pleasant scent. Bell- or tube-shaped in racemes, on rigid stalks above the mounds of foliage.

Leaf: Quite variable, ranging from narrow lanceolate to broad-round cordate, in the colors blue, gray, green, yellow, and white. The deep, longitudinal leaf veins add a pretty play of lines. Many of the large-leaved forms display handsome light yellow to golden yellow fall colors in October. In vases, the leaves are attractive and long-lasting.

Growth: In clumps, with a regular, hemispherical outline. Many dwarf species, however, are rather loose-growing and grassy.

Origin: Mostly Japan, some species also China and Korea. In mountain forests, alder and willow bushes, marsh meadows, and damp rock crevices.

Site: Light shade to shade, depending on leaf color. In partial shade, hostas develop fewer, but larger leaves. Cool, with evenly humid air and moist soil; many cultivars also partially in the sun or somewhat drier. Soil well-drained, humus, loam.

Care: Apply organic fertilizer occasionally, possibly by sprinkling well-aged bark chips or peat substitutes on soil. By all means, try to control slugs, especially in wet spring weather. No other procedures necessary. Old *Hosta* plants are best left undisturbed; they will live for decades.

Green-leaved Hostas
Hosta

White-leaved Hostas
Hosta

Blooming *Hosta* hybrid

Propagation: Possible by seed, but in some cases the seedlings differ greatly from the initial forms. Many hybrids are sterile. Division is preferable, best done in fall, also possible in spring—but be careful with the young, brittle shoots.

Use: At edges of bushes, under thin groups of trees, in shady beds, at edges of ponds, the small forms also in rock gardens out of sun.

Good Partners: Often the differently colored forms are most effective together. With the broad-leaved plants, these narrow-leaved partners are good: various woodland grasses like *Carex, Deschampsia,* and *Luzula,* or filigree ferns. Along with them, flowering woodland perennials, including *Aconitum, Astilbe, Cimicifuga, Kirengeshoma,* or *Tiarella.*

Classification: More than 100 cultivars and forms are available commercially. The nomenclature is confusing. To do justice to the diversity of the *Hosta* species, it is advisable to group the plants according to the principal leaf colors.

Hosta plantaginea 'Honeybells'

July–August
H 2–32 in. (5–80 cm)

Attractive, green-leaved perennials with decorative foliage.

Cultivars/Relatives:

Hosta elata, light blue-violet, July–August. Leaf large, broad ovate-cordate, prominently veined. Huge, broad clumps, 24–32 in. (60–80 cm).

Hosta fortunei 'Freising', white, July, large, broad, dark green leaves, dome-shaped clumps, 20–24 in. (50–60 cm).

Hosta lancifolia, narrow-leaved plantain lily, blue, July–August. Leaf narrow and ovate, glossy dark green. Pillow-like clumps, 12–20 in. (30–50 cm).

Hosta longissima, swamp plantain lily, blue, July–August, long, pointed, dark green leaves. Small clumps, 12 in. (30 cm). Only for moist to wet soils.

Hosta plantaginea, fragrant plantain lily, white, scented, free-flowering, July. Leaf vivid green, cordate. Large clumps, 20–28 in. (50–70 cm). For bright locations, very pretty!

Hosta tardiflora, light violet, free-flowering, September. Leaf lanceolate, olive green, leathery. Low clumps, 8–12 in. (20–30 cm).

Hosta ventricosa, blue plantain lily, lilac-violet, bell-shaped, July. Leaf round to cordate, glossy green. Clumps loose, hemi-spherical, 20–24 in. (50–60 cm). For bright, not overly sunny sites.

Hosta venusta, dwarf plantain lily, lilac, July. Leaves dainty, cordate. Produces runners, forms small mats, 2–6 in. (5–15 cm).

Hosta crispula

Hosta undulata 'Undulata'

July–August
H 8–24 in. (20–60 cm)

Some forms have green leaves and white leaf margins, others are white-leaved with green margins. The white areas turn brown if the sun is too strong.

Cultivars/Relatives:

Hosta crispula, giant white-edged plantain lily, lilac, July–August. Leaf long and pointed, cordate, prettily veined, margins white, curled, and wavy. Massive clumps, 20–24 in. (50–60 cm).

Hosta undulata, wavy-leaved plantain lily, lilac on long flower stems, July–August, leaves large.
• 'Undulata', flushes early, leaf pointed and elliptical, white with narrow green fringe, 8–12 in. (20–30 cm).
• 'Univittata', leaf center white, margin broad and green, 12–16 in. (30–40 cm).

Hosta sieboldii, white-edged plantain lily, lilac, July–August. Pointed, spoon-shaped green leaves with narrow white margins. Loose clumps, 12–24 in. (30–60 cm). Only in damp locations.

Yellow-leaved Hostas
Hosta

Hosta fortunei 'Aureo-Maculata'

July–August ◑
H 16–24 in. (40–60 cm)

Leaves uniformly golden green or yellow with green margins, also green leaves with yellow fringe. The yellow is most intense after initial growth.
Cultivars/Relatives:
Hosta fortunei 'Aurea', Fortune's plantain lily, flowers lilac in lush racemes, July. Leaf firm, uniformly cordate, prettily veined and ribbed. After initial growth, lustrous golden yellow; in summer, lemon-yellow. Magnificent clumps, 16–24 in. (40-60 cm).
• 'Aureo-Marginata', yellow-edged plantain lily, leaf green with yellow fringe.
Hosta sieboldiana 'Semperaurea', Siebold plantain lily, lilac, July–August. Broad, cordate leaves, faded yellow at first, in summer increasingly bright yellow. Clumps shallowly arched, 16–24 in. (40–60 cm).
Hosta ventricosa 'Aureo-Maculata', blue plantain lily, lilac, July. Leaf wavy, cordate, green with uneven yellow margin, in some cases striped with yellow, creamy yellow, and off-white. Strikingly colored only until early summer, then gradually turning green.

Blue-leaved Hostas
Hosta

Hosta sieboldiana 'Elegans'

June–August ◑
H 8–40 in. (20–100 cm)

In overly sunny spots the sun burns the leaves; in deep shade they turn green. The leaves are affected by drops falling from eaves or from trees, but not by rain. The blue color appears only in cool, humid shade. Do not let soil dry out.
Cultivars/Relatives:
Hosta sieboldiana, pale lilac, funnel-shaped, many-flowered, July–August. Leaf large, cordate, coarse, prominently ribbed, gray-green to blue-gray. Broad clumps, 20–32 in. (50–80 cm).
• 'Elegans', leaf steel-blue, clumps 24 in. (60 cm) tall. Reliable cultivar.
• 'Francis Williams', leaf steel-blue with yellow margin.
• 'Herkules', leaf blue-green, very large, almost plate-shaped. Clumps 32–40 in. (80–100 cm) tall.
Hosta fortunei 'Hyacinthina', hyacinth plantain lily, dark violet, July–August. Leaf cordate, dull gray-blue. Compact clumps, 16–20 in. (40–50 cm).
Hosta hybrids: There now exist dozens of cultivars in thrilling blue, mostly with broad or roundish, cordate leaves.
• 'Blaue Wolke', leaf deep blue, compact clumps, 16 in. (40 cm).

Hosta sieboldiana 'Francis Williams'

• 'Blue Boy', lilac, June. Leaf small, steel-blue. Clumps, 16 in. (40 cm) tall.
• 'Blue Cadet', lilac, June. Leaf round, small, gray-blue. Dwarf form, 10 in. (25 cm) tall.
Hosta x *tardiana*, dove plantain lily, lilac, July–August. Leaves cordate, coarsely leathery. Low, dove-colored to steel-gray, compact clumps, 8–16 in. (20–40 cm) tall.
• 'Blaue Venus', leaf deep blue, select cultivar.
• 'Hadspen Blue', wonderful, velvety blue cultivar.
• 'Halcyon', one of the best blue cultivars for uniformly shady places.

Evergreen Candytuft, Edging Candytuft
Iberis sempervirens

Cultivar 'Snowflake'

April–May	◯
H 6–12 in. (15–30 cm)	

Indispensable subshrub for rock gardens.
Flower: White, in dense terminal cymes.
Leaf: Narrow lanceolate, bright dark green, evergreen.
Growth: Low, spreading, cushion-shaped subshrub that can live for decades and grow to 60 in. (1.5 m).
Origin: Mediterranean region to southern Alps. On highland plateaus.
Site: Sun, warm. Soil dry to well-drained, permeable, humus-poor.
Care: Apply inorganic fertilizer from time to time. Cut back old, floppy cushions hard, to a shoot length of about 4 in. (10 cm). Alternatively (and preferably), after the bloom, regularly cut back by one-third. In winter, cover lightly with boughs.
Propagation: By cuttings.
Use: In rock gardens, on dry walls and slopes with southern exposure, in the front of borders with full sun.
Good Partners: *Alyssum, Aubrieta, Iris barbata-nana* hybrids—tulips—*Festuca*.
Cultivars/Relatives:
• 'Findel', 8 in. (20 cm).
• 'Snowflake', 12 in. (30 cm).
• 'Dwarf Snowflake', 6 in. (15 cm).
• *Iberis saxatilis*, white, blooms about two or three weeks before *I. sempervirens*. 4–6 in. (10–15 cm) tall, loose-growing stem trail, then grow vertically (decumbent) spreads out gradually.

Swordleaf Inula
Inula ensifolia 'Compacta'

Inula ensifolia 'Compacta'

July–August	◯ ✂
H 8–12 in. (20–30 cm)	

Compact-growing summer bloomer with masses of blossoms.
Flower: Golden yellow daisy-like flowers at the ends of erect stems. Blooms abundantly.
Leaf: Narrow linear, pointed at tip, matte dark green.
Growth: Compact, dense clumps.
Origin: Eastern Europe and Caucasus. On sunny mountain slopes and in dry grass.
Site: Full sun, warm. Soil moderately dry to well-drained, permeable, also nutrient-poor.
Care: Cut back in fall. No other procedures necessary.
Propagation: By division.
Use: In borders in rock gardens, on sunny slopes, and in roof gardens.
Good Partners: *Achillea, Anaphalis, Anchusa azurea, Echinops, Eryngium, Nepeta, Salvia, Stachys byzantina—Helictotrichon*.

Giant Inula
Inula magnifica

Inula magnifica

July–August	◯
H 56–72 in. (140–180 cm)	

Massive perennial, recommended only for relatively large gardens.
Flower: Lustrous yellow, daisy-like, with fine ray flowers in umbel-like inflorescences.
Leaf: Huge, broad ovate basal leaves and smaller, stemless leaves, matte green with slightly hairy undersides.
Growth: Enormous, erect, spreading clumps.
Origin: Caucasus. In thin birch woods and in tall perennial vegetation.
Site: Sun to light shade, cool, also warm. Soil well-drained to moist, permeable, nutrient-rich.
Care: Feed moderately from time to time. Cut back after the bloom, because the leaves turn brown.
Propagation: By seed and by division.
Use: In borders and on sunny slopes, in front of thin groups of woody plants.
Good Partners: *Aconitum, Campanula lactiflora, Rudbeckia, Solidago, Veronica virginica—Calamagrostis*.

BEARDED IRISES

Iris barbata Hybrids

Iris barbata-media 'Annikins' between evergreen candytuft (in front) and cushion spurge (in back)

May–June
H 4–8 in. (10–20 cm) ○

The *Iris* genus includes more than 200 species and countless breeds. Among them, the bearded iris category occupies a prominent position. Even for experts, it is difficult to get a clear view of the enormous commercial assortment of bearded irises. It is divided into three groups, according to mature height and blooming season:

• Tall bearded irises (*Iris barbata-elatior* hybrids), more than 28 in. (70 cm) tall, late-blooming from late May on. Peduncles branched.

• Intermediate bearded irises (*Iris barbata-media* hybrids), 16–28 in. (40–70 cm) tall, blooming after miniature bearded irises and before tall bearded irises.

• Low or dwarf bearded irises (*Iris barbata-nana* hybrids), about 6–12 in. (15–30 cm) tall and early blooming, from mid-April on.

Flower: In all shades except pure scarlet and orange-red, often bicolored. Falls (pendent sepals) are ornamented with conspicuous fuzz, the so-called beard. Scented. Stems are stiffly erect.

Leaf: Erect sword-shaped, firm, and stiff, gray-green, evergreen.

Growth: In clumps, with thick rhizomes that creep along beneath the surface of the soil.

Site: Full sun, warm, also hot. Soil dry to well-drained, permeable, nutrient-rich, mineral, humus-poor, lime-rich.

Care: Plant rhizomes horizontally, either at or just below the surface of the soil. Best planting time is after the bloom. If set too deep, bearded irises will be stunted. Remove leaves in spring. Cut back faded blosoms to prevent energy-consuming setting of seed. Apply inorganic fertilizer in spring.

Propagation: By division of the rhizomes with a knife or spade, after the bloom to late summer.

Use: In borders and in steppe gardens. Dwarf bearded irises, also in rock gardens and roof gardens.

Good Partners: *Anaphalis, Linum, Papaver orientale, Salvia, Stachys byzantina,* and other gray-leaved perennials.

Bearded Iris
Iris barbata Hybrids

Elatior hybrid 'Fresno Frolic'

Elatior hybrid 'Amethyst Flame'

Nana hybrid 'Tonya'

Iris barbata-elatior Hybrids
Tall bearded iris, May–July,
24–48 in. (60–120 cm):
White flowers:
- 'Cliffs of Dover', 32 in. (80 cm).
- 'White Knight', 28 in. (70 cm).
White-and-yellow flowers:
- 'Glacier Gold', 28 in. (70 cm).
- 'Tulip Festival', 28 in. (70 cm).
White-and-pink flowers:
- 'Crinoline', 28 in. (70 cm).
- 'Mod Mode', 32 in. (80 cm).
White-and-blue flowers:
- 'Mystique', 36 in. (90 cm).
- 'Stepping Out', 32 in. (80 cm).
Yellow flowers:
- 'Acapulco Gold', 32 in. (80 cm).
- 'Carolina Gold', 36 in. (90 cm).
- 'West Coast', 24 in. (60 cm).
Apricot-colored flowers:
- 'Peach Frost', with white center, 36 in. (90 cm).
- 'Sparkling Sunrise', with orange-red beard, 40 in. (100 cm).
Pink flowers:
- 'Heartbreaker', 32 in. (80 cm).
Velvety red flowers:
- 'Ruby Mine', 36 in. (90 cm).
- 'Spartan', 24 in. (60 cm).
Bronze-colored flowers:
- 'Happy Harvest', 28 in. (70 cm).
- 'Olympic Torch', 32 in. (80 cm).
Light blue flowers:
- 'Azure Apogee', 32 in. (80 cm).
- 'Blue Reflection', 36 in. (90 cm).
- 'Sea Bright', 36 in. (90 cm).
Medium blue flowers:
- 'Blue Luster', 32 in. (80 cm).

- 'Shipshape', 36 in. (90 cm).
- 'Tyrolean Blue', 28 in. (70 cm).
Dark blue flowers:
- 'Dusky Dancer', 32 in. (80 cm).
- 'Night Owl', 36 in. (90 cm).
Light and dark blue flowers:
- 'Dialogue', 32 in. (80 cm).
- 'Lord Baltimore', 32 in. (80 cm).
Violet flowers:
- 'Mysterious', 32 in. (80 cm).
- 'Spectabilis', 28 in. (70 cm).

Iris barbata-media Hybrids
Intermediate bearded irises,
May, 16–28 in. (40–70 cm):
White flowers:
- 'Avanelle', 20 in. (50 cm).
- 'Snow Festival', 24 in. (60 cm).
Yellow flowers:
- 'Dandelion', deep yellow, 20 in. (50 cm). • 'Frosted Cream', 24 in. (60 cm).
Apricot-colored flowers:
- 'Peachy Face', 20 in. (50 cm).
Pink flowers:
- 'Pink Kitten', 20 in. (50 cm).
- 'Sweetie', 16 in. (40 cm).
Velvety red flowers:
- 'Foxcote', 20 in. (50 cm).
- 'Vamp', 20 in. (50 cm).
Russet flowers:
- 'Brown Doll', 20 in. (50 cm).
Bronze-colored flowers:
- 'Boy Wonder', 24 in. (60 cm).
Light blue flowers:
- 'Bluekeeta', 24 in. (60 cm).
- 'Morgendämmerung', 24 in. (60 cm).
Dark blue flowers:
- 'Annikins', 20 in. (50 cm).
Light blue-violet flowers:
- 'Gypsy Jump', 24 in. (60 cm).

Iris barbata-nana Hybrids
Low bearded irises, dwarf bearded irises, April–May, 4–12 in.

(10–30 cm):
White flowers:
- 'Chalk Mark', 8 in. (20 cm).
- 'White Gem', 12 in. (30 cm).
White-and-violet flowers:
- 'Sky and Snow', 14 in. (35 cm).
Yellow flowers:
- 'Eyebright', dark-veined, 14 in. (35 cm). • 'Lemon Puff', 6 in. (15 cm). • 'Orange Caper', orange-yellow, 12 in. (30 cm).
Apricot-colored flowers:
- 'Melon Honey', 12 in. (30 cm).
Pink flowers:
- 'Little Dream', 12 in. (30 cm).
- 'Orchid Flair', 4 in. (10 cm).
Velvety red flowers:
- 'Fairy Ballet', 12 in. (30 cm).
- 'Lollipop', 12 in. (30 cm).
Bronze-colored flowers:
- 'Gingerbread Man', 10 in. (25 cm). • 'Little Bill', 8 in. (20 cm).
Light blue flowers:
- 'Himmelsauge', 4 in. (10 cm).
- 'Sapphire Gem', 10 in. (25 cm).
- 'Tinkerbell', 12 in. (30 cm).
Medium blue flowers:
- 'Baby Baron', 10 in. (25 cm).
- 'Puppet', 10 in. (25 cm).
Dark blue flowers:
- 'Demon', 12 in. (30 cm).
- 'Myra's Child', 8 in. (20 cm).
Violet-blue flowers:
- 'Cyanea', 6 in. (15 cm).
- 'Tease', 8 in. (20 cm).

Yellow Flag
Iris pseudacorus

Iris pseudacorus

May–June
H 32–48 in. (80–120 cm)

Indigenous *Iris* species, which even in gardens needs to be planted near water.
Flower: Yellow, the falls dark-veined, in loose racemes atop rigidly erect stems.
Leaf: Sword-shaped, large, fresh green, with slight waxy coating.
Growth: In clumps, spreads out heavily by means of rhizomes.
Origin: Europe to western Asia and North Africa. Along banks and wet ditches, in woodland swamps.
Site: Sun to light shade. Soil wet to moist, also submerged, nutrient-rich, preferably heavy, loamy soils.
Care: Tidy the clumps in spring. No other procedures needed.
Propagation: By division in spring.
Use: In shallow parts of ponds and pools, in damp beds, in natural gardens along banks of streams.
Good Partners: *Caltha, Ligularia, Lythrum, Trollius.*
Cultivars/Relatives:
• 'Bastardii', faded yellow.
• 'Beuron', medium yellow.

Siberian Iris
Iris sibirica

Iris sibirica 'Soft Blue'

May–June
H 16–36 in. (40–90 cm)

Iris species with many forms; for damp beds.
Flower: Bright violet-blue, in some cases with striking markings, scented.
Leaf: Grassy, in fall bronze or orange.
Growth: Dense clumps, above which the slender pedicles tower.
Origin: Europe to Siberia. In damp meadows.
Site: Sun to partial shade, cool, air humid. Soil well-drained to moist, nutrient-rich, loamy.
Care: Tidy the clumps in spring. Water generously and feed well.
Propagation: By division.
Use: In natural gardens, borders.
Good Partners: *Achillea ptarmica, Alchemilla, Polemonium, Primula japonica, Thalictrum, Trollius chinensis.*
Cultivars/Relatives:
• 'White Swirl', white, 28 in. (70 cm).
• 'Cambridge', light blue, large-flowered, 28 in. (70 cm).
• 'Strandperle', light blue, 32 in. (80 cm).
• 'Caesar', violet-blue, 36 in. (90 cm).

Spuria Iris, Spurious Iris, Seashore Iris
Iris spuria Hybrids

Hybrid 'Landscape Blue'

June–July
H 32–56 in. (80–140 cm)

Less well-known, gorgeous irises.
Flower: Violet, blue, yellow, white, or bronze, occasionally multicolored. Flowers on top of rigid stems.
Leaf: Sword-shaped, erect, and formal-looking, vivid green.
Growth: In clumps.
Site: Sun, warm. Soil well-drained, nutrient-rich, loamy.
Care: Plant 1–1.5 in. (5–8 cm) deep in fall. Tidy the clumps in spring. Feed regularly; water in dry spells. Cut off stems after the bloom. Moderately frost-hardy.
Propagation: By division in early fall.
Use: In borders.
Good Partners: *Alchemilla, Delphinium, Geranium.* White roses.
Cultivars/Relatives:
• 'Lydia Jane', white, 40 in. (100 cm).
• 'Chachie Owen', golden yellow, 40 in. (100 cm).
• 'Imperial Bronze', bright yellow to bronze, 32 in. (80 cm).
• 'Red Oak', red-brown, 32 in. (80 cm).
• 'Highline Lavender', lavender-blue with yellow, 36 in. (90 cm).

Wax Bell
Kirengeshoma palmata

Kirengeshoma palmata

July–September
H 24–36 in. (60–90 cm)

Splendid ornamental foliage perennial with showy, waxy leaves.
Flower: Light yellow, broad bell-shaped in loose, drooping cymes.
Leaf: Large, maple like, vivid green to yellowish green.
Growth: In clumps, erect.
Origin: Japan. On damp mountainsides and in fern-rich, humid beech forests.
Site: Light to partial shade, cool, air humid. Soil well-drained to moist, rich in humus and nutrients. <u>No compacted soils</u>!
Care: Protect from slug damage. Cut back in fall. Cover for light winter protection in cold zones.
Propagation: By division or by cuttings in spring.
Use: In light shade of woody plants and walls.
Good Partners: *Aconitum, Cimicifuga, Hosta, Rodgersia, Saxifraga cortusifolia, Tricyrtis—Carex morrowii, Dryopteris.*

Red-hot-poker, Poker Plant, Torch Lily
Kniphofia Hybrids

Kniphofia hybrid 'Alcazar'

July–September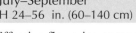
H 24–56 in. (60–140 cm)

Effective flowering perennial.
Flower: Yellow, orange, brick-red, scarlet, salmon-pink, also bicolored, tubular flowers in torch-like spadixes.
Leaf: Grassy, with sharp margin, gray-green, evergreen.
Growth: Clump-like tufts of leaves.
Origin: Cultivated form.
Site: Sun, warm, also hot. Soil well-drained, nutrient-rich, permeable.
Care: Plant in spring. Apply inorganic fertilizer with potassium. Cut off pedicles in fall, leave evergreen foliage. Moderately frost-hardy; use dry winter protection.
Propagation: By division.
Use: In small groups in borders and on slopes.
Good Partners: *Nepeta, Salvia, Sedum, Stachys.*
Cultivars/Relatives:
• 'Canary', light yellow, 24 in. (60 cm).
• 'Fyrwerkery', orange, 36 in. (90 cm).
• 'Abendsonne', orange, late blooming, 48 in. (120 cm).
• 'Safranvogel', salmon, early blooming, 32 in. (80 cm).
• 'Royal Standard', scarlet, lower flowers yellow, 36 in. (90 cm).
• 'Alcazar', red, 32 in. (80 cm).

Spotted Dead Nettle
Lamium maculatum

Cultivar 'Chequers'

May–June
H 6–16 in. (15–40 cm)

Naturalized wild perennial.
Flower: Lilac-purple labiate flowers in whorls.
Leaf: Ovate, toothed, with white spots.
Growth: Creeps by means of runners without becoming rampant.
Origin: Europe to Asia Minor. In riverside woods, along edges of woods.
Site: Light to partial shade, cool. Soil well-drained to moist, loose, nutrient-rich.
Care: Add humus occasionally. Can be mowed down.
Propagation: By division and by cuttings.
Use: In small areas in light shade of walls and woody plants.
Good Partners: *Brunnera, Polygonatum, Pulmonaria, Tiarella, Waldsteinia—Luzula.*
Cultivars/Relatives:
• 'Album', white, leaves heavily marked with silvery white.
• 'Silbergroschen', light violet with silvery white leaves.
• *Lamiastrum galeobdolon* 'Florentinum', Florentine yellow archangel, yellow, June–July, 8–12 in. (20–30 cm) tall. In undergrowth of woody plants, rampant as ground cover.

Spring Vetchling
Lathyrus vernus

Lathyrus vernus

April–May ◑
H 8–12 in. (20–30 cm)

Indigenous spring bloomer for shady areas of the garden.
Flower: Bicolored crimson to purple-red and blue-violet flowers, popular with butterflies.
Leaf: Pinnate with narrow leaf segments, at first light green, then grass-green, glossy.
Growth: Small, bushy clumps.
Origin: Europe to Siberia. In beech forests and mixed forests.
Site: Light to partial shade. Soil moderately dry to well-drained; humus, with average nutrient content, also lime-rich.
Care: Let grow undisturbed; cut back fast-growing neighbors.
Propagation: By seed, the cultivars by division. Self-sowing.
Use: Undemanding, rewarding perennial for shady natural gardens, also in light shade of walls.
Good Partners: *Anemone apennina* and *Anemone nemorosa* 'Plena'—*Epimedium, Pulmonaria saccharata—Carex.*
Cultivars/Relatives:
• 'Alboroseus', white-and-pink.
• 'Roseus', pink.

True Lavender
Lavandula angustifolia

Cultivar 'Hidcote Blue'

June–August ○
H 12–32 in. (30–80 cm)

Aromatic subshrub.
Flower: Violet-blue to lilac, sweet-scented labiate flowers in long-stemmed spikes.
Leaf: Linear, silvery gray, aromatic, evergreen.
Growth: Cushion-shaped, becoming floppy when old.
Origin: Common throughout southern Europe as a cultivated plant.
Site: Full sun, warm to hot. Soil dry to well-drained, permeable, gravelly or sandy-loamy, moderately nutrient-rich, lime-rich.
Care: Cut back regularly in spring. The plant is only moderately frost-hardy.
Propagation: By cuttings.
Use: Beside patios, in scented gardens and herb gardens, as cut flowers, in country gardens, among paving stones.
Good Partners: Drought-tolerant perennials or subshrubs, also with roses.
Cultivars/Relatives:
• 'Alba', white, 20 in. (50 cm).
• 'Rosea', lilac-pink, 16 in. (40 cm).
• 'Munstead', deep blue, 16 in. (40 cm), compact, reliable.
• 'Hidcote Blue', violet-blue, 16 in. (40 cm), compact, reliable.

Spike Gayfeather, Liatris, Blazing Star
Liatris spicata

Liatris spicata

July–September ○ ✂
H 16–36 in. (40–90 cm)

Prairie perennial with extravagant flower spikes.
Flower: Violet-pink, in slender candles resembling bottle brushes. Occasionally unstable.
Leaf: Linear, dark green.
Growth: Grassy clumps.
Origin: North America. On prairies and rock ledges.
Site: Sun, warm, hot. Soil moderately dry to well-drained, permeable, nutrient-rich. Rots in heavy, wet soils.
Care: Tidy the clumps in spring. Feed well. Cut back flower spikes after bloom finishes. Voles like to eat the rootstock.
Propagation: By division in early spring.
Use: In beds, on slopes, in gravel beds, in rock gardens.
Good Partners: *Anaphalis, Echinacea, Gypsophila, Salvia, Sedum.*
Cultivars/Relatives:
• 'Floristan', white, 36 in. (90 cm).
• 'Kobold', violet-pink, 16 in. (40 cm).
• 'Floristan Violett', lustrous violet, 32 in. (80 cm).

PERENNIALS

155

Bigleaf Golden-ray
Ligularia dentata

Candle Groundsel
Ligularia przewalskii

Ligularia dentata

Ligularia hybrid 'Zepter'

August–September ◐
H 40–48 in. (100–120 cm)

July–August ○◐
H 40–60 in. (100–150 cm)

Large perennials that flourish only in damp places.
Flower: Orange-yellow, daisy-like, in loose, nosegay-like cymes.
Leaf: Large, round to kidney-shaped, cordate at base, with sharp-toothed margin, coarsely leathery, dark green.
Growth: Impressive erect, bushy clumps.
Origin: China and Japan. In tall perennial vegetation and along stream banks.
Site: Partial shade to light shade, cool, air humid. Soil moist to wet, nutrient-rich.
Care: Excellent water and nutrient supply; plant wilts after even a brief period of dryness. Protect from slug damage. Cut back in fall.
Propagation: By division, the species also by seed.
Use: At water's edge, in swampy gardens, along damp edges of woods.
Good Partners: *Alchemilla— Miscanthus.*
Cultivars/Relatives:
• 'Othello', light orange with purple-brown leaves.
• 'Desdemona', bright orange-yellow with purple-red leaves.
• *Ligularia* x *hessei*, golden yellow with green leaves, July.

Companion piece to bigleaf golden-ray, with erect, candle-shaped inflorescences.
Flower: Rich yellow, tiny heads, each with two star-like flowers, in erect candle shapes.
Leaf: Deeply notched in palmate pattern, dark green, with long, blackish stems.
Growth: Large, erect clumps.
Origin: Northern China. Along edges of banks.
Site: Full sun to partial shade, cool. The plant is sensitive to heat and drought. Soil moist to wet, nutrient-rich.
Care: Protect flush from slug damage. Good water and nutrient supply. Cut back in fall.
Propagation: By division or by seed. Occasionally self-sowing.
Use: In damp beds, beside edge of streams or ponds. Suitable for all locations with standing water, which otherwise are hard to find plants for.
Good Partners: *Alchemilla, Chrysanthemum maxlmum, Ligularia dentata, Lysimachia, Rodgersia, Tradescantia andersoniana* hybrids—*Miscanthus.* Bamboo, *Molinia.*

Cultivars/Relatives:
• 'The Rocket', yellow, columnar inflorescences, 72 in. (180 cm).
• *Ligularia* hybrid 'Weihenstephan', golden yellow, with five star-shaped blossoms per capitulum in slightly wider flower spikes, 56–68 in. (140–170 cm). Very pretty, vigorous form for damp borders.
• *Ligularia stenocephala*, yellow, inflorescences like those of *Ligularia przewalskii*, July–August. Leaves cordate to kidney-shaped, strikingly saw-toothed, not notched. Native to East Asia, where it grows in damp mountain meadows.

Narbonne Flax
Linum narbonense

Washington Lupine
Lupinus polyphyllus Hybrids

Linum perenne

Lupinus polyphyllus hybrid 'Schlossfrau'

May–June ○
H 12–20 in. (30–50 cm) .

Pale blue perennial for dry places.
Flower: Blue plate-shaped flowers in loose bunches.
Leaf: Narrow lanceolate, light blue-green.
Growth: Clumps that seem diaphanous.
Origin: Mediterranean area. On stony-rocky inclines.
Site: Full sun, warm to hot. Soil moderately dry, permeable, nutrient-poor.
Care: Mostly short-lived; replace every four to five years.
Propagation: By seed; the cultivars by cuttings in August.
Use: In sunny beds, in rock and terraced gardens. On the south side of walls, in gravel beds, and for roof gardens.
Good Partners: *Alyssum, Anaphalis, Iberis sempervirens, Iris barbata-elatior* hybrids, *Papaver orientale, Stachys byzantina—Festuca ovina.*
Cultivars/Relatives:
• 'Heavenly Blue', dark, rich azure.
• *Linum perenne,* perennial flax, short-lived, indigenous species with light blue, smaller, nodding flowers and almost needle-shaped leaves.
• *Linum perenne* 'Album', white.

June–July ○
H 32–40 in. (40–100 cm)

Extremely common perennial for borders; has abundant flowers.
Flower: Blue, violet, white, yellow, pink, brick-red, crimson, in some cases bicolored, lightly scented, large flowers popular with butterflies, in dense, cylindrical racemes borne on erect stalks.
Leaf: Palmately divided with lanceolate segments, dull blue-green.
Growth: Erect, in clumps, occasionally unstable. Dies back after bloom.
Origin: Cultivated form.
Site: Sun, warm. Soil moderately dry to well-drained, permeable, sandy humus, acid. No extremely lime-rich soils!
Care: Deadhead faded flowers regularly. Cut back completely after bloom to encourage new growth and less abundant second bloom. Unpruned plants die back soon after primary bloom. Older specimens cannot be transplanted.
Propagation: By seed or by division of younger plants, also by basal cuttings.
Use: In borders in rhythmically recurring small groups. Place in middle of border, because these plants die back.

Good Partners: Combine various cultivars. *Alchemilla, Geranium* x *magnificum. Paeonia lactiflora.*
Cultivars/Relatives:
• 'Fräulein', creamy white.
• 'Schlossfrau', bicolored pink-and-white.
• 'Kastellan', bicolored blue-and-white.
• 'Kronleuchter', yellow.
• 'Mein Schloss', brick-red.
• 'Edelknabe', crimson.
• 'Rote Flamme', crimson.

Maltese Cross, Jerusalem Cross, Scarlet Lightning
Lychnis chalcedonica

Lychnis chalcedonica

June–July ○ ✂
H 32–40 in. (80–100 cm)

Perennial for use in borders, has fiery red flowers.
Flower: Brilliant scarlet, star-shaped, in terminal, umbrella-like flower clusters.
Leaf: Ovate, dark green, slightly shiny.
Growth: In clumps, erect, and somewhat formal in appearance.
Origin: Western Russia to northern China. In thin woods with moist soil.
Site: Sun, cool to moderately warm. Soil well-drained, rich in nutrients and humus.
Care: Long-lived if fed well and watered adequately. Does not tolerate lengthy dry spells. After primary bloom cut back completely; new growth with less abundant second bloom will result.
Propagation: By seed, the cultivars by division.
Use: As companion plant in perennial borders. Keep the intense blue flower color in mind when making combinations!
Good Partners: *Cosmos bipinnatus* 'Unschuld', *Nicotiana sylvestris, Salvia farinacea—Chrysanthemum maximum, Delphinium.*
Cultivars/Relatives: None of the following cultivars attains the beauty and brilliance of the species.
• 'Alba', white, 32 in. (80 cm)
• 'Rauhreif', white, 40 in. (100 cm), can also be propagated by seed. 'Rosea', pale pink, 32 in. (80 cm). 'Carnea', flesh-colored, 32 in. (80 cm).

Japanese Crosswort, Loosestrife, Shepherd's-crook
Lysimachia clethroides

Lysimachia clethroides

July–September ○ ◐
H 28–40 in. (70–100 cm)

Perennial with unusual, wavy racemes and striking fall colors. Very popular with butterflies.
Flower: Pure white, small, star-shaped flowers with slight scent, in narrowly tapering racemes, which at first are curved downward, then gradually become upright as blossoming progresses.
Leaf: Ovate to lanceolate, green, with pleasing, light orange-brown fall color.
Growth: In erect clumps with many shoots.
Origin: East Asia. In damp meadows and in mountain forests.
Site: Sun to light shade, cool, air humid. Soil moist to well-drained, nutrient-rich.
Care: Tidy the clumps in early spring. Water adequately and sprinkle water over plants in dry spells. Feed well.
Propagation: By division in spring and by seed.
Use: Along edge of woody plants, at edge of pond, in damp borders.
Good Partners: *Aconitum, Filipendula rubra, Geranium pratense, Ligularia, Lysimachia punctata, Tradescantia.*
Cultivars/Relatives:
• *Lysimachia ephemerum,* also white, but with erect, loose racemes and narrow lanceolate leaves with a gray shimmer. Moderately frost-hardy.

Yellow Loosestrife
Lysimachia punctata

Lysimachia punctata

June–September ○ ◐
H 32–48 in. (80–120 cm)

Magnificently flowering perennial that spreads out thickly in suitable sites.
Flower: Golden yellow, delicately scented, funnel-shaped, in elongated racemes.
Leaf: Ovate to broad lanceolate, dull green, hairy.
Growth: Erect, spreads in thicket-like fashion by means of runners.
Origin: Central Europe to Asia Minor. In riverside meadows, along banks, at edges of woods.
Site: Sun to partial shade, cool to moderately warm. Soil well-drained to moist, nutrient-rich; preferably loam or clay-rich.
Care: Using your spade and starting at the edges, repeatedly reduce size of clumps to give neighboring plants room to grow.
Propagation: Easily possible by division in spring and fall, also by seed.
Use: At edge of pond and beside garden pool, in damp borders, in light shade among woody plants; in large areas let grow untended in natural meadows.
Good Partners: *Aconitum, Alchemilla, Geranium, Geum—Miscanthus.*

Purple Loosestrife, Spiked Loosestrife
Lythrum salicaria

Lythrum salicaria

July–September ◯ ◗
H 32–56 in. (80–140 cm)

Indigenous perennial for damp areas of the garden. Popular with bees and butterflies.
Flower: Violet-red, star-shaped, small, very numerous, in dense, candle-shaped spikes.
Leaf: Lanceolate, green, with red fall color.
Growth: Rigidly erect clumps.
Origin: Europe and Asia. In wet meadows, on banks.
Site: Sun to partial shade. Soil well-drained to wet, also submerged; nutrient-rich, vigorous.
Care: Water and feed well. Cut off faded spikes at once to keep seed from being sown. Mowing is possible.
Propagation: By cuttings in early summer.
Use: At edge of ponds and garden pools, in borders.
Good Partners: *Alchemilla, Filipendula rubra, Hemerocallis—Miscanthus.*
Cultivars/Relatives:
• 'Stichflamme', purple-pink, 56 in. (140 cm).
• 'Zigeunerblut', lustrous dark red, 48 in. (120 cm).

Monarda, Bee Balm
Monarda Hybrids

Monarda hybrid 'Fish'

July–September ◯ ✄
H 28–52 in. (70–130 cm)

Midsummer bloomer with unusual flowers and aromatic foliage. Favorite of bees and butterflies.
Flower: Crimson, purple-red, scarlet, pink, violet-blue, or white labiate flowers with aromatic fragrance in terminal shallow whorls.
Leaf: Narrow ovate, coarsely toothed, dark blue-green, with aromatic, mint-like scent.
Growth: In clumps, rigidly erect, in some cases unstable.
Origin: Cultivated form, the parent species from North America.
Site: Sun to light shade, warm. Soil well-drained, nutrient-rich. In heavy soils, unstable and short-lived.
Care: Water in dry spells in order to prevent mildew. Feed well. Cut back in fall.
Propagation: By division and cuttings in spring.
Use: In sunny borders. Make sure the hues of the cultivars are carefully coordinated with those of the partner plants.
Good Partners: *Campanula persicifolia, Erigeron* hybrids, *Gypsophila paniculata, Iris spuria* hybrids—*Miscanthus sinensis.*

Monarda hybrid 'Cambridge Scarlet'

Monarda hybrid 'Blaustrumpf'

Cultivars/Relatives:
• 'Schneewittchen', white, 40 in. (100 cm)
• 'Croftway Pink', delicate salmon-pink, 44 in. (110 cm).
• 'Mrs. Perry', light red, 30 in. (75 cm).
• 'Squaw', scarlet, 40 in. (100 cm).
• 'Präriebrand', lustrous dark crimson, 48 in. (120 cm).
• 'Cambridge Scarlet', scarlet, 48 in. (120 cm).
• 'Blaustrumpf', dark lilac, 44 in. (110 cm). Also for heavy soils.

PERENNIALS

Mauve Catnip
Nepeta mussinii (= N. racemosa)

Nepeta mussinii

May–September ○
H 8 in. (20 cm)

Aromatic perennial whose scent attracts cats.
Flower: Lavender-blue labiate flowers in loose whorls.
Leaf: Broad cordate-ovate, gray, with pungent fragrance.
Growth: Low cushions.
Origin: Asia Minor and Caucasus. In mountain pastures.
Site: Full sun, warm. Soil dry to well-drained, not wet in winter. No heavy soils!
Care: Apply inorganic fertilizer from time to time. After the first bloom in July, cut back by one-half to obtain second bloom and more compact growth.
Propagation: By division and cuttings in May.
Use: In rock gardens, on slopes, in gravel beds, in containers, and for roof gardens.
Good Partners: *Achillea, Anaphalis, Lavandula, Phlomis, Salvia, Santolina—Helictotrichon.* Roses.
Cultivars/Relatives:
• *Nepeta* x *faassenii*, long-term bloomer with narrower leaflets, May–September, 12 in. (30 cm).
• *Nepeta* x *faassenii* 'Six Hills Giant', over 16 in. (40 cm) tall.

Young's Sundrops, Northern Sundrops

Oenothera tetragona 'Sonnenwende'

June–August ○
H 16–28 in. (40–70 cm)

Indigenous yellow midsummer bloomer with long blooming season.
Flower: Canary-yellow saucer-shaped flowers in bunches; scented.
Leaf: Oval, blue-green, with reddish fall color.
Growth: Erect, in clumps.
Origin: Eastern North America. Damp meadows and edges of woods.
Site: Sun, warm. Soil well-drained, nutrient-rich.
Care: Good nutrient supply. Deadhead faded flowers regularly.
Propagation: By division and tip cuttings in May.
Use: In sunny borders and on slopes with southern exposure.
Good Partners: *Monarda, Veronica—Calamagrostis.*
Cultivars/Relatives:
• 'Fryverkeri', golden yellow, buds and stems red, 16 in. (40 cm).
• 'Hohes Licht', canary-yellow, 24 in. (60 cm).
• 'Sonnenwende', golden yellow with dark green foliage, 24 in. (60 cm).
• *Oenothera missouriensis,* Ozark sundrops, with lemon-yellow, scented, saucer-shaped flowers, up to 5 in. (12 cm) across, opening only in the evening. June–September, 8–12 in. (20–30 cm) tall. For sunny rock gardens, gravel beds, dry walls, and roof gardens. Soil moderately dry and permeable. Can also be propagated by seed.

Creeping Forget-me-not, Venus's Navelwort
Omphalodes verna

Omphalodes verna

March–April ◑
H 6–10 in. (15–25 cm)

Spring bloomer with flowers resembling forget-me-nots.
Flower: Lustrous medium blue with white center, small, in loose racemes.
Leaf: Ovate, pointed, vivid green.
Growth: Forms mats by means of runners. Thick-growing, overruns weaker neighbors.
Origin: Southeastern Alps to Romania, naturalized in central Europe. Damp mountain forests.
Site: Light to partial shade, warm. Soil well-drained to moist, any loose soil.
Care: In late winter, cover shallowly with humus or humus-rich soil mix. If neighboring plants lack room, use your spade to reduce the size of the creeping forget-me-not.
Propagation: Possible by division throughout the year.
Use: As ground cover under woody plants. Not sensitive to layer of fallen leaves in autumn. In light shade of walls.
Good Partners: *Epimedium, Lamium maculatum, Tiarella, Vinca, Waldsteinia. Carex.*
Cultivars/Relatives:
• *Omphalodes cappadocica,* sky-blue, April–May. Less rampant, produces only short runners. Moderately frost-hardy.

Chinese Peony
Paeonia lactiflora

Paeonia lactiflora 'Mme Claude Tain' (white), 'Sarah Bernard' (pink), and 'Gold Medal' (red)

May–June
H 20–44 in. (50–110 cm)

One of the most important perennials, with magnificent flowers and foliage that is ornamental throughout the year, is represented by a colossal number of cultivars. Peonies are easy-to-tend, long-lived garden plants that can grow in the same spot for decades. In China, home of the original form, cultivars were being bred over one thousand years ago. The first Chinese peonies came to the western world only in the late nineteenth century, but today we could not imagine our gardens without them. A great many cultivars are of French origin.

Flower: White, pink, velvety red, blood-red, or wine-red; single, semidouble, or double. Double-flowered cultivars bloom longer than singles. The strength of the fragrance varies. It is most intense in light-colored, double-flowered cultivars.
Leaf: Two sets of three, with elliptical to lanceolate segments, very decorative. Bright green, during flush reddish brown, in many cultivars coppery red in fall.
Growth: Spreading and clump-like. Sometimes requires staking.
Origin: Cultivated form.
Site: Sun, moderately warm. Soil moderately dry to well-drained, nutrient-rich, vigorous. No compacted soils!

Paeonia lactiflora 'Pomponette'

Chinese Peony
Paeonia lactiflora Hybrids

Paeonia lactiflora 'Karl Rosenfield'

Cultivar 'Sarah Bernard'

Cultivar 'Ball of Beauty'

Care: Plant in early fall. Set shallowly, covering with no more than 1 in. (3 cm) of soil, to ensure good leaf growth and flower production. In spring, before growth, apply a moderate amount of well-aged organic fertilizer like bone meal or compound fertilizer with low a percentage of nitrogen. Tidy the clumps in early spring. No thick mulch layer; it often causes stem rot! Deadhead faded flowers to prevent energy-consuming setting of fruit. In September, feed moderately again, to promote development of tuber-like roots. Leave undisturbed for years as the plants develop their full beauty only after three to four years.
Propagation: By division in fall. Only a few offspring can be obtained from each mother plant.
Use: In borders, as cut flowers. Color combinations are possible with the fall colors of the leaves, as well as with the flowers.
Good Partners: *Alchemilla,* early blooming *Delphinium* hybrids and *Erigeron* hybrids, *Geranium* x *magnificum, Salvia nemorosa.* Fall-blooming perennials to go with the fall colors of the leaves: *Aster, Chrysanthemum serotinum, Vernonia.*

White cultivar 'Jan van Leeuwen'

Cultivars/Relatives:
Single flowers:
• 'Dürer', white, early blooming, 32 in. (80 cm).
• 'Holbein', pink, blooms in midseason, 40 in. (100 cm).
• 'L'Etincelante', pink, blooms in midseason, 40 in. (100 cm).
• 'Hogarth', purple-red, early blooming, 40 in. (100 cm).
• 'Torpilleur', purple-red, early blooming, 36 in. (90 cm).
Semidouble flowers:
• 'Lady Alexander Duff', pink, blooms in midseason, 36 in. (90 cm).
Double flowers:
• 'Avalanche', white, blooms in midseason, heavily scented, 36 in. (90 cm).
• 'Le Cygne', white, early blooming, 40 in. (100 cm).
• 'Madame de Verneville', creamy white, early blooming, 40 in. (100 cm).

• 'Reine Hortense', pink, early blooming, 28 in. (70 cm).
• 'Wiesbaden', pink, early blooming, 32 in. (80 cm).
• 'La Perle', pink, late blooming, 32 in. (80 cm).
• 'Sarah Bernard', pink, late blooming, 40 in. (100 cm), yields very good cut flowers.
• 'Solange', pink, late blooming, 40 in. (100 cm).
• 'Bunker Hill', crimson, early blooming, 32 in. (80 cm).
• 'Felix Crousse', crimson, blooms in midseason, 40 in. (100 cm).
• 'Monsieur Martin Cahuzac', velvety red, darkest cultivar, blooms in midseason, 40 in. (100 cm).
Warning: Peonies contain poisonous substances!

Hybrid Peonies
Paeonia Hybrids

Hybrid 'Claire de Lune'

May–June
H 28–48 in. (70–120 cm)

Through crossings with Chinese and other peony species and cultivars, breeders developed a group of new forms with extraordinary colors and, in some cases, huge flowers up to 10 in. (25 cm) across.
Flower: Various yellow, pink, and red tones, as well as white; single, semidouble, or double; large.
Leaf: As in Chinese peonies.
Growth: Erect, spreading and clump-like.
Origin: Cultivated form.
Site, Care, Propagation, and Use: As for Chinese peonies.
Cultivars/Relatives:
• 'Chalice', creamy white, single, gigantic saucer-shaped flowers, early blooming. Very vigorous, up to 48 in. (120 cm).
• 'Coral Charm', salmon-pink to salmon-orange in variable color, semidouble, 28 in. (70 cm).
• 'Carina', scarlet, semidouble, early blooming, 32 in. (80 cm).
• 'Blaze', brilliant red, single flowers, early blooming, 32 in. (80 cm).
Warning: Peonies contain poisonous substances!

Common Peony
Paeonia officinalis

Paeonia officinalis

May
H 20–40 in. (40–100 cm)

Long-lived healing plant, in cultivation since ancient times. Blooms about two weeks before Chinese peonies. The double cultivars are typical country garden plants.
Flower: Blood-red, scented, large saucer-shaped flowers with striking yellow stamens on rigid stems in the species.
Leaf: Two sets of three, firm, dark green with light gray sheen, decorative.
Growth: Erect, broad and clump-like; in some cases—especially the double cultivars—require staking. Long-lived.
Origin: Southern Europe and southern Central Europe, with emphasis on the Italian Alps. In thin Spanish chestnut woods, on rocky mountain slopes, in dry mountain meadows, usually in limy soils.
Site: Sun to light shade, warm. Soil moderately dry to well-drained, deep, nutrient-rich, lime-rich.
Care: Plant in early fall. Tidy the clumps in spring. Feed regularly. Cut off spent stems to prevent energy-consuming seed production. Stake weak-stemmed forms with dry, branched brushwood. As peonies display their

Paeonia officinalis 'Rubra Plena'

full beauty only after several years, leave them in one place as long as possible, transplanting them only if the flowers become less abundant.
Propagation: By division in early fall.
Use: In borders, along edge of shrub plantings, in country gardens, as cut flowers.
Good Partners: *Campanula glomerata, Cerastium tomentosum, Geranium* x *magnificum, Iberis sempervirens,* blue and white *Iris barbata-elatior* hybrids, *Scabiosa caucasica*—tall *Allium* species.
Cultivars/Relatives:
• 'Alba Plena', white, double-flowered.
• 'Rosea Plena', rose-pink, double-flowered.
• 'Mollis', dark pink, single, 24 in. (60 cm).
• 'China Rose', brilliant salmon-red, single, 40 in. (100 cm).
• 'Crimson Globe', brilliant crimson, single, 24 in. (60 cm).
• 'Rubra Plena', blood-red, double-flowered.
Warning: Peonies contain poisonous substances!

Oriental Poppy
Papaver orientale

Papaver orientale 'Catharina'

Papaver orientale 'Feuerriese'

May–June ○ ☠
H 12–40 in. (30–100 cm)

Perennial with enormous, brilliant flowers, which compensate for the short blooming season of this species.

Flower: Brilliant orange, scarlet, pink, or white saucer-shaped flowers with black pollen-bearing stamens. Flowers up to 8 in. (20 cm) in diameter. Solitary on rigidly erect stems.

Leaf: Large, deeply and pinnately cut, dull green, densely covered with bristly hairs, juice poisonous.

Growth: In clumps, many cultivars not strong-stemmed.

Origin: Caucasus, northeastern Turkey, and northern Iran. On rocky hillsides, in dry alpine meadows at altitudes of 1 to nearly two miles (2000–2800 m).

Site: Full sun, warm to hot. Soil dry to well-drained, permeable, nutrient-rich. No wet sites or heavy soils, where the taproots will rot.

Care: Apply inorganic fertilizer regularly. Cut back after blooming to encourage new growth; otherwise, the old leaves turn yellow. Because of the deep-reaching taproot, only small specimens can be transplanted. Voles enjoy eating the roots, so set out traps in time.

Propagation: By root cuttings after blooming or in winter; some cultivars also by seed.

Use: Singly or in small groups in sunny borders and on slopes. Don't plant in the foreground, because the plants leave unsightly gaps after they die down. Partners with restrained colors make the best choices, because the brilliantly colored flowers outdo almost all other perennials. Blue- and white-flowered plants or perennials with decorative gray foliage are good.

Good Partners: *Anchusa azurea,* blue- and white-flowered *Iris barbata-elatior* hybrids, *Lavandula, Linum narbonense, Salvia nemorosa* and *Salvia officinalis, Stachys byzantina.*

Cultivars/Relatives:
• 'Perry White', muted white with black-red spots at the base, 28 in. (70 cm).
• 'Karine', pink with dark, velvety red spots at the base, small-flowered, 24 in. (60 cm).
• 'Catharina', salmon-pink, large-flowered, 32 in. (80 cm).
• 'Kleine Tänzerin', salmon-pink, flowers small but abundant, only 12–20 in. (30–50 cm).
• 'Marcus Perry', brilliant orange, 24 in. (60 cm).
• 'Feuerriese', brick-red, erect, very vigorous cultivar, 32 in. (80 cm).
• 'Aladin', brilliant red with black spots at base and wavy petals, large-flowered, 36 in. (90 cm).
• 'Beauty of Livermere', dark scarlet, long-flowering, 40 in. (100 cm). Highly recommended, extremely strong-stemmed cultivar, which can be propagated by seed.
• 'Türkenlouis', flaming red with black spots at the base and fringed flower margins, 28 in. (70 cm), one of the prettiest cultivars.

Warning: The entire plant is mildly poisonous!

Russel's Jerusalem Sage
Phlomis russeliana

Phlomis russeliana

June–August ○ ◑
H 24–32 in. (60–80 cm)

Extremely easy-to-grow ground cover for sunny settings. Garden centers usually sell it under the name *Phlomis samia*.

Flower: Pale yellow labiate flowers, in groups in dense whorls that are arranged in tiers, one above the other, and form a loose inflorescence 8–16 in. (20–40 cm) long. Fruits look wonderful covered with frost and snow.

Leaf: Large, pointed cordate, dull green with a tinge of ocher, grows early.

Growth: Spreads out slowly but steadily by means of runners. The basal leaves form a dense mat, above which the erect flower shoots rise.

Origin: Southern Europe to Asia Minor. In pine and cedar woods, in stands of evergreen bushes.

Site: Full sun to abundant sun, warm, also hot. Soil moderately dry to well-drained, for any garden soil.

Care: Cut off fruit structures in spring. Using your spade, reduce the size of mats grown overly large.

Propagation: By division, also by seed.

Use: In terraced gardens and pebble gardens, on sunny slopes, and in gravel beds.

Good Partners: *Echinops, Eryngium, Oenothera missouriensis, Salvia nemorosa, Santolina, Verbascum—Festuca mairei.*

PHLOX
Phlox paniculata

The cultivars 'Schneeferner' (white), 'Rosa Pastell' (pink), and 'Flamingo' (red)

The *Phlox* genus includes about 50 perennials and a few annuals, all indigenous to North America. Within the genus, two groups can be differentiated:

• Low, mostly cushion-shaped species. They bloom in spring and are drought-tolerant. In addition to plants that are decidedly for connoisseurs, this class also includes the familiar *Phlox subulata* hybrids. These undemanding perennials for rock gardens have a variety of forms.

• Taller-growing, clump-like species that bloom from early summer until fall. Unlike the smaller species, they always require well-drained soil.

Phlox paniculata occupies a prominent position within this group. Through great efforts of breeders, a broad-ranging, colorful assortment of spectacular perennials for borders was developed from a species with modest, variably colored flowers.

Because of their susceptibility to mildew and stem nematodes, these lush bloomers are not always easy to grow in gardens. The first symptom of nematodes is crinkling and browning of the lower leaves, and the infestation can result in the loss of the plants. Afflicted clumps have to be removed. For a period of years, avoid planting phloxes in places infested by nematodes, in order to prevent reinfestation. The susceptibility of phlox to nematodes and mildew is increased by poor aeration and water and nutrient deficiencies. Consequently, don't plant too close together, between tall partners, or in front of walls providing shelter from the wind!

Garden Phlox, Summer Perennial Phlox
Phlox paniculata

Cultivar 'Landhochzeit'

Cultivar 'Graf Zeppelin'

June–September ○
H 20–60 in. (50–150 cm)

Splendid, well-known perennial for borders.

Flower: White, pink, salmon-pink, brick-red, crimson, purple-red, or light violet, also bicolored, scented, plate-shaped, with long, thin tube, in dense, dome-shaped corymbs.

Leaf: Lanceolate to narrow, ovate, grass-green.

Growth: Erect clumps.

Origin: Cultivated form. The parents from eastern North America. In well-drained, thin woods and along river banks.

Site: Sun, predominantly cool, sheltered from wind. Soil well-drained to moist, permeable, nutrient- and humus-rich. No hot sites or easily drying, nutrient-poor soils, which intensify nematode infestations.

Care: Always keep moist, water regularly. Along with optimal site conditions, that is the best way to prevent stem nematodes and mildew. At the same time, it keeps the flowers from wilting rapidly on warm days. If you cut back the stalks by one-third in mid-June, the blooming season will be postponed until September. By so doing, and by choosing appropriate cultivars, you can extend the blooming period substantially. Remove faded inflorescences to prevent self-sowing. The seedlings have smaller flowers in paler colors, but they are very vigorous and quickly overgrow the cultivars.

Propagation: By division and cuttings in spring, by root cuttings in winter.

Use: In sunny borders, in country gardens. The flower colors are not always easy to combine, and cultivars with showy salmon-red and orange-red blossoms should be tied into your garden with white or pale blue neighboring plants, as well as perennials with ornamental foliage.

Good Partners: Groups of different cultivars in harmonizing colors look pretty. Be sure to space the individual clumps far enough apart. *Chrysanthemum parthenium, Lobularia—Achillea ptarmica, Chrysanthemum maximum, Delphinium, Monarda* hybrids, *Physostegia, Veronica longifolia*—grasses like *Pennisetum.*

Cultivars/Relatives:
Early blooming cultivars:
• 'Frauenlob', light pink with velvety red eye, 48 in. (120 cm).
• 'Württembergia', intense pink, old country garden cultivar and still one of the best, 32 in. (80 cm).
• 'Sommerfreude', pink with velvety red eye, 36 in. (90 cm).
• 'Düsterlohe', dark violet-red, 48 in. (120 cm).
• 'Look Again', violet, 44 in. (110 cm).
Cultivars that bloom in midseason:
• 'Schneeferner', white, 40 in. (100 cm).
• 'Schaumkrone', white with crimson eye, 40 in. (100 cm).
• 'Dorffreude', pink with purple-red eye, 48 in. (120 cm).
• 'Landhochzeit', light violet-pink with bright red eye, 56 in. (140 cm). One of the best breeds.
• 'Starfire', brilliant red, 36 in. (90 cm).
• 'Kirchenfürst', dark crimson, 44 in. (110 cm).
• 'Frau Alfred von Mauthner' (= 'Spitfire'), brick-red with crimson eye, signal-light color effective from a distance, 40 in. (100 cm).
• 'Aida', violet-red, 36 in. (90 cm).
• 'Violetta Gloriosa', lightest blue-violet with white eye, 56 in. (140 cm), very vigorous.
• 'Sternhimmel', light violet with white eye, 40 in. (100 cm).
Late blooming cultivars:
• 'Pax', white, 36 in. (90 cm).
• 'Nymphenburg', white, 56 in. (140 cm).
• 'Kirmesländler', white with blood-red eye, 48 in. (120 cm).
• 'Orange', brilliant orange-red, signal-light color, 56 in. (140 cm).
• 'Flammenkuppel', bright rose-pink, 40 in. (100 cm).

Moss Pink, Ground Pink, Moss Phlox
Phlox subulata Hybrids

Hybrid 'Ronsdorfer Schöne'

April–May ○
H 2–6 in. (5–15 cm)

Free-flowering, cushion-shaped perennials.
Flower: Lilac-blue, violet, white, pink, crimson, eye often of contrasting color, scented, star-shaped.
Leaf: Linear, matte green.
Growth: Cushion-shaped to mat like.
Origin: Cultivated form.
Site: Sun, warm. Soil moderately dry to well-drained, permeable, nutrient-rich.
Care: After the bloom, cut back to about two-thirds of the original size.
Propagation: By division or by small plant segments.
Use: In rock gardens and on wall cornices.
Good Partners: *Aubrieta, Gypsophila, Iberis.*
Cultivars/Relatives:
• 'White Delight', pure white, vigorous, the best white-flowered cultivar.
• 'Avalanche', white.
• 'Moerheimii', pink with velvety red eye.
• 'Samson', salmon-pink.
• 'Daisy Hill', pink.
• 'Atropurpurea', crimson.
• 'G. F. Wilson', light lilac-blue.
• 'Thomasini', violet-blue.
• *Phlox douglasii* hybrids, very similar, with shallower flowers, hemispherical cushions, growth less dense.
• 'Red Admiral', crimson.
• 'Crackerjack', brilliant crimson, best cultivar.
• 'Georg Arends', lilac-pink with dark eye.
• 'Lilac Cloud', lilac-blue.

Crosswort
Phuopsis stylosa

Phuopsis stylosa

June–August ○ ◐ ☠
H 6–10 in. (15–25 cm)

Vigorous, undemanding small perennial.
Flower: Old-rose, scented, tiny star-shaped flowers in hemispherical false umbels.
Leaf: Lanceolate, in whorls, fresh green; in some cases rampant.
Origin: Northern Caucasus and northern Iran. In thin woods.
Site: Sun to light shade, warm. Soil moderately dry to well-drained, loose, otherwise any soil will do.
Care: Cut back completely in fall. Occasionally sprinkle with light amounts of humus. Trim overly abundant mats with spade.
Propagation: By division.
Use: Two-dimensionally, in large rock gardens, beneath light stands of woody plants, on slopes, and in scented gardens.
Good Partners: Don't combine with slow-growing partners. *Aruncus* and *Geranium* are suitable.
Cultivars/Relatives:
• 'Purpurea', purple-pink flowers.
Warning: Mildly poisonous.

Cape Fuchsia
Phygelius capensis

Phygelius capensis

July–September ○
H 32–48 in. (80–120 cm)

Exotic perennials with long blooming season in midsummer.
Flower: Brick-red, tubular, up to 2 in. (5 cm) long, hangs in a loose, broad conical panicle.
Leaf: Broad ovate, margins scalloped, dark green.
Growth: In clumps, lignifies in its native habitat.
Origin: South Africa. On rocks, along watercourses, and on damp hillsides in mountainous regions.
Site: Sun, warm to hot. Soil moderately dry to well-drained, permeable, nutrient-rich.
Care: Cut back in spring. Feed occasionally. In winter, cover lightly with boughs.
Propagation: By cuttings in early summer, by division in spring, or by seed in a hothouse.
Use: In sunny borders, also as espalier on south walls.
Good Partners: In mats of gray-leaved perennials like *Nepeta* or *Stachys byzantina*. Also with *Agapanthus, Euphorbia griffithii,* and *Kniphofia.*

Obedience, Virginia Lion's-heart, False Dragonhead
Physostegia virginiana

Cultivar 'Bouquet Rose'

July–September ○ ✂
H 24–48 in. (60–120 cm)

Indigenous perennial with flowers that can move around the stems into new positions.
Flower: Light pink, tubular labiate flowers in terminal spikes.
Leaf: Narrow lanceolate, notched, grass-green, shiny.
Growth: Erect, produces short runners.
Origin: Eastern North America. Riverside meadows, river banks.
Site: Sun, with intermittent shade. Soil well-drained to moist, nutrient-rich, vigorous.
Care: Water and feed well. Stake weak shoots. Cut back in fall. Cut off portions of overly large clumps to reduce size.
Propagation: By division and by cuttings.
Use: In borders and near ponds.
Good Partners: *Eupatorium, Filipendula, Geranium, Phlox, Tradescantia.*
Cultivars/Relatives:
• 'Summersnow', pure white, 32 in. (80 cm).
• 'Vivid', purple-pink, 24 in. (60 cm).
• 'Bouquet Rose', violet-pink, 32 in. (80 cm), valuable cultivar.

Balloonflower, Chinese Bellflower
Platycodon grandiflorus

Platycodon grandiflorus

July–August ○
H 8–28 in. (20–70 cm)

A summer-blooming member of the *Campanulaceae* with unusual, balloon-shaped flower buds.
Flower: Medium blue, in the cultivars also white or pink, broad bell shapes in loose racemes at the ends of densely leaved stems.
Leaf: Lanceolate to narrow ovate, margin toothed, leathery, bluish green.
Growth: From a fleshy rootstock, produces erect clumps, sometimes unstable, growth begins late.
Origin: Northeastern Asia. Mountain meadows.
Site: Sun. Soil moderately dry to well-drained, permeable, nutrient-rich.
Care: Water and feed moderately. Cut back in fall.
Propagation: By seed in early spring, also possible with cultivars.
Use: In borders; also in rock gardens, where it is one of the few summer bloomers.
Good Partners: *Gypsophila paniculata, Liatris, Saponaria* x *lempergii.*
Cultivars/Relatives:
• 'Album', white with blue veining, 24 in. (60 cm).
• 'Perlmutterschale', pearly pink, 24 in. (60 cm).
• 'Mariesii', blue, free-flowering, 20 in. (50 cm).
• 'Apoyama', violet-blue, 8 in. (20 cm), dwarf cultivar for rock gardens.

Dwarf Jacob's-ladder, Richardson's Jacob's-ladder
Polemonium x richardsonii

Polemonium x *richardsonii*

May–June/September ○ ◐
H 16–28 in. (40–70 cm)

Spring bloomer with leaves that resemble a ladder.
Flower: Sky-blue, sweet-scented, broad bell-shaped in terminal clusters.
Leaf: Pinnate, vivid green.
Growth: In clumps with dense leaf tufts and erect pedicles.
Origin: Europe to Asia. In riverside woods, in damp meadows, and in shallow marshes.
Site: Sun to partial shade, cool, air humid. Soil moist, nutrient-rich. No soils that dry out easily!
Care: After the bloom, cut back completely; result is strong new growth and second bloom. Can be mowed down.
Propagation: By division, except during blooming season; by seed; by basal cuttings.
Use: In damp beds, at edges of ponds, along damp edges of woody plants, scattered in mosaic pattern in natural garden.
Good Partners: *Brunnera, Iris sibirica, Trollius.*
Cultivars/Relatives:
• 'Album', white, 16 in. (40 cm)
• 'Superbum', violet-blue, 20 in. (50 cm).
• *Polemonium foliosissimum*, lavender-blue, May–August, 24–32 in. (60–80 cm). More vigorous species that tolerates more dryness and is beautiful with peonies.

Solomon's Seal
Polygonatum Hybrid
'Weihenstephan'

Hybrid 'Weihenstephan'

May–June ◐ ☠
H 24–40 in. (60–100 cm)

Unusual woodland perennial
Flower: Milky white, scented,
tubular, arising from leaf axils of
drooping stems.
Leaf: Broad lanceolate, parallel
veins.
Growth: With many shoots,
arching.
Origin: Cultivated form.
Site: Light shade to partial
shade, with sufficient soil moisture also sun. Soil well-drained
to moist, loose, humus-rich.
Care: Water in dry spells. Protect from slug damage.
Propagation: By division, by
rhizome cuttings.
Use: In front of woody plants
and walls.
Good Partners: *Brunnera,
Epimedium, Hosta, Omphalodes,
Symphytum grandiflorum, Waldsteinia—Convallaria.*
Cultivars/Relatives:
• *Polygonatum multiflorum,*
common Solomon's seal, greenish white, May–June 12–24 in.
(30–60 cm). Indigenous perennial from mixed forests, for
woods-like plantings in humus-
rich soil. Slug damage is a seri-
ous threat!
Warning: The entire plant is
poisonous.

Himalayan Fleeceflower
Polygonum affine

Polygonum affine

June–September ○ ◐
H 6–10 in. (15–25 cm)

Short-lived ground cover.
Flower: Whitish when flower
opens, later pink. Tiny flowers in
dense terminal spikes. Plant
blooms less abundantly when
old.
Leaf: Lanceolate, grass-green, in
fall bronze.
Growth: Mat-like, gradually
developing gaps. Growth begins
late.
Origin: Himalayas. In mountain
meadows and on rocky hillsides.
Site: Light to partial shade, cool,
air humid. Soil well-drained to
moist, nutrient-rich.
Care: Prune brown leaves in
spring. Cut off portions of overly
large mats. Fill gaps in mat with
soil, then fertilize; alternatively,
divide and replant.
Propagation: By division and
by cuttings.
Use: In small areas in the front
of borders.
Good Partners: Combine only
with plants whose growth is vigorous. *Campanula persicifolia,
Eupatorium fistulosum, Filipendula purpurea* 'Elegans', *Veronica virginica.*
Cultivars/Relatives:
• 'Superbum', light pink.
• 'Darjeeling Red', deep red
with compact growth.

Mountain Fleece
Polygonum amplexicaule

Polygonum amplexicaule

August–October ○ ◐
H 32–48 in. (80–120 cm)

Fall bloomer for sites with well-
drained soil.
Flower: Ruby-red, in elongated,
terminal spikes.
Leaf: Broad lanceolate, green,
with yellow fall color.
Growth: Erect clumps that
spread out over time.
Origin: Himalayas. In mountain
meadows and along waterways.
Site: Sun to partial shade, cool.
Soil well-drained to moist, nutri-
ent-rich.
Care: Water and feed well. Cut
back in late fall. If necessary,
reduce size of clumps by cutting
off portions.
Propagation: By division.
Use: In borders, at edge of pond.
Good Partners: *Aconitum, Chelone, Eupatorium, Filipendula,
Lysimachia—Miscanthus.*
Cultivars/Relatives:
• 'Firetail', brilliant wine-red.
• *Polygonum bistorta,* snakeweed, pink, in cylindrical, long-
stemmed inflorescences,
May–June. Indigenous. For
moist soils. Tends to become
rampant, 20–36 in. (50–90 cm),
pretty in natural gardens.

169

Primula # PRIMROSE

Japanese primroses like damp sites with partial shade.

The *Primula* genus includes about 550 species, most of which are native to Europe and Asia, and some of which are among the best-known harbingers of spring, both in our gardens and in the wild.

In addition to the indigenous species, countless others can be planted in gardens without any difficulty. Many of them belong to the standard assortment available in garden centers. However, there exists a rather large number of species with very special site requirements, plants that should be used only by die-hard primula fanciers with plenty of experience.

As for the following profiles, only the most important species and groups are presented. They usually can be cultivated without significant difficulties.

The plate- to funnel-shaped flowers of the primroses narrow to a slender tube. They come in a wide range of colors. Apart from pure gentian-blue, almost all shades are found among the numerous species and breeds.

The strap- to tongue-shaped leaves are typical of many primroses. Frequently they are conspicuously wrinkled. Holes and slimy trails left by slugs are often seen on leaf blades. Now and then entire plants are eaten, with only the leaf ribs remaining. It is essential to protect the plants from damage by slugs.

Among the diverse species and forms, there are no spectacular ornamentals for borders. As a rule, primroses are fairly uncompetitive plants that are best used at the edges of thin stands of woody plants, beside water, in sparse grass, and in rock gardens. As partners or neighbors, primroses do best in the company of other fairly uncompetitive perennials.

Warning: Primroses contain poisonous substances that can severely irritate sensitive skin. When handling the plants, wear gloves to avoid allergic reactions.

Himalayan Primrose
Primula denticulata

Primula denticulata

April–May
H 6–10 in. (15–25 cm)

Spring bloomer.
Flower: Light to dark lilac; in the cultivars also white. Globe-shaped heads on rigidly erect stems.
Leaf: Elongated, obovate or spatulate, wrinkled, with saw-toothed margins, matte light green. Grows to full size only after blooming.
Origin: Himalayas to western China. In damp mountain meadows.
Site: Light or partial shade; with moist soils also sunny, cool settings. Soil well-drained to moist, humus, loam. No hot sites!
Care: Water in dry spells. Sprinkle with compost now and then.
Propagation: By seed in winter, the cultivars by root cuttings.
Use: In light shade of trees and walls, at edge of pond.
Good Partners: *Muscari*, narcissuses—*Cardamine trifolia*, *Primula juliae* hybrids. Small almond trees.
Cultivars/Relatives:
• 'Alba', white.
• 'Rubin', ruby-red.

Oxlip Primrose
Primula elatior

Primula elatior

March–May
H 6–10 in. (15–25 cm)

Indigenous primrose that sows itself.
Flower: Light yellow, in many-flowered umbels.
Leaf: Tongue-shaped, wrinkled, with wavy or scalloped margin, light green.
Growth: Produces leaf rosettes.
Origin: Europe and Asia Minor. In woods and damp meadows.
Site: Light or partial shade; with sufficient soil moisture also sun; cool. Soil well-drained to moist, nutrient-rich, loamy.
Care: Water if dry. Let grow undisturbed.
Propagation: By seed or by division.
Use: In natural gardens, in light shade of walls, at edges of ponds, in sparse grass.
Good Partners: Narcissuses—*Brunnera*, *Dicentra spectabilis* 'Alba', *Omphalodes*, *Pulmonaria*.
Cultivars/Relatives:
• *Primula elatior* hybrids, white, yellow, pink, scarlet, and brown. Flowers are larger and closer together, blooms April–May.
• *Primula veris*, cowslip, indigenous, golden yellow with orange spots and pleasant scent, April–May. For drier sites, suitable for rock gardens or for sunny slopes.

Japanese Primrose
Primula japonica

Primula japonica

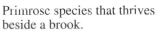
May–July
H 12–24 in. (30–60 cm)

Primrose species that thrives beside a brook.
Flower: Crimson, in tiered whorls, one above the other.
Leaf: Large, elongated, obovate, vivid green.
Growth: Basal leaf rosettes.
Origin: Japan, Taiwan. In damp valleys.
Site: Light to partial shade; with sufficient moisture also sun, cool, air humid. Soil well-drained to moist, loose, humus.
Care: Water adequately and apply humus-rich soil mix regularly. Protect from slug damage.
Propagation: By seed (cold-temperature germinator) or by division of large specimens; self-sowing.
Use: In rather large clusters beside streams or in light shade of woody plants.
Good Partners: *Epimedium*, *Rodgersia*—*Carex morrowii*, ferns. Rhododendrons.
Cultivars/Relatives:
• 'Alba', white with red eye.
• *Primula bullesiana* hybrids, Bulle's primrose, colors ranging from red, salmon-red, crimson, and lilac to violet, June–July.

Julia Primrose
Primula juliae Hybrids

Primula juliae hybrid

March–May ◐
H 2–6 in. (5–15 cm)

Dainty spring bloomers.
Flower: Violet, purple-red, pink, or white, about 1 in. (2 cm) across. Short-stemmed umbels.
Leaf: Small, obovate to roundish, margin markedly scallopped, rich green.
Growth: Creeping to grassy, forms small mats.
Site: Light shade, cool. Soil well-drained, moderately nutrient-rich. No hot sites!
Care: Water in dry spells. Regularly apply a weak solution of organic fertilizer.
Propagation: By division after the bloom.
Use: In rock gardens with light shade and in the shade of walls.
Good Partners: *Muscari,* narcissuses—*Cardamine trifolia, Primula denticulata, Saxifraga arendsii* hybrids, *Viola odorata.*
Cultivars/Relatives:
• 'Schneewittchen', white.
• 'Blütenkissen', crimson.
• 'Frühlingsbote', velvety red.
• 'Gartenmeister Bartens', brilliant purple-red.
• 'Gruss an Königslutter', purple-violet.

Siebold Primrose, Japanese Star Primrose
Primula sieboldii

Primula sieboldii

May–June ◐
H 8–12 in. (20–30 cm)

Spring-blooming primrose that long has been cultivated in Japan, with many cultivars.
Flower: White, pink, crimson to violet with small white eye, in terminal umbels on short stems.
Leaf: Tongue-shaped, wrinkled, light green.
Growth: Creeping. The leaves die down soon after the bloom.
Origin: Northeastern Asia. In swampy meadows.
Site: Light to partial shade, cool, air humid. Soil well-drained, loose, humus-rich.
Care: Water in dry spells. Apply leaf mold from time to time. As the plants are mostly short-lived, they have to be replaced fairly often.
Propagation: By division in spring.
Use: Only in small areas, in light shade of woody plants and walls.
Good Partners: *Cardamine trifolia, Epimedium, Saxifraga* x *urbium, Tiarella—Carex morrowii,* ferns, rhododendrons.
Cultivars/Relatives:
• 'Snow Flakes', white.

English Primrose, True Primrose
Primula vulgaris

Primula vulgaris

February–April ○ ◐
H 4 in. (10 cm)

Early spring bloomers with a great many forms and colors.
Flower: White, yellow, pink, red to blue-violet, in bunches.
Leaf: Spatulate, fresh green.
Growth: Cushion like.
Origin: Europe and Asia Minor. On shady hillsides and in woods.
Site: Sun to partial shade, cool. Soil well-drained, permeable, nutrient-rich.
Care: Water in dry spells. Feed regularly.
Propagation: By seed.
Use: In sunny beds, beneath deciduous, fairly uncompetitive trees.
Good Partners: *Chionodoxa, Puschkinia,* white narcissuses or tulips.
Cultivars/Relatives:
• *Primula vulgaris* ssp. *sibthorpii,* pink, red, or purple, with smaller flowers. Sensitive to summer drought; water regularly. Grows wild by self-sowing and migrates from partial shade of woody plants to scraggly patches of grass.

Cowslip Lungwort, Blue Lungwort
Pulmonaria angustifolia 'Azurea'

Pulmonaria angustifolia 'Azurea'

March–May
H 8–12 in. (20–30 cm)

Early spring bloomer with gentian-blue flowers.
Flower: Blue, funnel-shaped, in groups at the ends of erect stems.
Leaf: Lanceolate to narrow ovate, matte dark green, rough-haired.
Growth: Creeping, forms dense mats.
Origin: Cultivated form.
Site: Light shade to shade, cool. The plant is affected by heat. Soil moist to well-drained, loose, humus.
Care: Water in dry spells. <u>Don't remove foliage</u>! Let grow undisturbed.
Propagation: Easily possible by division.
Use: In small areas in undergrowth of woody plants and in light shade of walls.
Good Partners: *Epimedium, Galium odoratum, Lathyrus vernus, Waldsteinia—Carex, Luzula, Polystichum.*
Cultivars/Relatives:
• *Pulmonaria rubra,* red lungwort, brick-red, free-flowering, April–May. Leaves light green, large, forms less-dense mats and grows almost in thin clumps, 12 in. (30 cm).

Bethlehem Sage
Pulmonaria saccharata

Pulmonaria saccharata

March–May
H 6–12 in. (15–30 cm).

Beautiful ornamental flowering and foliage plant for shady gardens.
Flower: Matte crimson, violet when fading, funnel-shaped in clusters at the ends of erect, leafy stems.
Leaf: Large, narrow ovate, dull green with striking silver-mottled leaves. The summer leaves appear after the bloom.
Growth: By creeping; gradually forms mats.
Origin: Southeastern France and northern Apennines. In woods and bushes.
Site: Partial shade to shade, moderately warm. Soil well-drained to moderately dry, loose, humus-rich. The plant is sensitive to heat and compacted soil.
Care: Water in dry spells. Apply humus regularly. If necessary, cut off pieces of the mat with your spade.
Propagation: Easily possible by division, also by seed right after seeds ripen.
Use: In small areas in undergrowth of deciduous woody plants, in light shade or partial shade of shrubs and walls.

Cultivar 'Sissinghurst White'

Cultivar 'Mrs. Moon'

Good Partners: *Galium odoratum, Hepatica, Lamium maculatum, Polygonatum, Pulmonaria angustifolia.*
Cultivars/Relatives:
• 'Cambridge Blue', light blue.
• 'Sissinghurst White', pure white, strikingly marked.
• 'Mrs. Moon', red-violet, splendid ornamental foliage plant with showy leaves, the silvery spots are clearly delineated.
• *Pulmonaria officinalis,* common lungwort, indigenous, blue-violet, flowers are more restrainted, with fewer spots on leaves, March–April, 6–12 in. (15–30 cm). For natural gardens.

Pasqueflower
Pulsatilla vulgaris

Bronzeleaf, Bronzeleaf Rodgers'-flower
Rodgersia podophylla

Pulsatilla vulgaris

March–April	○ ☠
H 6–10 in. (15–25 cm)	

Early spring bloomer; retains its charm a long while by virtue of its attractive buds, flowers, and fruit structures.

Flower: Violet-blue to red, bell-shaped with golden yellow stamens. Bud covered with striking, silky white hair; the feather-like fruits are especially effective against the light.

Leaf: Finely pinnate, first with silky white hair, later dull green.

Growth: In clumps. The leaves develop in the blooming season and die down soon thereafter.

Origin: Europe. On stony hillsides and in limestone districts with sparse grass.

Site: Full sun, warm. Soil moderately dry, permeable, nutrient-poor.

Care: Plant with ball in spring. Not very competitive; keep vigorous neighbors in check.

Propagation: By seed as soon as seeds are ripe. Self-sowing in suitable sites.

Use: In rock gardens, and on slopes facing south.

Good Partners: <u>Don't combine with highly vigorous neighbors!</u> *Adonis vernalis, Saxifraga* x *apiculata—Festuca ovina, Helictotrichon.*

Warning: The entire plant is poisonous.

Rodgersia henryci

Rodgersia podophylla

June–July	◐ ●
H 32–72 in. (80–180 cm)	

Imposing woodland perennials whose gigantic leaves are major attention-getters.

Flower: Creamy white, in huge, branching, loosely drooping panicles.

Leaf: Palmately divided, with five obovate segments, slightly lobed at the sides. Bronze during initial growth, later dark green.

Growth: In clumps.

Origin: Japan and Korea. In damp mountain forests.

Site: Light to partial shade; also predominantly sun with sufficient soil moisture; cool, air humid, sheltered from wind. Soil well-drained to moist, permeable, nutrient- and humus-rich.

Care: Tidy the clumps in spring. Water regularly and apply organic fertilizer. Cut off spent panicles.

Propagation: By division in spring, by root cuttings from late fall to end of winter, and by seed.

Use: As solitary plant and feature perennial in light shade of woody plants and walls, beside ponds.

Good Partners: *Astilbe, Epimedium, Galium odoratum, Hosta, Tiarella—Carex morrowii, Carex pendula, Luzula sylvatica, Matteuccia,* and other ferns—Rhododendrons and other evergreen woody plants.

Cultivars/Relatives:
• 'Rotlaub', young leaves striking red-brown in color.
• 'Smaragd', young leaves also vivid green.
• *Rodgersia aesculifolia,* western China, white, June–July. With similar leaves, but usually seven segments, less sinuous and resembling horse chestnut, 36–56 in. (90–140 cm).
• *Rodgersia henryci* (formerly *Rodgersia pinnata* 'Superba'), light pink panicles and wine-red fruits, June–July. Foliage divided into six to nine broad lanceolate segments, flush purple with prominent veining, 20–40 in. (50–100 cm).
• *Rodgersia sambucifolia,* creamy white, with large pinnate leaves, 28–40 in. (70–100 cm).

Rudbeckia CONEFLOWERS

Orange coneflower (left and right) and brown-eyed Susan (center), between them violet ageratum

We all are familiar with them— the glowing coneflower species that can magically bring a touch of sunshine to gardens even on overcast days. The genus includes 30 to 40 species, all indigenous to North America. Those species, varying greatly in terms of their life spans, have been introduced into our gardens and parks.

Although annuals like *Rudbeckia hirta* and biennials like *Rudbeckia triloba,* are garden standards, it is principally the long-lived perennials *(Rudbeckia fulgida, laciniata,* and *nitida)* that continue to captivate us with their masses of flowers.

All of them have in common the lustrous, bright yellow ray flowers that are arranged in a ring around a tall-domed black, dark brown, or green center. The individual species range widely in height.

The giants among them, like the cut-leaved coneflower, need a corresponding amount of room in the garden and can be used only in wide borders or as solitary plants.

Shorter species like *Rudbeckia fulgida* are suitable even for small gardens.

In regard to site and care requirements, all the plants described in the profiles are quite easily satisfied. They need only a sunny place and adequate moisture; otherwise, they are content in any garden soil.

Most species yield long-lasting cut flowers. If you remove the yellow petals, the remaining centers of *Rudbeckia fulgida* 'Goldsturm' can be dried and put to excellent use as floral accessories in dried wreaths and bouquets.

Rudbeckia coneflowers can be propagated without difficulty. For most species and breeds, division is possible at almost any time of year. If you need only a few young plants, it is easy to cut off pieces with a spade. The short-lived *Rudbeckia triloba* is propagated by seed, which germinates easily and quickly.

Orange Coneflower, Showy Coneflower
Rudbeckia fulgida 'Goldsturm'

Cutleaf Coneflower
Rudbeckia laciniata 'Goldball'

Brown-eyed Susan
Rudbeckia triloba

Rudbeckia fulgida 'Goldsturm'

Rudbeckia laciniata 'Goldball'

Rudbeckia triloba

July–September
H 20–32 in. (50–80 cm)

August–September
H 64–80 in. (160–200 cm)

July–September
H 40–56 in. (100–140 cm)

Free-flowering, long-blooming, easy-to-tend perennial.
Flower: Golden yellow, slender-petaled flowers around a black-brown, globe-shaped center, at the ends of branching stems. Black-brown, button-shaped fruit structures are effective, particularly with frost and powdery snow.
Leaf: Ovate, dark green.
Growth: Broad clumps, strong-stemmed.
Origin: Cultivated form.
Site: Sun, warm. Soil well-drained, nutrient-rich, loamy.
Care: Water in dry spells; plant is affected by heat and drought. If the faded stalks are pruned, the blooming season will be prolonged.
Propagation: By division or by seed.
Use: In sunny borders.
Good Partners: Asters, *Coreopsis, Delphinium, Helenium, Heliopsis,* white-flowered *Phlox paniculata, Solidago—Calamagrostis.*

Old-fashioned, extremely tall country garden perennial with cascades of lustrous yellow flower globes.
Flower: Golden yellow, heavily petaled double flowers, globe-shaped, at the ends of branching stems.
Leaf: Three to seven parts, stem leaves lobed, green.
Growth: Spreads out by means of short runners. Tall-growing, not strong-stemmed.
Origin: Cultivated form.
Site: Sun to light shade, warm. Soil well-drained, nutrient-rich.
Care: Water and feed well. Cutting back by one-half in July makes plant more stable. Cut back completely in fall.
Propagation: By division.
Use: In sunny borders, best in front of fences against which the plants can lean.
Good Partners: *Helenium, Heliopsis, Solidago—Panicum virgatum.*
Cultivars/Relatives:
• *Rudbeckia nitida* 'Herbstsonne', single-flowered, golden yellow, backward pointing, tongue-shaped flowers around a green, cylindrical center, August–October, 80 in. (200 cm) tall.

Gorgeous, extremely free-flowering perennial; short-lived, it often is treated as an annual.
Flower: Yellow with button-shaped black center, in great profusion at the ends of many-branched stems.
Leaf: Lower leaves are divided into three parts; others are ovate, dark green.
Growth: Erect, spreading and bushy, sometimes weak-stemmed.
Origin: North America. On prairies.
Site: Full sun, warm. Soil moderately dry to well-drained, loose, nutrient-rich.
Care: Prompt cutting back just as the bloom finishes can extend the plant's life span. Otherwise, let the seeds ripen and collect them.
Propagation: By seed.
Use: In sunny borders, together with midsummer and fall bloomers.
Good Partners: *Cosmos bipinnatus* 'Unschuld', *Rudbeckia hirta, Verbena bonariensis—Aster, Delphinium, Helianthus—Calamagrostis* x *acutiflora, Panicum.*

Violet Sage
Salvia nemorosa

Salvia nemorosa 'Mainacht'

May–August/September ○
H 16–32 in. (40–80 cm)

Perennial sage with long-lasting blooming season.
Flower: Light to dark violet, labiate flowers in dense whorls in candle-shaped spikes.
Leaf: Elongated ovate, wrinkled, dull green; aromatic.
Growth: Erect, clump-like, sometimes weak-stemmed.
Origin: Central Europe to western Asia. In dry grass and steppe heaths.
Site: Sun, warm, also hot and briefly dry. Soil moderately dry to well-drained, permeable, nutrient-rich. In heavy soils, plant is unstable and rots.
Care: Cutting back completely when primary bloom finishes results in second bloom in late summer. Can be mowed down. Remove seedlings.
Propagation: By cuttings in early summer.
Use: In sunny borders, on sunny slopes, in sunny natural gardens.
Good Partners: Very versatile; can be combined with, for example, *Anaphalis, Anthemis, Coreopsis, Erigeron, Iris barbata* hybrids, *Paeonia*—roses.
Cultivars/Relatives:
• 'Blauhügel', medium blue.
• 'Ostfriesland', violet-blue, extremely free-flowering.
• 'Mainacht', dark violet-blue, early blooming.

Common or Garden Sage
Salvia officinalis

Salvia officinalis

June–July ○
H 12–24 in. (30–60 cm)

Aromatic subshrub, used primarily as ornamental foliage plant. Long grown as a healing plant and for culinary use.
Flower: Somber violet blue, small labiate flowers in loose spikes.
Leaf: Elongated, ovate, wrinkled, velvety, grayish, evergreen; aromatic scent.
Growth: Erect subshrub, forms small bushes.
Origin: Spain, southern France, and western Balkans. Old cultivated plant, naturalized in Central Europe. On stony hillsides, in thin stands of pine and juniper.
Site: Sun, warm to hot. Soil dry to moderately dry, quite permeable, moderately nutrient- and lime-rich.
Care: After the bloom, cut back by two-thirds to keep the plants compact. Young plants especially need to be covered in severe winters, as plant is frost-tender.
Propagation: By cuttings in early summer and in fall.
Use: In the front of sunny beds, on sunny slopes, in rock beds, shaped brick walls, herb gardens, and scented gardens.

Salvia officinalis 'Berggarten'

Good Partners: *Achillea, Gypsophila paniculata, Lavandula, Santolina, Helictotrichon*—also with roses and blue-leaved mat-forming juniper.
Cultivars/Relatives:
• 'Berggarten', with roundish leaves, grows compact. Attractively shaped, vigorous cultivar.
• 'Purpurascens', foliage heavily tinged with purple, slow-growing.
• 'Tricolor', with multicolored foliage, leaves gray-green in the center and white to creamy yellow at the margins, in some cases entire surface tinged with purple. Frost-tender cultivar.
• 'Variegata', with yellow-spotted foliage, needs winter protection.
• *Salvia lavandulifolia*, lavender-leaved sage, also a subshrub, resembles garden sage, but with narrower leaves.
• *Salvia sclarea*, clary sage, short-lived, aromatic. The first year, a leaf rosette made up of wrinkled, dark green leaves is produced. The second year, the impressive, many-branched inflorescences with numerous violet, pink, or even white single flowers make their appearance. Can be propagated by seed, self-sowing in favorable places, 32–40 in. (80–100 cm).

Lavender Cotton
Santolina chamaecyparissus

Santolina chamaecyparissus

July–August
H 12–20 in. (30–50 cm)

Free-flowering, aromatic sub-shrub.
Flower: Yellow, globular flower heads.
Leaf: Finely pinnate, silvery gray, evergreen; aromatic.
Growth: Compact subshrub with upward-arching shoots.
Origin: Southern Europe. In dry, warm heaths of juniper and small shrubs.
Site: Full sun, warm, also hot. Soil dry to moderately dry, highly permeable, also nutrient-poor. No waterlogged soils!
Care: After the bloom, cut back by one-third to keep the plants from becoming floppy.
Propagation: By cuttings in summer.
Use: In sunny borders, on sunny slopes, in rock gardens, scented gardens, and herb gardens, in gravel beds. As an austere edging and ornamental plant in gardens of geometric design.
Good Partners: *Aster amellus, Lavandula, Nepeta, Salvia, Stachys byzantina.*

Soapwort
Saponaria x lempergii

Saponaria x lempergii

July–September
H 12–16 in. (30–40 cm)

Rock garden plant that blooms both late and long.
Flower: Crimson, star-shaped, in clusters on stems that are branched like forks.
Leaf: Lanceolate to narrow ovate, small, dull dark green.
Growth: In clumps, with arching shoots.
Origin: Cultivated form, the parent species from southeastern Europe.
Site: Sun, warm. Soil moderately dry to well-drained, also dry for brief periods. Any highly permeable garden soil.
Care: Cut back hard in fall.
Propagation: By cuttings in late spring.
Use: In rock gardens, in the front of sunny borders, on sunny slopes, on wall crests, and in paving crevices.
Good Partners: *Calamintha nepeta, Campanula poscharskyana, Centranthus, Satureja montana, Silene schafta, Thymus.*
Cultivars/Relatives:
• 'Max Frei', pink. Large-flowered. Growth less compact.

Rock Soapwort
Saponaria ocymoides

Saponaria ocymoides

May–July/September
H 4–8 in. (10–20 cm)

Free-flowering, colorful, as well as undemanding perennial for rock gardens.
Flower: Rose-pink, scented, small, star-shaped, in numerous false umbels on forked stems.
Leaf: Narrow, obovate to linear, dull green.
Growth: Loose cushions, almost matlike by virtue of long, decumbent shoots.
Origin: Southern European mountains, Alps. On sunny hillsides and limestone rocks.
Site: Sun, moderately warm. Soil moderately dry to well-drained, highly permeable, moderately nutrient- and lime-rich. No wet and heavy soils!
Care: After the bloom, cut back plants by one-third to keep them compact. The pruning also will stimulate a less abundant second bloom in September.
Propagation: By seed in summer, by division.
Use: In rock gardens, in gravel and pebble beds, in dry walls.
Good Partners: *Campanula garganica, Cerastium tomentosum, Iberis saxatilis, Veronica spicata* ssp. *incana.*

Saxifraga SAXIFRAGE, BREAKSTONE

Saxifraga arendsii hybrids

The large *Saxifraga* genus includes almost 400 species and countless varieties and hybrids. It owes its Latin name, saxifrage, which means rock-breaking, to its manner of growth. At times growing in even the tiniest crevices in the rocks, alpine varieties seem almost to break the stone apart in their persistent struggle to emerge. In addition to alpine plants, the genus includes a great many other species that occur in totally different kinds of natural habitats. Their appearance varies, depending on their particular adaptation to the habitat. For this reason, botanists divide the genus into groups, or sections. Of significance to gardeners are the mossy saxifrages, shade-tolerant saxifrages, and woodland saxifrages.

The mossy saxifrages (*Dactyloides* section) are notable for their vivid green, soft-leaved rosettes. They form low, dense cushions by means of lateral runners. They include the *Saxifraga arendsii* hybrids, with cultivars of many colors.

The shade-tolerant or leaf-rosette saxifrages (*Robertsoniana* section) are also quite popular in gardens. They are evergreen perennials that live in woodlands. Mostly they form gradually increasing mats by means of runners, as does London-pride saxifrage (*Saxifraga* x *urbium*).

The woodland saxifrages (*Diptera* section), indigenous to East Asia where they also occur in woodland settings, belong to the third garden-worthy group. Like *Saxifraga cortusifolia*, they bloom in late summer or fall.

The "true" alpine saxifrages are difficult to grow in the lowlands; they require special care and specially prepared sites. They are of value only to plant collectors.

Crusted Saxifrage
Saxifraga x apiculata

Moss Saxifrage
Saxifraga arendsii Hybrids

London-pride Saxifrage
Saxifraga x urbium

Saxifraga x apiculata

Saxifraga arendsii hybrid

Saxifraga x urbium

| March–April | ◯ ◑ |
| H 24 in. (5–10 cm) | |

Free-flowering saxifrage species for rock gardens.
Flower: Light yellow flower clusters.
Leaf: Narrow lanceolate, stiff, fresh green, evergreen.
Growth: Continually produces new rosettes, forming shallow cushions.
Origin: Cultivated form.
Site: Out of sun to light shade, cool, air humid. Soil well-drained, permeable, stony. Crevices in stone. Only after the plants have developed deep-reaching roots are they able to tolerate short-term heat and drought.
Care: Plant rosettes in crevices. Cut back after bloom finishes.
Propagation: By cuttings and by detaching offshoots.
Use: In rock gardens, dry walls.
Good Partners: *Aubrieta* hybrids, *Iberis,* other rosette-forming *saxifrages.*
Cultivars/Relatives:
• *Saxifraga juniperifolia,* juniperleaf saxifrage, bright yellow, April–May. Firm cushions of stiff, needle-shaped leaves for sun to partial sun.
• *Saxifraga juniperifolia* ssp. *sancta,* sacred saxifrage, lemon-yellow, April–May. Forms wide, globular cushions.

| May–June | ◑ |
| H 2–8 in. (5–20 cm) | |

Mossy, cushion-shaped perennial.
Flower: Pink, crimson, velvety red, white, light yellow, saucer-shaped, on thin stems.
Leaf: Small, deeply incised, evergreen.
Growth: Shallow cushions, becoming bare at the center.
Origin: Cultivated form.
Site: Partial to light shade, cool, air humid. Soil well-drained, permeable with humus.
Care: Sprinkle in dry spells. Plant is short-lived; divide and replant every four to five years.
Propagation: By division, by rosette cuttings.
Use: In bright shade of walls and woody plants, in rock gardens.
Good Partners: *Cardamine trifolia, Heuchera, Saxifraga* x *urbium—Carex,* ferns.
Cultivars/Relatives:
• 'Biedermeier', white.
• 'Schneeteppich', white.
• 'Rosenzwerg', pink, 4 in. (10 cm).
• 'Blutenteppich', pink.
• 'Leuchtkäfer', blood-red.
• 'Triumph' bright ruby-red.

| May–June | ◑ |
| H 6–12 in. (15–30 cm) | |

Form with funnel-shaped leaf rosettes.
Flower: White, pink in the center, star-shaped, in veil-like panicles.
Leaf: Broad spatulate, green, leathery, evergreen.
Growth: Dense mats.
Origin: Cultivated form.
Site: Light shade, cool, air humid. Soil well-drained to moist, permeable, humus.
Care: Apply humus from time to time.
Propagation: By division.
Use: In small areas as ground cover for undergrowth in light shade; in shade of walls. Not very competitive!
Good Partners: *Astrantia, Epimedium, Hosta, Tiarella— Carex, Luzula,* ferns.
Cultivars/Relatives:
• 'Elliots Variety', pink.
• *Saxifraga cortusifolia* var. *fortunei,* white, April–October. Deciduous, 8–12 in. (20–30 cm). Use light winter protection. The flowers will freeze in the first frosts. Use with woody plants that have fall color and with late blooming perennials like *Aconitum* and *Tricyrtis.*

Pincushion Flower, Caucasian Scabious, Scabiosa
Scabiosa caucasica

Cultivar 'Clive Greaves'

June–September ○ ✂
H 20–32 in. (50–80 cm)

Versatile perennial with pale blue flowers.

Flower: Light blue, large, saucer-shaped.

Leaf: Basal leaves elongated lanceolate, stem leaves deeply incised, pinnate.

Growth: Broad, tuft-like clumps, occasionally weak-stemmed.

Origin: Caucasus, northern Iran, and northern Turkey. In mountain meadows and on rocky hillsides.

Site: Full sun, warm. Soil moderately dry to well-drained, permeable, nutrient-rich. No heavy or moist soils, where it will rot.

Care: Use inorganic fertilizer. Keep cutting back inflorescences; that will extend the blooming season into fall. Cut back completely in fall.

Propagation: By division.

Use: In borders, on slopes, in large rock gardens, as cutting flower.

Good Partners: *Achillea* hybrids, *Anaphalis, Aster amellus, Aster pyranaeus,* and *Aster sedifolius, Oenothera missouriensis, Salvia nemorosa.*

Cultivars/Relatives:
• 'Miss Willmott', creamy white.
• 'Clive Greaves', light blue.
• 'Blauer Atlas', dark blue.
• 'Nachtfalter', bright violet-blue.

STONECROP, SEDUM, LIVE-FOREVER
Sedum

Sedum spectabilis 'Carmen' and *Aster dumosus*

Like cactuses, stonecrops also have water storage organs that enable them to colonize inferior, parched sites where other plants cannot follow. In the *Sedum* species, however, only the leaves are thick with water-filled tissues (succulent), while in cactuses the entire shoot is thick. In normal beds, stonecrops are unable to compete with neighboring plants. In moist or overly nutrient-rich soil, they rot easily or exhaust themselves by excessive seed production.

Leaf: In the short species, more or less cylindrical; in the tall-growing species, roundish oval and fleshy. In excessive heat and drought, many forms turn reddish or bronze-brown. If conditions improve again, the original leaf color is restored.

Site: Full sun, occasionally light shade, also hot. Soil dry to well-drained, permeable, moderately nutrient-rich, humus-poor, sandy-gravelly or gravelly-loamy. For taller-growing species, moderately dry soil mixes with somewhat greater nutrient content.

Care: Feed moderately every three to four years. No other procedures necessary.

Propagation: By cuttings. All *Sedum* species take root with extraordinary ease. Short pieces of shoot are sufficient to produce new plants quickly, and with the large-leaved forms even individual leaves will do the job. Division is possible.

Use: In rock gardens and steppe gardens, in sunny crevices in paving and walls, in roof gardens, and in other stony settings.

Good Partners: The short forms are best with other plants tolerant of drought, including *Dianthus, Geranium, Gypsophila repens, Linum, Nepeta, Saxifraga, Sempervivum,* and *Stachys.* The tall-growing forms are better combined with bedding perennials and cushion-forming grasses.

Worm-grass
Sedum album

Cultivar 'Coral Carpet'

Sedum sexangulare 'Weisse Tatra'

May–June
H 2–4 in. (5–10 cm)

Undemanding plant for rock gardens.
Flower: White to whitish pink, star-shaped, umbel like.
Leaf: Cylindrical, usually dull green, reddish under stress.
Growth: In shallow mats.
Origin: Europe to Asia, North Africa. On rocks, stony hillsides, and walls.
Site: See page 181.
Care: No procedures required.
Propagation: By cuttings and by division. See page 181.
Use: See page 181.
Good Partners: See page 181.
Cultivars/Relatives:
• 'Coral Carpet', has few flowers, forms pretty mats. Leaves coppery red, particularly in winter.
• *Sedum acre,* gold-moss stonecrop, yellow, free-flowering, May–June, 2–6 in. (5–15 cm).
• *Sedum sexangulare,* hexagon stonecrop, yellow, free-flowering, June 2–3 in. (5–8 cm). Leaves olive-green, narrow cylindrical, spreading, evergreen. In mats.

Golden Sedum
Sedum floriferum
'Weihenstephaner Gold'

Cultivar 'Weihenstephaner Gold'

July–September
H 4–6 in. (10–15 cm)

Free-flowering, pretty, easy-to-tend mat former that always looks attractive.
Flower: Lustrous yellow, star-shaped, in shallow, umbel-like racemes on orange-red stems.
Leaf: Lanceolate, rich green.
Growth: Low cushions to extensive mats.
Origin: Cultivated form.
Site: See page 181.
Care: No procedures needed.
Propagation: By cuttings and by division. See page 181.
Use: See page 181.
Cultivars/Relatives:
• *Sedum spurium,* two-row stonecrop, pink, in shallow, umbel-like racemes, June–July. Leaves blunt oval, often arranged densely, one above another, so that the shoots appear cylindrical. Forms shallow cushions to grasslike mats, 4–6 in. (10–15 cm). Origin: Caucasus; damp rocky hillsides. Site: Sun to partial shade, cool. Soil moderately dry to moist, also submerged for short periods, moderately nutrient-rich, sandy loam or sandy humus. As ground cover and for edging.
• 'Album Superbum', white.
• 'Fuldaglut', crimson, free-flowering, with dark red leaves that turn green in shade.

Purple Sedum
Sedum telephium

Cultivar 'Herbstfreude'

July–September
H 16–24 in. (40–60 cm)

Important late summer and fall bloomer.
Flower: Pink to purple-red, star-shaped, in shallow false umbels. The fruit structures are also enchanting.
Leaf: Large, oval, fleshy, gray-green, with beautiful yellow fall color.
Growth: Spreading and in clumps.
Origin: Europe to Asia. Rocky hillsides with loose grass, patches of rock debris, sunny edges of bushes.
Site: See page 181.
Care: No procedures needed.
Propagation: By cuttings and by division. See page 181.
Use: In sunny beds and in stony settings.
Good Partners: White- and silver-leaved ground covers *Anaphalis* and *Stachys byzantina,* drought-tolerant bedding perennials or subshrubs like *Caryopteris*—blue-leaved grasses. Red-leaved shrubs like *Berberis* and *Cotinus coggygria.*
Cultivars/Relatives:
• 'Herbstfreude', copper-red to pink-purple, August–September. Dependable late bloomer.
• 'Unstead Red', mahogany-red, August–September, black-red leaves. Strikingly dark plant.
• *Sedum spectabile,* showy sedum, pink to purple, August–September, gray-green, broad oval leaves, 16 in. (40 cm).
• *Sedum cauticolum* 'Robustum', crimson, September–October. Leaves blue-green, 8 in. (20 cm), cushion-forming.

Houseleeks, Hens and Chickens
Sempervivum

Hybrid 'Mt. Kenia'

June–July ○
H 4–10 in. (10–25 cm)

Extremely undemanding plant.
Flower: Pink, crimson, or ruby-red, star-shaped.
Leaf: Lanceolate to spatulate, evergreen. Green, brown, and gray shades, also silvery white, with metallic shimmer.
Growth: In tightly packed, globe-shaped rosettes. Offsets form on margins. Slow-growing, dense cushions, more rarely small mats. Each individual rosette dies back after the bloom.
Origin: Europe to western Asia. On rock faces, on wall crests and rooftops.
Site: Sun, warm to hot. Soil dry to moderately well-drained, nutrient-poor, gravelly-stony.
Care: None.
Propagation: By detaching offsets.
Use: In cracks in walls and paving, crevices of rocks in boulder garden, in containers, in roof gardens.
Good Partners: No very vigorous plants! *Dianthus, Saxifraga, Sedum.*
Cultivars/Relatives:
• *Sedum arachnoideum*, cobweb houseleek, crimson-pink, extremely slow-growing, in small, white, globe-shaped rosettes.
• *Sedum tectorum*, common houseleek, pink, in large rosettes of green leaves with reddish tips.
• *Sempervivum* hybrids, pink, crimson to ruby-red, splendid rosettes up to 6 in. (15 cm) across, in many colors.

Moss Campion, Schafta Campion
Silene schafta

Silene schafta

August–September ○
H 2–6 in. (5–15 cm)

Valuable rock garden plant because of its late blooming season.
Flower: Bright pink, star-shaped, solitary or in groups at the ends of branching stalks.
Leaf: Lanceolate, small, matte green.
Growth: Shallow, cushion-shaped to loose grassy.
Origin: Caucasus, on hillsides covered with rock debris.
Site: Sun or light shade, moderately warm. Soil moderately dry to well-drained, any permeable garden soil. No damp sites!
Care: Water in dry spells. Cut back after the bloom.
Propagation: By seed or by division.
Use: In rock gardens and on wall crests.
Good Partners: Not highly competitive; don't combine with very vigorous neighbors. *Aster sedifolius* 'Nanus', fall-blooming *Gentiana* species, *Saponaria, Scabiosa caucasica—Festuca cinerea.*
Cultivars/Relatives:
• 'Splendens', crimson, free-flowering.

False Solomon's-seal, Wild Spikenard
Smilacina racemosa

Smilacina racemosa

May–June
H 24–36 in. (60–90 cm)

Indigenous decorative perennial for shade.
Flower: Creamy white, scented, small, star-shaped, in conical panicles on densely leaved, arching stalks. Ornamental light red berries.
Leaf: Broad lanceolate, with prominent parallel venation, green, yellow in fall.
Growth: Broad, heavily bent, dense clumps from slowly creeping rhizomes.
Origin: North America. Damp deciduous, coniferous, and riverside forests.
Site: Light shade to shade, cool, air humid. Soil well-drained, permeable, loamy humus.
Care: Water in dry spells. Occasionally supply with leaf mold.
Propagation: By division.
Use: In light shade of woody plants and walls.
Good Partners: *Cardamine trifolia, Epimedium, Hosta, Tiarella*— ferns.
Cultivars/Relatives:
• *Smilacina stellata*, starry Solomon's-seal, with larger flowers in a loose raceme, dark red berries, 16 in. (40 cm). For places with partial shade, where it spreads out heavily.

Hybrid Goldenrod
Solidago Hybrids

Solidago hybrid

Lamb's-ears, Woolly Betony
Stachys byzantina

Stachys byzantina 'McQueen'

July–September	◯ ✂
H 20–32 in. (50–80 cm)	

Yellow midsummer bloomer.
Flower: Golden yellow, with pungent odor. In dense terminal panicles.
Leaf: Lanceolate, green.
Growth: In clumps, not rampant; sometimes weak-stemmed.
Origin: Cultivated form.
Site: Sun. Any well-drained to moist, nutrient-rich garden soil.
Care: Water in dry spells. Feed well. After the bloom, cut back to prevent self-sowing.
Propagation: By division.
Use: In borders.
Good Partners: *Campanula persicifolia, Chrysanthemum, Monarda, Physostegia virginiana* 'Sommersnow', *Rudbeckia, Tradescantia.*
Cultivars/Relatives:
• 'Goldwedel', light yellow, early-blooming, with loosely nodding branches of panicles.
• 'Goldenmosa', golden yellow, late-blooming, with mimosa-like inflorescences and light green foliage.
• 'Strahlenkrone', golden yellow, shallow flower panicles, rigidly erect. The best cultivar.

July–August	◯
H 4–12 in. (10–30 cm)	

Valuable, highly versatile perennial with gray, ornamental foliage.
Flower: Inconspicuous pale rose labiate flowers, in dense, downy gray candle shapes.
Leaf: Broad ovate, covered with dense, silvery, woolly hair, velvety soft.
Growth: Forms dense, low mats by means of runners. Flower stems occasionally weak.
Origin: Asia Minor and Caucasus. On ledges of rock, on hillsides covered with rock debris, in juniper bushes.
Site: Full sun, warm, also hot. Soil dry to well-drained, permeable, nutrient-poor. In nutrient-rich soils the plant is short-lived; if wet, it rots.
Care: Plant in spring. Cut off faded stalks. If necessary, curtail growth with spade.
Propagation: Easily possible by division.
Use: In small areas in the front of borders, in rock gardens and terraced gardens, in paving crevices, in front of south-facing walls, and for roofs. Very versatile, as the silver-gray coloring of the leaf mats makes an excellent link between flowers of different colors.

Good Partners: *Achillea* hybrids, *Alyssum, Anaphalis, Anthemis, Campanula glomerata, Lavandula, Nepeta, Salvia nemorosa,* and *Salvia officinalis, Yucca—Achnatherum calamagrostis, Festuca cinerea, Helictotrichon.*
Cultivars/Relatives:
• 'Silver Carpet', seldom blooms, 8 in. (20 cm) tall with flowers. Long-lived, forms unbroken mats of leaves 2 in. (5 cm) tall.
• 'Cotton Ball' (= 'Sheila McQueen'), compact with dense, woolly flower globes, 4 in. (10 cm).

Big Betony, Woundwort
Stachys grandiflora 'Superba'

Stachys grandiflora 'Superba'

June–July ○ ◐ ✂
H 16–24 in. (40–60 cm)

Showy flowering perennial, not easy to combine with other perennials because of the brilliant color of the blossoms.
Flower: Purple-pink labiate flowers in cylindrical spikes.
Leaf: Elongated cordate, wrinkled, margins scalloped, matte dark green, stays attractive for a long while.
Growth: Broad-set, clump like.
Origin: Caucasus, northern Turkey, and northern Iran. Damp mountain meadows, rocky hillsides with many bushes.
Site: Out of sun, with sufficient soil moisture also sun, cool. Soil well-drained, deep, loamy humus.
Care: Tidy the clumps in spring, water in dry spells. Feed occasionally. After the bloom, cut back the stalks.
Propagation: By division.
Use: In borders with partial shade, with well-drained soil in sunny beds.
Good Partners: *Alchemilla, Campanula persicifolia, Chrysanthemum maximum, Geranium.*

Comfrey
Symphytum grandiflorum

Symphytum grandiflorum

April–May ○ ◐ ●
H 8–12 in. (20–30 cm)

Easy-to-grow ground cover for shady garden spots.
Flower: Creamy yellow, tubular, rather inconspicuous, in terminal clusters.
Leaf: Ovate, dark green, rough-haired.
Growth: Forms dense mats by means of numerous runners.
Origin: Caucasus. In mixed forests in mountains.
Site: Light shade, partial shade to shade, with sufficient moisture also sun, cool, fresh, also briefly dry. Best in humus-rich, loamy soils, fairly undemanding.
Care: Easy to tend; almost no weeds appear in the dense mats. Water in prolonged dry spells. Occasionally apply compost.
Propagation: Easily possible by detaching runners and by division.
Use: Two-dimensionally in shade of woody plants and walls.
Good Partners: Only with highly competitive neighbors. *Brunnera, Epimedium, Hosta, Waldsteinia.*
Cultivars/Relatives:
• 'Hidcote Blue', blue-and-white, May, wide and clump like, 12–16 in. (30–40 cm). Good for damp beds. Pretty with *Iris sibirica, Polemonium,* and *Trollius.*

Feathered Columbine, Columbine Meadow Rue
Thalictrum aquilegifolium

Thalictrum aquilegifolium

May–July ○ ◐ ✂
H 32–48 in. (80–120 cm)

Meadow perennial with unusual, feathery inflorescences.
Flower: Pink to pale violet. Many-rayed by virtue of numerous, long stamens. In loose false umbels.
Leaf: Pinnate, like those of columbine, matte blue-green.
Growth: In clumps, erect, often weak-stemmed.
Origin: Europe. In riverside woods, tall perennial vegetation, and damp meadows.
Site: Partial shade, in moist soils also sun. Soil well-drained to wet, also submerged, nutrient-rich, with humus, loam, or clay.
Care: If not watered in dry spells, plant is prone to infestation by aphids. Feed well. Support shoots. Can be mowed down.
Propagation: By seed; by division in spring.
Use: Beside pond, in borders, in natural gardens.
Good Partners: *Achillea ptarmica, Chrysanthemum maximum, Filipendula, Iris sibirica, Tradescantia—Molinia.*
Cultivars/Relatives:
• 'Album', milky white.

Thyme
Thymus doerfleri 'Bressingham Seedling'

'Bressingham Seedling'

May–July	○
H 2–4 in. (5–10 cm)	

Perennial for rock gardens.
Flower: Pink labiate flowers in dense, almost hemispherical whorls located just above the foliage.
Leaf: Narrow, spatulate, small, hairy; aromatic.
Growth: Low mats that turn bare from the center.
Origin: Cultivated form.
Site: Full sun, warm, also hot. Soil dry to moderately dry, permeable, moderately nutrient-rich, stony or sandy. No wet, nutrient-rich soils, where it is short-lived.
Care: Cut back after the bloom.
Propagation: By division.
Use: In small areas in rock or terraced gardens, on sandy slopes, and for roofs.
Good Partners: *Aster alpinus, Campanula poscharskyana, Sedum.* Species of *Allium, Crocus,* and tulips that rise from the mats—*Festuca.*
Cultivars/Relatives:
• *Thymus serpyllum,* wild thyme, forms less-dense mats, June–September, 2–4 in. (5–10 cm).
• 'Albus', with white flowers.
• 'Coccineus', crimson.

Foamflower, Allegheny Foamflower
Tiarella cordifolia

Tiarella cordifolia

May–June	◐ ●
H 6–12 in. (15–30 cm)	

Indigenous ground cover for plantings of the woodland type.
Flower: Milky white, lightly scented, star-shaped, in erect spikes that have a foamy effect when massed.
Leaf: Oval to cordate, lobed, linden-green, with red fall color.
Growth: Forms dense mats by means of runners, but does not become a nuisance.
Origin: North America. In thin woods with well-drained soil.
Site: Light shade to shade, cool. Soil well-drained, permeable, humus-rich. No compacted soils, no hot, dry sites!
Care: Occasionally apply humus or leaf mold. Otherwise, let grow undisturbed.
Propagation: By division or by detaching runners.
Use: In small areas in the shade of root-tolerant woody plants and walls.
Good Partners: *Corydalis cava, Hosta, Saxifraga* x *urbium, Tricyrtis—Carexmorrowii—*rhododendrons.

Spiderwort
Tradescantia andersoniana
Hybrids

Hybrid 'Blue Stone'

June–August	○
H 16–24 in. (40–60 cm)	

Long-blooming perennials.
Flower: Blue or violet, crimson, white, tripartite, in clusters.
Leaf: Grassy, sticking out horizontally from the culms, green.
Growth: Erect clumps.
Origin: Cultivated form.
Site: Sun, warm. Soil well-drained to moist, nutrient-rich, definitely not sandy.
Care: Cut back after the primary bloom to encourage reblooming. That also prevents self-sowing.
Propagation: By division in spring.
Use: Beside water, in damp, sunny borders.
Good Partners: *Alchemilla, Chrysanthemum maximum, Filipendula, Geranium pratense, Veronica virginica.*
Cultivars/Relatives:
• 'Gisela', pure white.
• 'Karminglut', crimson.
• 'I. C. Weguelin', light blue.
• 'Blue Zwanenburg', dark blue, best cultivar.
• 'Blue Stone', bright blue.

Hairy Toad-lily
Tricyrtis hirta

Tricyrtis hirta

| September–October ◑ |
| H 20–36 in. (50–90 cm) |

Little-known fall bloomer with extravagant flowers.
Flower: Milky white, heavily dotted with purple-violet, funnel- to star-shaped, orchid like, in racemes on leafy stems.
Leaf: Narrow ovate, pointed, dark blue-green.
Growth: In clumps, erect.
Origin: Japan. Beside shady rocks in thin woods.
Site: Partial shade to light shade, cool, air humid. The plant is weak-stemmed in heavy shade; it is affected by heat. Soil well-drained, permeable, humus-rich.
Care: Water adequately in dry spells. Occasionally supply with leaf mold. Protect from slug damage.
Propagation: By division and by cuttings in spring. By seed (cold-temperature germinator).
Use: In light shade of trees and walls.
Good Partners: Don't combine with very vigorous plants! *Saxifraga cortusifolia* var. *fortunei*, *Tiarella*—*Carex morrowii*—*Adiantum*.

Globeflower
Trollius Hybrids

Trollius hybrid 'Helios'

| April–June ○ ◑ ☠ |
| H 16–28 in. (40–70 cm) |

Brilliant spring and early summer bloomer for damp borders.
Flower: Yellow or yellow-orange, globular, solitary on erect stems.
Leaf: Palmately divided, the segments more or less deeply incised, lush green. The leaves die back soon after the bloom.
Growth: In clumps, bushy.
Origin: The current form is cultivated; the parents are from the moderate latitudes of the northern hemisphere.
Site: Sun to partial shade, cool. Soil well-drained to wet, nutrient-rich, loamy humus. The moister the soil, the sunnier the place for planting may be. No hot sites!
Care: Water adequately. After the bloom, cut back completely, then feed and water well in order to encourage new growth, with a less abundant second bloom, in September.
Propagation: By division in spring.
Use: In damp beds and beside ponds. Don't plant in the front of borders, as globeflowers leave unsightly gaps when the foliage dies back after blooming. Excellent as cut flowers.

Trollius chinensis 'Golden Queen'

Good Partners: Don't plant in the immediate vicinity of highly competitive woody plants! *Geranium pratense*, *Geum* hybrids, *Iris pseudacorus*, *Iris sibirica*, *Symphytum grandiflorum* 'Hidcote Blue'.
Cultivars/Relatives:
• 'Earliest of All', golden yellow, earliest cultivar, often blooms as early as latter half of April.
• 'Maigold', golden yellow, with pretty, globe-shaped flowers.
• 'Goldquelle', yellow-orange, hemispherical flowers, late blooming cultivar.
• *Trollius europaeus*, common globeflower, indigenous, with golden yellow globe-shaped flowers, May–June, 12–20 in. (30–50 cm). One of the parent species of the *Trollius* hybrids.
• *Trollius chinensis* 'Golden Queen', orange-yellow, saucer-shaped, with nectar producing structures rising high above the flower, June–August, 32–40 in. (40–100 cm). This late blooming species, indigenous to northern China, also played a role in the development of the *Trollius* hybrids.
Warning: All globeflowers are poisonous.

Mullein
Verbascum bombyciferum

Ironweed
Vernonia crinita

Verbascum hybrid

Vernonia crinita

June–August ○
H 48–72 in. (120–180 cm)

August–October ○ ✂
H 60–100 in. (150–250 cm)

Short-lived perennial.
Flower: Yellow, from white, woolly buds. Dense flower spikes with few branches.
Leaf: Large, broad oval, and pointed; covered with gray, downy to white, woolly hair.
Growth: Dense basal leaf rosettes, above which the immense peduncle towers.
Origin: Asia Minor. In dry, stony places.
Site: Full sun, warm, also hot and dry. Soil dry to moderately dry, highly permeable, nutrient-poor.
Care: Prune peduncles after the bloom so plant will live longer.
Propagation: By seed; self-sowing in favorable spots.
Use: On slopes, in terraced gardens.
Good Partners: *Anaphalis, Anthemis, Nepeta, Santolina, Salvia—Helictotrichon.*
Cultivars/Relatives:
• *Verbascum olympicum,* yellow, June–August, up to 80 in. (2 m) tall.
• *Verbascum phoenicum,* purple mullein, purple-violet, May–July, green-leaved, 16–32 in. (40–80 cm). Long-lasting species for more vigorous, well-drained soil.

Indigenous enormous, fall-flowering perennial for damp parts of the garden.
Flower: Purple-violet heads one-half to one inch (1–2 cm) across, up to 100 in large, loose umbel like panicles on erect, leafy stems.
Leaf: Elongated ovate, large, dark green, rough-haired.
Growth: Loosely structured, tall-growing clumps, in some cases large in diameter. Despite size, quite strong-stemmed.
Origin: Eastern North America. In damp meadows, in reed banks, in riverside bushes.
Site: Sun, warm places. Soil well-drained to moist, also occasionally wet, nutrient-rich, loamy. In all good garden soils.
Care: Cut the fruit structures to the ground in fall or, at the latest, in spring. Can be transplanted at any time without difficulty, but best in spring.
Propagation: By division and cuttings in early spring; by seed.
Use: On pond banks, in damp beds. Good cut flowers.

Good Partners: *Aster novi-belgii, Eupatorium, Ligularia, Rudbeckia nitida. Chelone, Chrysanthemum serotinum*—tall ornamental grasses—woody plants with fall color.
Cultivars/Relatives:
• *Vernonia noveboracensis,* New York ironweed, purple-red, more rarely white, umbels with up to 50 blossoms. August–September. Leaves lanceolate, dark green. Tall- and broad-growing, up to 80 in. (200 cm). Not quite as strong-stemmed as the previous form. Robust perennial, long-lived species for sunny, warm situations. Loves moist to wet, nutrient-rich, loamy soils. Prefers sites sheltered from wind. Good with *Chrysanthemum serotinum, Eupatorium, Ligularia, Lysimachia clethroides.*

Austrian Speedwell
Veronica austriaca ssp. *teucrium*

Veronica austriaca ssp. *teucrium*

May–June
H 10–20 in. (25–50 cm)

Speedwell in brilliant blue.
Flower: Medium blue, star-shaped, in dense spikes.
Leaf: Elongated ovate, margins scalloped, lush green.
Growth: In clumps, slowly becomes larger by means of creeping rootstock; occasionally weak-stemmed.
Origin: Europe, Caucasus, Asia Minor, and Siberia. Edges of woods, semidry grass.
Site: Sun, warm. Soil moderately dry, permeable, moderately nutrient-rich. No wet sites!
Care: Cut off the faded blossoms.
Propagation: By division, the species also by seed.
Use: In the front of sunny borders, in rock gardens, terraced gardens, and heath gardens.
Good Partners: *Armeria maritima, Cerastium tomentosum, Geranium dalmaticum, Helianthemum* hybrids, *Iris barbata, Stachys byzantina.*
Cultivars/Relatives:
• 'Kapitan', gentian-blue, 10 in. (25 cm), stronger-stemmed.
• 'Knallblau', brilliant gentian-blue, 16 in. (40 cm)

Clump Speedwell
Veronica longifolia

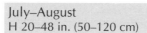

Veronica longifolia

July–August
H 20–48 in. (50–120 cm)

Tall speedwell species with slender inflorescences.
Flower: Medium blue, small, funnel-shaped, in dense, slender spikes on branched stems.
Leaf: Elongated lanceolate, dark green.
Growth: In clumps, erect.
Origin: Europe to East Asia. In damp meadows, in ditches, and on banks.
Site: Sun, warm. Soil well-drained to moist, nutrient-rich. Best are vigorous loamy soils.
Care: Water thoroughly in dry spells. Feed adequately. Cut off spikes after the bloom.
Propagation: By division in spring.
Use: In well-drained borders, at edges of ponds.
Good Partners: *Achillea ptarmica, Alchemilla, Chrysanthemum maximum, Hemerocallis,* low *Solidago* hybrids.
Cultivars/Relatives:
• 'Schneeriesin', white, 40 in. (100 cm).
• 'Blauriesin', medium blue, 44 in. (110 cm).
• 'Blaubart', deep blue, 20 in. (50 cm).

Spike Speedwell, Woolly Speedwell
Veronica spicata ssp. *incana*

Veronica spicata ssp. *incana*

June–August
H 8–16 in. (20–40 cm)

Species with attractive, silver-gray leaf mats.
Flower: Dark blue, star-shaped, in slender spikes on erect stems.
Leaf: Elongated ovate, silvery gray.
Growth: Forms grassy, gray mats by means of runners.
Origin: Eastern Europe to northern Asia. In dry meadows, steppes.
Site: Full sun, warm, also hot. Soil moderately dry to well-drained, permeable, moderately nutrient-rich.
Care: Cut back stalks after they fade.
Propagation: By division.
Use: In sunny, dry borders and on slopes, in rock gardens and heath gardens.
Good Partners: *Campanula carpatica* 'Weisse Clips', *Gypsophila repens, Saponaria—Festuca, Helictotrichon.*
Cultivars/Relatives:
• *Veronica spicata* var. *spicata,* violet-blue, gray-and-green foliage, taller-growing, July–September, 14–20 in. (35–50 cm).
• 'Heidekind', wine-red, 8 in. (20 cm).
• 'Blaufuchs', dark blue, 12 in. (30 cm).

Culver's-root
Veronica virginica

Veronica virginica 'Alborosea'

July–September ○
H 48–80 in. (120–200 cm)

Indigenous enormous perennial with candelabra-shaped inflorescences.
Flower: Medium blue with pink, star-shaped; protruding stamens. In dense spikes.
Leaf: Lanceolate, lush green, always in groups in whorls.
Growth: Large clumps, stalks arched, not always stable.
Origin: Eastern North America. In damp meadows, in woods and bushes.
Site: Sun, warm. In shady places, the clumps become floppy. Soil well-drained to moist, nutrient-rich. Best are vigorous loamy soils.
Care: Water well and feed generously. Stake if support is required.
Propagation: By division.
Use: Beside water, at edge of pond, in borders.
Good Partners: *Hemerocallis, Ligularia, Lysimachia punctata, Filipendula purpurea* 'Elegans'—*Miscanthus sinensis.*
Cultivars/Relatives:
• 'Alba', white, erect, 48 in. (120 cm), strong-stemmed.
• 'Rosea', pink, otherwise like 'Alba'.

Periwinkle, Lesser
Periwinkle, Myrtle
Vinca minor

Vinca minor

April–May ◐ ● ☠
H 4–8 in. (10–20 cm)

Evergreen ground cover for shady garden areas.
Flower: Light blue, plate- to star-shaped, on short stems arising from leaf axils.
Leaf: Lanceolate to narrow ovate, leathery, shiny dark green, evergreen.
Growth: Forms mats by means of layers.
Origin: Europe to Asia Minor. In woods and bushes.
Site: Partial shade to shade, cool to moderately warm. The plant is affected by heat. Soil moderately dry to moist, loose.
Care: Water in dry spells. Apply organic fertilizer from time to time.
Propagation: By division or by detaching layers. Easy to do.
Use: Beneath woody plants and in the shade of walls.
Good Partners: Combine only with very vigorous plants. *Aruncus, Campanula latifolia, Hosta, Rodgersia, Symphytum grandiflorum, Waldsteinia—Carex—Dryopteris.*
Cultivars/Relatives:
• 'Bowles Variety', blue, large-flowered.
• 'Gertrude Jekyll', white, free-flowering.
• 'Rubra', purple, not very vigorous.
• 'Variegata', light blue, with white-variegated foliage.

Tufted Pansy, Horned Violet
Viola cornuta Hybrids

Viola cornuta hybrid

April–May ○
H 4–8 in. (10–20 cm)

Small, unobtrusive perennials with flowers resembling faces.
Flower: Violet-blue, blue, yellow, or white pansy-like flowers on leafless stems.
Leaf: The leaves near the ground round, the stem leaves ovate or elongated ovate and slightly scalloped, dark green, somewhat shiny.
Growth: In clumps, spreads out gradually by means of creeping rootstock.
Origin: Cultivated form. The parent species is native to the Pyrenees.
Site: Sun, cool to moderately warm. The plant is sensitive to heat. Soil well-drained, not wet; loamy humus or sandy loam.
Care: Water in dry spells. After the primary bloom in May/June, cut back to stimulate reblooming in fall. Use light winter protection; moderately frost-hardy.
Propagation: By division or by cuttings.
Use: In the front of borders, in rock gardens and country gardens. Cutting flower.
Good Partners: *Geum coccineum, Veronica spicata.*
Cultivars/Relatives:
• 'White Superior', pure white.
• 'Alona', creamy white.
• 'Bouillon', yellow.
• 'Blaue Schonheit', medium blue.

Sweet Violet, Garden Violet, Florist's Violet
Viola odorata

Cultivar 'Königin Charlotte'

March–April/September ◐
H 4–6 in. (10–15 cm)

Violet renowned for its scent.
Flower: Violet, sweet-smelling. Small, with five segments.
Leaf: Broad ovate to cordate or almost round, grass-green.
Growth: In clumps, gradually becomes mat-shaped by means of creeping rootstock.
Origin: Western Europe, Mediterranean region to Caucasus. Along edges of woods, in deciduous hedges and bushes.
Site: Light to partial shade; the plant loves warmth. Any well-drained, loose garden soil.
Care: Let grow undisturbed.
Propagation: By detaching runners, by seed immediately after seed collection. The fruits are spread by ants, so that the scented violet pops up everywhere in the garden.
Use: Beneath well-spaced deciduous shrubs; plant is not very competitive.
Good Partners: *Chionodoxa, Galanthus, Puschkinia.*
Cultivars/Relatives:
• 'Königin Charlotte', dark blue-violet, blooms a second time in September.

Barren-strawberry, False-strawberry
Waldsteinia geoides

Waldsteinia geoides

April–May ◐ ●
H 8–12 in. (20–30 cm)

Strawberry-like perennial.
Flower: Golden yellow, saucer-shaped, about 1 in. (2 cm) across, on branched stems.
Leaf: Three- to five-lobed, bright green during initial growth, later dark green.
Growth: Broad and clump like.
Origin: Eastern Central Europe to Ukraine. In woods.
Site: Partial shade to shade, moderately warm. Soil moist to moderately dry. For all soils that are not compacted or nutrient-poor.
Care: Water in prolonged dry spells. Apply organic soil mix.
Propagation: By division.
Use: In small areas or in alternation with other perennials as a ground cover in shady places of all kinds.
Good Partners: *Brunnera, Hellebora* hybrids, *Hosta, Pulmonaria angustifolia, Symphytum grandiflorum, Vinca—Carex morrowii.*
Cultivars/Relatives:
• *Waldsteinia ternata*, yellow, April–May, forms mats by means of layers. Good evergreen ground cover that flourishes even in deep shade, 6–8 in. (15–20 cm).

Adam's Needle
Yucca filamentosa

Yucca filamentosa

July–September ○
H 48–80 in. (120–200 cm)

Large, native perennial.
Flower: Milky white, scented, bell-shaped, in large, branched panicles on strong stems. First flowers appear several years after planting.
Leaf: Sword-shaped, leathery, fibrous, blue-green, evergreen.
Growth: Clump-like, dense tuft of leaves.
Origin: Eastern North America. Sandy areas, rocky cliffs, dry pine woods.
Site: Full sun, warm, also hot. Soil dry to moderately dry, permeable, also stony, nutrient-rich.
Care: Apply inorganic fertilizer in spring. Keep dry during winter by covering.
Propagation: By detaching offsets.
Use: Singly or in small groups. In rock gardens, on the south side of walls, and in gravel beds.
Good Partners: *Lavandula, Nepeta, Santolina, Stachys byzantina*—Blue juniper cultivars.
Cultivars/Relatives:
• 'Schneefichte', with slimmer flowers and leaves.
• *Yucca glauca*, soapweed, perennial with ornamental foliage. Flowers only in warm years, July–September, up to 80 in. (200 cm).

BULBS

Spring-flowering bulbs thrive in the shelter of thin woody plants.

AND TUBERS

What Are Bulbs and Tubers?

Bulbs and tubers—or bulbous and tuberous plants—are technically perennials, although they are classified separately; they too are herbaceous plants that live for several years. Unlike other perennials, however, they have underground storage organs—the bulbs and tubers—or transitional forms with elements of each. Because these survival organs are located in the ground, they are known also as geophytes ("earth plants"). During their vegetative period they stockpile reserves in these storage organs, and by so doing they are able to survive adverse conditions, such as dry spells and poor light.

Proper Planting and Care

The wild species—the plants that breeders have not adapted—need conditions like those in their natural habitat. You can plant them and let them grow wild in areas of your garden that approximate those conditions. Such plants include lilies of the valley, daffodils, and wild tulips.

Plant list:
① *Lunaria annua*
② *Narcissus pseudonarcissus 'Ice Follies'*
③ *Narcissus poeticus 'Actaea'*
④ *Lunaria annua*
⑤ *Cornus alba 'Sibirica Elegantissima'*
⑥ *Doronicum orientale*
⑦ *Fritillaria imperialis 'Lutea Maxima'*

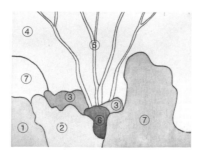

Multiflowered tulip, *Tulipa tarda*

The hybrids are splendid ornamental forms that thrive only in well-prepared beds. This category includes the large commercial assortments of tulips, lilies, dahlias, and gladioluses.

The planting time is October or November for spring bloomers, summer for fall-flowering cultivars. Early May is the best time to plant montbretias, dahlias, and gladioluses.

The planting depth depends on the size of the bulb, as well as on the soil. As a basic rule plant the bulbs in the ground at a depth equal to three times their diameter. In sandy soils you can plant them slightly deeper, in heavy soils slightly shallower.

Fertilize—but how? Adjust the feeding to the plants' rhythm of growth; that is, apply a weak solution of fertilizer in spring during the initial growth, and in fall when the roots begin to grow.

Tips on care. Cut off faded stalks, to keep the plants from expending energy unnecessarily on fruit production.
Important: Don't cut back green leaves. They help the plants assimilate and store reserves needed for bulb production.

Allium ALLIUMS

Allium giganteum, the giant onion, can reach a height of 60 in. (150 cm)

The *Allium* genus not only gives us several kinds of garden vegetables—including onions, garlic, leek, spring onions, shallots, and chives—but also provides a host of marvelously beautiful ornamental plants.

Overall, the genus includes over 500 species, of which some 50 play a role in gardening. The garden treasures we have chosen to present in this book are representative of the great diversity found among the commercially available species. All are easy to cultivate and are commonly grown.

The lasting popularity of the *Allium* species in gardens is due not least to the fact that they, unlike many other bulbous plants, are spurned by voles and other little rodents.

Within the overall group of bulbous plants, some *Allium* species are notable for their relatively late blooming season. These plants, distinctly spring to early summer bloomers, display their flowers at a time when tulips and narcissuses have long since left the garden stage.

The tall *Allium* species make excellent cut flowers, and the ball-shaped fruit structures are also extremely popular with florists. For example, *Allium giganteum,* the giant onion, has purple-violet flowers and can reach 60 in. (150 cm) in height. It blooms about two weeks after *Allium aflatunense,* and is a good partner for peonies.

Persian Allium
Allium aflatunense

Allium aflatunense

May–June
H 28–40 in. (70–100 cm)

Brightly colored cutting flower.
Flower: Purple-violet. Dense, globular umbels about 4–6 in. (10–15 cm) across. Fruit structures green, long-lasting.
Leaf: Strap-shaped, blue-green. Turns yellow during blooming season.
Growth: One-stemmed, with rigid flower stalks.
Origin: Northern Iran to central China.
Site: Sun. Soil moderately dry to well-drained. Best are permeable loamy soils with good nutrient supply.
Care: Feed once a year, as soon as the leaves put forth. After the bloom, cut off the stems and removed yellowed foliage.
Propagation: By seed and by detaching bulblets (daughter bulbs).
Use: In loose groups with low companion plants. In the middle or at the back of sunny borders, where the yellowing foliage is not so noticeable.
Good Partners: *Geranium renardii, Iberis, Nepeta*—very pretty in front of lilacs.
Cultivars/Relatives:
• 'Purple Sensation', bright purple-violet, outstanding cutting flower.
• *Allium rosenbachianum,* light violet, blooms at the same time as *Allium aflatunense,* 24 in. (60 cm) tall.

Star-of-Persia
Allium christophii

Turkestan Onion
Allium karataviense

Moly, Lily Leek, Golden Garlic
Allium moly

Allium christophii

Allium karataviense

Allium moly

Star-of-Persia

May–July
H 16–24 in. (40–60 cm)

Allium species with gigantic, globe-shaped inflorescences.
Flower: Amethyst with metallic shine. Globular umbel with diameter that can exceed 8 in. (20 cm). The bizarre, silver-gray fruits are good in dried bouquets.
Leaf: Lanceolate, blue-green, undersides white-haired.
Growth: One-stemmed, with rigidly erect flower stalk and three to seven leaves.
Origin: Asia Minor to Central Asia. On sunny, stony mountain slopes.
Site: Sun, warm. Soil moderately dry to dry, permeable. Short-lived in heavy soils.
Care: Apply inorganic fertilizer occasionally.
Propagation: By seed and by detaching bulblets.
Use: In small groups in rock gardens, on sunny slopes, and in stony places. Not a very competitive species.
Good Partners: Gray-leaved perennials like *Nepeta, Stachys byzantina—Festuca cinerea, Helictotrichon.*

Turkestan Onion

May–June
H 6–10 in. (15–25 cm)

Because of its beautiful leaves, this low-growing allium stays attractive even after the blooming season, well into fall.
Flower: Silvery white with old-rose shimmer. Dense globular umbels. The fruit structures are suitable for dried bouquets.
Leaf: Each plant has two tongue-shaped, blue-green leaves spread out just above the ground.
Growth: One-stemmed bulbous plant.
Origin: Central Asia. In lime-rich gravel.
Site: Sun; warm places with no relatively heavy vegetation. Soil dry to well-drained, permeable, also nutrient-poor.
Care: Very vigorous neighbors have to be cut back to give the allium elbow room.
Propagation: By seed and by detaching bulblets.
Use: In small groups in rock gardens, in gravel beds, and on stony slopes.
Good Partners: *Anaphalis, Arabis, Aubrieta, Cerastium—Festuca.*

Moly, Lily Leek, Golden Garlic

May–June
H 8–12 in. (20–30 cm)

Undemanding, colony-forming allium with showy golden yellow flowers.
Flower: Golden yellow single flowers in shallow, umbrella like clusters.
Leaf: Broad linear, blue-green.
Growth: Quickly forms largish colonies by means of bulblets.
Origin: Southwestern Europe. In places on rocky mountain hill-sides with light shade.
Site: Sun to light shade. Soil moderately dry to well-drained. No extremely sandy or heavy clay soils!
Care: Feed occasionally. If the colonies become too large, use your spade.
Propagation: By detaching bulblets and by seed. Self-sowing is common in gardens, and moly crops up around the yard.
Use: In groups in rock gardens, beneath thin woody plants, and in borders. Don't plant in the front of borders, as moly's yellowing foliage after the bloom ruins the look of the planting.
Good Partners: *Campanula carpatica, Campanula portenschlagiana, Geranium renardii, Viola cornuta—Allium.*

BULBS/TUBERS

195

BULBS/TUBERS

Windflower
Anemone blanda

Cultivar 'Blue Shades'

March–May ○ ☠
H 8–10 in. (20–25 cm)

Pretty early spring bloomer.
Flower: Sky-blue. Solitary, shallow ray flowers.
Leaf: Divided into three parts, deeply lobed, grass-green, dies back early.
Growth: Colony-forming tuberous plant.
Origin: Eastern Mediterranean region, Balkans, Asia Minor. In stony places and in scrub.
Site: Sun, or in a bright place in spring. Soil moderately dry to well-drained, permeable, humus-rich.
Care: None.
Propagation: By brood tubers.
Use: In small areas beneath deciduous woody plants, in woodland type plantings.
Good Partners: *Hepatica nobilis—Anemone nemorosa* and *Anemone ranunculoides.*
Cultivars/Relatives:
• 'White Splendour', white.
• 'Radar', crimson.
• 'Atrocaerulea', violet-blue.
• *Anemone apennina,* Apennine anemone, resembles *Anemone blanda,* but blooms three weeks later.
Warning: The entire plant is mildly poisonous.

European Wood Anemone, Lady's-nightcap, Cuckoo Spit
Anemone nemorosa

Anemone nemorosa

March–April ○ ☠
H 6–10 in. (15–25 cm)

In gardens, wood anemone grows best in undisturbed places beneath woody plants.
Flower: White, at times pink, saucer-shaped.
Leaf: Divided into three parts, deeply notched, grass-green, dies back after the bloom.
Growth: Forms colonies by means of secondary or daughter rhizomes.
Origin: Europe to Asia. In deciduous forests and shady meadows.
Site: Bright in spring, warm, windless. Soil well-drained, humus-rich.
Care: Apply humus occasionally. Any other care hinders the plant's development.
Propagation: By detaching secondary rhizomes.
Use: In largish numbers beneath deciduous woody plants, in woodland areas of the garden.
Good Partners: *Hepatica nobilis, Lathyrus vernus— Anemone blanda* and *Anemone ranunculoides—Luzula sylvatica.*
Cultivars/Relatives:
• 'Alba Plena', double white flowers that appear somewhat later and last a very long time.
• 'Rosea', pink.
• 'Robinsoniana', lilac.
• *Anemone ranunculoides,* yellow wood anemone, also indigenous and quite similar, but with golden yellow flowers.
Warning: The entire plant is mildly poisonous.

Glory of the Snow
Chionodoxa luciliae

Chionodoxa gigantea

March–April ○ ◐ ✂
H 6 in. (15 cm)

Early spring bloomer that forms colonies of countless star-like flowers.
Flower: Lilac-blue star-shaped flowers with white eye, in loose racemes.
Leaf: Linear, grass-green, dies back after the bloom.
Growth: Colony-forming small bulbous plant.
Origin: Western Turkey. In hilly country up to 1 mile (2000 m), on stony subsoil.
Site: Sunny in spring, warm. Soil moderately dry to well-drained, permeable, nutrient-rich.
Care: Apply a weak solution of fertilizer during blooming season. No other care is needed.
Propagation: By seed, by detaching bulblets. The seeds are spread by ants.
Use: In rather large numbers beneath thin stands of deciduous woody plants or on the fringe of hedges.
Good Partners: *Cyclamen coum, Eranthis,* narcissuses.
Cultivars/Relatives:
• *Chionodoxa gigantea* is larger in all its parts than *Chionodoxa luciliae*; 6–8 in. (15–20 cm), spreads less thickly.
• *Chionodoxa sardensis,* bright azure, 6 in. (15 cm) tall.

Lily of the Valley
Convallaria majalis

Convallaria majalis

May–June   🌓 ✂ ☠
H 6–10 in. (15–25 cm)

Scented woodland plant.
Flower: Small, white, heavily scented, bell-shaped, in racemes. Fruits poisonous, bright red berries.
Leaf: Elliptical to broad lanceolate, dark green.
Growth: Covers areas of ground by means of runner-producing rhizomes.
Origin: Europe to western Asia. In deciduous and mixed forests.
Site: Light shade, in well-drained soil also sun. All moderately dry to well-drained, loose soils.
Care: Occasionally fertilize with compost. If growth is too vigorous, cut off parts.
Propagation: Easily possible at any time by detaching runners.
Use: In small groups in light shade of woody plants and walls.
Good Partners: *Epimedium, Hosta, Omphalodes, Pulmonaria, Waldsteinia.*
Cultivars/Relatives:
• 'Grandiflora' is the form usually found on the market. Larger flowers.
Warning: All parts of the plant are poisonous. Watch children carefully! The poisonous red berries are enticing.

Corydalis
Corydalis cava

Corydalis cava

April–May   🌓
H 6–10 in. (15–25 cm)

Pretty, spring bloomer, excellent for letting run wild.
Flower: Purple-pink or milky white, spurred, in dense terminal racemes.
Leaf: Bipinnate with three segments, bluish green, dies back soon after the bloom.
Growth: Tuberous plant, forms largish stands in congenial areas by means of self-sowing.
Origin: Europe. In well-drained soil in deciduous woods and bushes.
Site: Bright in spring (beneath deciduous woody plants). Soil well-drained to moist, humus-rich, loose.
Care: Add leaf compost occasionally. No other care needed.
Propagation: By seed, right after the seed harvest.
Use: Two-dimensionally, in rather large numbers, beneath deciduous woody plants.
Good Partners: *Hosta—Chionodoxa luciliae, Crocus tommasinianus, Galanthus.*
Cultivars/Relatives:
• *Corydalis solida*, resembles the previous species, but has small, firm tubers and finger-like leaflets under the single flowers.

Montbretia
Crocosmia x crocosmiiflora

Cultivar 'Lucifer'

July–September   ⚪ ✂
H 24–32 in. (60–80 cm)

Exotic bulbous plant.
Flower: Orange, scented, funnel-shaped, in dense spikes.
Leaf: Narrow sword-shaped, overhanging. Fresh green.
Growth: Bulbous plant, almost in a clump owing to numerous bulblets and runners.
Origin: Cultivated form, the parent species from South Africa.
Site: Full sun, warm. Soil well-drained to moderately dry, permeable, nutrient-rich.
Care: Occasionally apply inorganic fertilizer. Protect from frost and winter damp! Covering with leaves and evergreen boughs as winter protection is preferable to digging up the plants and overwintering them dry. Don't cut back completely until early spring.
Propagation: By division of the bulb clumps in spring.
Use: In groups in borders.
Good Partners: *Agapanthus, Kniphofia, Salvia, Stachys byzantina.*
Cultivars/Relatives:
• *Crocosmia masoniorum*, orange-red, July–August, all parts larger.
• 'Lucifer', bright orange-red.
• 'Firebird', brilliant orange.

197

Crocus CROCUS

Crocus
Crocus chrysanthus

Hybrid 'Victor Hugo' among *Erica carnea*

Cultivar 'E. P. Bowles'

February–March ○
H 2–4 in. (5–10 cm)

Crocuses are popular, colorful garden flowers. There are some 100 different species, most of which are indigenous to the Mediterranean area and Asia Minor. Along with the well-known harbingers of spring, there are also some less common, marvelously beautiful species that bloom in fall.

One of them, the saffron crocus *(Crocus sativus),* enjoyed enormous popularity even in ancient times. From its dried stigmas comes saffron, which is prized as a medication, a seasoning, and a dye.

In gardens, crocuses always should be used in relatively large groups. Plant them in irregular drifts, never in geometric patterns. Crocuses are not able to compete with grasses, and in well-tended green areas they soon vanish. They can hold their own only in sparse grass or at the edge of shrubs. Don't mow the grass in such areas until late May, when the foliage of the crocuses is already turning yellow.

Many species propagate by means of brood bulbs (small bulblets that form on a parent bulb) and seeds that are spread by ants. Consequently, crocuses appear even in areas of the garden where they were never planted.

The yellow stigmas of the bulbous plants provoke attacks by blackbirds, which bend the stems or disturb the petals. Mice are another "enemy" of crocuses. For these little rodents, the bulbs of the garden plants are special treats. The threat is greatest when the bulbs are in storage. If the occasion arises, you need to take appropriate protective measures.

Crocuses with a variety of forms; they bloom soon after the snow melts.

Flower: Depending on the cultivar, creamy yellow, yellow, bronze, light blue to purple-violet, in some cases also white-striped flowers on short stems.
Leaf: Narrow linear, grass-green with white median stripe.
Growth: Bulbous (cormous) plant with single stem, produces few brood bulbs and does not spread widely in gardens.
Origin: Southeastern Europe to Asia Minor. Dry, stony mountain slopes and alpine grass.
Site: Sun; warm places with no heavy growth of vegetation. Soil moderately dry, stony or sandy, permeable. No wet sites!
Care: No tending needed.
Propagation: By detaching brood bulbs, though the yield is small.
Use: In groups in rock gardens and on sunny slopes.
Good Partners: A variety of other cultivars together—*Festuca ovina.*
Cultivars/Relatives:
• 'Snowbunting', white.
• 'Cream Beauty', creamy yellow.
• 'Goldilocks, golden yellow.
• 'E. P. Bowles', golden yellow with dark purple stripes.
• 'Zwanenburg Bronze', outside bronze, inside yellow.
• 'Prinz Claus', light blue.
• 'Blue Peter', violet-blue, inside lighter, large-flowered.

Dutch Yellow Crocus
Crocus flavus

Crocus flavus

February–March ○
H 2–4 in. (5–10 cm)

Highly competitive crocus for rock gardens and terraced gardens.
Flower: Dazzling orange-yellow, on short stems.
Leaf: Narrow linear, grassy green with white median stripe.
Growth: Bulbous plant that gradually forms large stands by means of brood bulbs.
Origin: Southeastern Europe to Asia Minor. Dry, stony mountain slopes and alpine grass.
Site: Sun, warm. Soil moderately dry, stony or sandy, permeable. No wet sites!
Care: No tending needed.
Propagation: Propagates itself without coaxing, by means of brood bulbs and self-sowing.
Use: In groups in rock gardens and terraced gardens.
Good Partners: Cushion-forming rock garden plants—Blue cultivars of *Crocus chrysanthus*—low grasses like *Carex montana* or *Festuca ovina*.

Hybrid Crocuses, Garden Crocuses
Crocus Hybrids

'Jeanne d'Arc' (white), 'Pickwick' (lilac)

March–April ○
H 4–6 in. (10–15 cm)

Large-flowered crocuses; initially they sow few seeds and frequently fall victim to nibbling rodents.
Flower: White, yellow, light violet, bright violet-blue, violet-and-white. The large, wide funnel-shaped blossoms do not begin to appear until late March.
Leaf: Narrow linear, grass-green, with white median stripe. Turns yellow after blooming and dies back.
Growth: Bulbous plant; propagates itself to only a slight extent by brood bulbs.
Origin: Cultivated form.
Site: Sun to partial shade, warm, with little competition. Soil well-drained, dry in summer, permeable. No clay soils!
Care: Feed in late winter.
Propagation: Tedious and not worthwhile. Self-sowing only after several years.
Use: In rather large, irregular groups in sparse grass, in areas with little vegetation in front of and beneath solitary woody plants.
Good Partners: Use a combination of the variously colored cultivars.
Cultivars/Relatives:
• 'Grosser Gelber', rich golden yellow, doesn't spread its own seeds, is often pulled up by birds.
• 'Vanguard', light lilac with gray-white shading, blooms very early and abundantly.
• 'Striped Banner', white-and-violet striped.
• 'Queen of the Blues', bright violet-blue.

Showy Crocus
Crocus speciosus

Crocus speciosus

September–November ○ ◑
H 4–6 in. (10–15 cm)

Spectacular fall-blooming crocus with large flowers.
Flower: Violet-blue, large funnel-shaped flowers with dark veining and golden yellow stamens.
Leaf: Narrow linear, grass-green, with white median stripe. The leaves appear only after the bloom.
Growth: One-stemmed bulbous plant; sometimes forms large stands through brood bulbs and by self-sowing.
Origin: Asia Minor. In thin woods and bushes, on stony hills.
Site: Sun to light shade, places without heavy vegetation. Soil well-drained, permeable. No sites that are hot in summer!
Care: Feed occasionally in fall. No other care.
Propagation: By seed and by removal of brood bulbs. You also can remove individual clumps from a larger stand and replant them.
Use: In groups in rock gardens between and among low cushion-and mat-forming plants, beneath woody plants, in sparse grass.
Good Partners: *Cerastium, Saponaria* x *lempergii, Thymus*.
Cultivars/Relatives:
• 'Oxonian', dark violet-blue, large-flowered.

Tommasinian Crocus
Crocus tommasinianus

Crocus tommasinianus

February–April
H 4 in. (10 cm)

The best crocus for naturalizing beneath shrubs.
Flower: Light violet funnel-shaped flowers.
Leaf: Narrow linear, grass-green, with white median stripe. Leaves develop at blooming season and die back in May.
Growth: Bulbous plant; forms large colonies by sowing its own seed.
Origin: Western Balkans. Woods and shady hills over limestone rock.
Site: Garden areas with sun to partial shade in spring. Any well-drained to moderately dry garden soil.
Care: Feed in blooming season. No other care needed. The bulbs can be transplanted at any time.
Propagation: Self-sowing on a large scale.
Use: In large groups in sparse grass, beneath shrubs, and in other places with light to partial shade.
Good Partners: Yellow crocuses, *Cyclamen coum, Eranthis, Galanthus.*
Cultivars/Relatives:
• 'Whitewell Purple', showy purple-violet, free-flowering, larger than the species.

Atkins' Cyclamen
Cyclamen coum

Cyclamen coum

February–April
H 4 in. (10 cm)

Garden treasure with delightful, but frost-tender, flowers.
Flower: Pink to crimson or white, scented.
Leaf: Round to kidney-shaped, matte dark green, faintly marked. Leaves die back after the bloom and put forth again in fall.
Growth: Low, long-lived tuberous plant, forms colonies by self-sowing.
Origin: Western Asia. Deciduous woods and bushes that are damp in spring, dry in summer. Soil moderately dry to well-drained, must be permeable, humus-rich.
Care: Plant the tubers about 2 in. (5 cm) deep, with the root swelling pointing downward. For soil mix, see *Cyclamen hederifolium.* In winter cover loosely with boughs. Cover flowers at night to protect from relatively heavy frosts.
Propagation: By seed after the seeds ripen; tedious.
Use: In largish groups beneath thin stands of deciduous woody plants.
Good Partners: Other bulbous and tuberous plants. <u>Don't mix with very vigorous plants</u>!

Baby Cyclamen, Neapolitan Cyclamen
Cyclamen hederifolium

Cyclamen hederifolium

September–October
H 4 in. (10 cm)

Fall-blooming counterpart of *Cyclamen coum.*
Flower: Crimson, pink, or white, scented.
Leaf: Pointed cordate, coarsely saw-toothed, dark green, with attractive silvery markings. The leaves appear after the bloom and die back the next spring.
Growth: Low, colony-forming tuberous plant.
Origin: Mediterranean region. In pine and certain evergreen forests, in hilly and mountainous country.
Site: In bright shade, warm. Soil well-drained to moderately dry, permeable, humus-rich.
Care: As the tubers are rooted at the top, the roots have to point upward when planted. Set about 4 in. (10 cm) deep in a 70:30 blend of composted leaf mold and loam. Light winter protection with boughs is advisable.
Propagation: Propagates by self-sowing without coaxing. By seed after seeds ripen in May.
Use: In groups beneath shrubs and in thin stands of woody plants.
Good Partners: Fall-blooming crocus species like *Crocus speciosus.* <u>No highly vigorous, rampant neighbors</u>!

Dahlia DAHLIA

Formal decorative dahlia 'Yvonne', with flowers like water lilies, among *Aster novae-angliae*

July–October
H 12–64 in. (30–160 cm)

For a long time, dahlias have ranked among the best-known and best-loved garden flowers. Brought to Europe some 200 years ago, intensive breeding efforts turned the tiny, inconspicuous wild plants into an enormous assortment with a great variety of flower colors and shapes.

Flower: Almost all colors—except pure blue—in single, semi-double, or double flower forms.
Leaf: Ovate, dark green; in various cultivars also dark purple.
Growth: Erect, bushy, sometimes not altogether stable.
Origin: The current cultivated form arose from the parent species from Mexico.
Site: Sun; also in light, shifting shade. Soil well-drained, permeable, moderately nutrient-rich. No wet sites!

Care: Plant tubers from late April to early May. Water in dry spells. Choose fertilizer with emphasis on potassium, not nitrogen. Stake weak-stemmed cultivars. Protect from slug damage. Deadhead faded flowers to prolong blooming season.

After the first frost, cut back plants and dig up tubers. Let tubers dry, with the remainder of the stalk pointing downward; clean off the soil; overwinter them free from frost, at about 39°F (4° C). If the overwintering quarters are too dry, cover the tubers with sand or peat. During the winter, check on the plants often and remove any diseased tubers.

Propagation: By division of tubers with a sharp knife in spring. Alternatively, take cuttings (see pages 72–73). To do

so, bring the tubers indoors in late winter or early spring and force them, then cut off the first shoots and stick them at once.
Use: To make tending easier, dahlias often are planted in beds by themselves or along with gladioluses. Frequently, however, that practice results in visually monotonous, awkward rows of various cultivars.

As successful examples show, however, you also can combine the showy bloomers with perennials or annuals by fine-tuning the color choices. In this way, the dahlias become the principal vehicles for color in the beds. They have to be given partners whose leaf size and flower form make an exciting contrast with those of the dahlias.

Single dahlia 'Feuerrad'

Collarette dahlia 'Grand Duc'

Don't use too many different colors, however! The neighboring plants need to pick up the hues of the dahlias and harmonize with

Pompon dahlia 'Kaiser Wilhelm'

them. Don't use starkly contrasting colors under any circumstances. Harsh transitions can be toned down by white-flowered or gray-leaved partners.

Good Partners: Different dahlia cultivars, or with gladioluses. *Chrysanthemum parthenium, Cosmos, Salvia farinacea* and *Salvia uliginosa—Chrysanthemum maximum, Chrysanthemum serotinum, Delphinium, Lythrum, Physostegia, Vernonia, Veronica longifolia*—yellow, orange, and red cultivars with *Crocosmia—Calamagrostis, Miscanthus, Panicum.*

Cultivars/Relatives:
Single Flowers:
• 'Schneekönigin', white, 40 in. (100 cm).
• 'Feuerrad', brilliant scarlet with yellow stamens, foliage dark purple, 40 in. (100 cm).
Dwarf Mignon Dahlias (Top Mix Dahlias), also single, 8–12 in. (20–30 cm):
• 'White Lilliput', white.

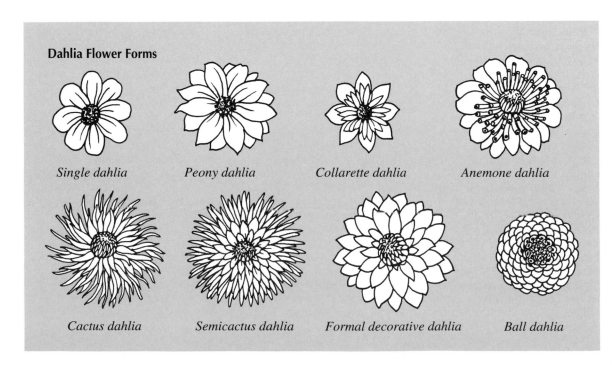

Dahlia Flower Forms

Single dahlia   Peony dahlia   Collarette dahlia   Anemone dahlia

Cactus dahlia   Semicactus dahlia   Formal decorative dahlia   Ball dahlia

Decorative dahlia 'Berliner Kleene'

Cactus dahlia 'Schwarze Prinzessin'

Cactus dahlia 'Walhalla'

- 'Andrea', yellow.
- 'Bonne Esperance', pink.

Mignon Dahlias, 16 in. (40 cm):
- 'Anna-Karina', white.
- 'Irene', yellow.
- 'Roxy', wine-red.

Tall Mignon Dahlias, 24 in. (60 cm) tall and over:
- 'Gartenparty', yellow-orange.
- 'Parkprinzess', pink.

Semidouble Flowers:

Duplex Dahlias, with several rings of ray flowers.
- 'Olympic Fire', orange-red, 44 in. (110 cm).
- 'Bishop of Llandaff', fire-red, foliage purple, 40 in. (100 cm).

Collarette Dahlias have two rings of ray flowers; the inner ring petals are notched and are a different color from those of the outer ring.
- 'Cricket', inside red, outside yellow, 36 in. (90 cm).
- 'Libretto', inside purple, outside white, 40 in. (100 cm).

- 'Rondo', inside lilac, outside white, 44 in. (110 cm).

Anemone Dahlias: In these cultivars, shallow ray flowers encircle a group of larger tubular flowers. They have a dainty, slightly old-fashioned look.
- 'Monsieur Dupont', purple-pink, 32 in. (80 cm).

Double Flowers:

They are filled almost completely with ray flowers of various forms, covering the few remaining tubular flowers.

Cactus Dahlias: In these classic dahlia cultivars, the petals of the ray flowers are rolled up into elongated cones.
- 'Golden Horn', orange, small-flowered, 32 in. (80 cm).
- 'Vulkan', fiery orange-red, 40 in. (100 cm).
- 'Marianne Strauss', purple-pink, small-flowered, 44 in. (110 cm).

Formal Decorative Dahlias have spatula- to spoon-shaped ray flowers; because of their regular arrangement they also are described as "water lily dahlias."
- 'Frau Edith Daniel', white, 44 in. (110 cm).
- 'Wilhelm Tell', salmon-orange, 48 in. (120 cm).
- 'Mairo', violet, 40 in. (100 cm).

Ball Dahlias have almost globular flowers composed of regularly arranged, broad ovate to kidney-shaped ray flowers with rounded tips.
- 'Vader Abraham', yellow, 52 in. (130 cm).
- 'Annette', pink, 48 in. (120 cm).
- 'Ruby Wedding', dark crimson, 44 in. (110 cm).

Pompon Dahlias resemble ball dahlias, but have smaller, daintier, more compact flowers that are excellent as cut flowers.
- 'Schneeflocke', white, 40 in. (100 cm).
- 'Golden Fiz', golden yellow, 40 in. (100 cm).
- 'Amusing', orange, 44 in. (110 cm).
- 'Robina', ruby-red, 40 in. (100 cm).
- 'Franz Kafka', violet, 40 in. (100 cm).

Winter Aconite
Eranthis hyemalis

Eranthis hyemalis

February–March ◑ ●
H 4 in. (10 cm)

Along with snowdrops, the first messengers of spring.
Flower: Lustrous yellow, lightly scented, saucer-shaped flowers on a ruff-like bract.
Leaf: Palmately divided and deeply slit, fresh green. Leaves appear during the bloom, soon die back.
Growth: Tuberous plant, forms rather large mats by means of short runners.
Origin: Southern Europe. Edges of woods that are damp in spring.
Site: Shade to partial shade, bright in spring. Soil well-drained to moderately dry. No dry and compacted soils!
Care: None. Commercially available tubers are often dried out and will not grow. Mail-order as early as possible, and plant immediately upon receipt. Long storage results in total loss. Transplanting possible at any time.
Propagation: By direct sowing right after seed harvest. Winter aconites pop up all over the garden, as the seeds often are carried by ants.
Use: Beneath solitary shrubs, in stands of deciduous woody plants, in sparse grass.
Good Partners:
Crocus tommasinianus, Galanthus.

Giant Desert Candle, Giant Foxtail Lily
Eremurus robustus

Eremurus robustus

June–July ○ ✂
H 80–100 in. (200–250 cm)

Striking plant with imposing candles of flowers.
Flower: White, in a 40-in. (1 m) raceme on a rigid stem.
Leaf: Sword-shaped, blue-green, turns yellow during the bloom.
Growth: One-stemmed, with starfish-shaped rootstocks.
Origin: Turkestan. In steppes.
Site: Sun, warm. Soil dry to well-drained, very permeable, nutrient-rich. No wet sites!
Care: Plant carefully, to avoid injuring brittle rootstocks. Place 6 in. (15 cm) deep on a drainage layer of coarse sand. Apply inorganic fertilizer in spring.
Propagation: By seed after seed collection: tedious. By careful division in fall.
Use: In borders and in steppe gardens.
Good Partners: *Achillea, Anthemis, Nepeta, Stachys byzantina, Thymus.*
Cultivars/Relatives:
• *Eremurus stenophyllus*, yellow, June–July, more than 40 in. (100 cm).
• *Eremurus himalaicus*, white, blooms in May, 60 in. (150 cm).
• *Eremurus* Shelford hybrids, white, orange, pink, June–July, 48–72 in. (120–180 cm).

Crown Imperial, Imperial Fritillary

Cultivar 'Lutea Maxima'

April ○
H 24–40 in. (60–100 cm)

Old country-garden plant.
Flower: Orange, brick-red, or yellow, bell-shaped, several whorled at end of stem, with tuft of leaves rising above.
Leaf: Narrow ovate, pointed, grass-green.
Growth: One-stemmed, erect.
Origin: Iran to Himalayas. In stony places in thin scrub.
Site: Sun, warm. Soil well-drained, nutritious, and permeable. Short-lived in heavy or nutrient-poor soils.
Care: Plant from July to September. Feed regularly in spring. After the bloom, cut off the stalks to the leaves. Remove yellowed foliage in late spring.
Propagation: By removal of brood bulbs.
Use: In small groups in borders.
Good Partners: *Myosotis, Viola wittrockiana* hybrids—low *Sedum* species—tulips.
Cultivars/Relatives:
• 'Lutea Maxima', golden yellow.
• 'Aurora', brilliant orange.
• 'Rubra Maxima', bright brick-red.

Guinea Hen Flower, Snakehead, Checkered Lily
Fritillaria meleagris

Fritillaria meleagris

April–May ◑
H 8–12 in. (20–30 cm)

Indigenous, now rare bulbous plant that owes one of its common names, checkered lily, to the light-and-dark checkered marking of the flowers.
Flower: Brown-violet with a checkerboard-like pattern, broad bell-shaped, on drooping stems.
Leaf: Narrow linear, gray-green, dies back soon after the bloom.
Growth: One-stemmed bulbous plant with erect stalk. In favorable places, forms small stands by means of brood bulbs.
Origin: Europe. In damp meadows and pastures.
Site: Partial to light shade, cool, damp, temporarily even wet. Soil nutrient-rich with humus or loam.
Propagation: By seed after the seeds ripen, but germinates with difficulty. Alternative: By removal of brood bulbs, but this can be tedious.
Use: In small groups near ponds and in damp flowery meadows.
Good Partners: *Leucojum*— bamboo, *Carex pendula*.
Cultivars/Relatives:
• 'Aphrodite', pure white.
• 'Emperor', gray-and-violet checkered.

Common Snowdrop
Galanthus nivalis

Snowdrops are content beneath deciduous woody plants.

February–April ◑
H 4–6 in. (10–15 cm)

Easy-to-tend spring bloomer.
Flower: White, inside corolla green-and-white-striped, scented.
Leaf: Narrow linear, dark green. The leaves appear with the flowers and die back after the blooming season.
Growth: One-stemmed bulbous plant, forms colonies by means of brood bulbs and self-sowing. The seeds are spread by ants.
Origin: Central and southern Europe to Caucasus. Riverside woods and thin bushes, in the Alps also in meadows.
Site: Bright in spring, cool. Soil well-drained to moist; humus-rich loamy soils are especially good, No sandy, dry soils!
Care: No special procedures needed. Shortly after the bloom, specimens can be removed from larger stands with a digging fork and replanted elsewhere.
Propagation: By removal of brood bulbs.
Use: Beneath deciduous woody plants and in woods-like stands of woody plants.
Good Partners: *Anemone, Crocus tommasinianus, Cyclamen, Eranthis—Helleborus*.

Cultivars/Relatives:
• *Galanthus elwesii*, giant snowdrop, has larger flowers, leaves, and bulbs than *Galanthus nivalis* and blooms earlier. Leaves gray-green. The flowers exude a delicate, sweetish scent. The giant snowdrop is preferable to the indigenous species only in soils that are dry in summer. *Galanthus nivalis* spreads itself more heavily and forms larger stands. There are a great many cultivars, often hybrids between the two species listed above. Many are self-sterile; that is, they produce seed only when other snowdrop cultivars grow nearby. They grow nest like by producing a profusion of brood bulbs.

Gladiolus
Gladiolus Hybrids

Hybrid 'Sweet Dreams'

Hybrid 'May Love'

Baby gladiolus 'Nymph'

June–September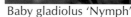
H 16–56 in. (40–140 cm)

Popular tuberous plant that yields excellent cut flowers.
Flower: Almost all shades except pure blue, often also bicolored or multicolored. Funnel like, in dense terminal racemes.
Leaf: Sword-shaped, fresh green.
Growth: One-stemmed, erect-growing tuberous plant. Occasionally unstable.
Origin: Cultivated form.
Site: Sun, warm. Soil well-drained to moist, nutrient-rich, permeable. No wet sites or soils that dry out easily!
Care: In early May plant the tubers about 4 in. (10 cm) deep. In light, sandy soils plant slightly deeper for greater stability. Apply inorganic fertilizer with emphasis on potassium. Water well. Support tall cultivars. Dig up tubers in late October, cut off foliage and stalks to 2 in. (5 cm), clean, remove outer skin, and overwinter dry and frost-free at about 41°F (5°C), with the cut part downward. Check frequently for evidence of disease; remove any damaged tubers.
Propagation: By brood tubers.
Use: In cutting flower beds and in borders.

Good Partners: Different gladiolus cultivars or dahlias to make tending easier. Coordinate the colors carefully, to keep the planting from looking clumsy and garish. Also with suitably colored annuals, including *Ageratum, Chrysanthemum frutescens, Cosmos bipinnatus, Heliotropium, Salvia farinacea,* and *Salvia uliginosa*—in addition, perennials like *Chrysanthemum maximum, Chrysanthemum serotinum,* white *Phlox paniculata.*
Cultivars/Relatives:
Large-flowered Gladiolus, 40–56 in. (100–140 cm), with dense flower candles.
• 'White Goddess', pure white, fringed, blooms moderately early.
• 'Nova Lux', pure yellow, blooms moderately early.
• 'Jester', yellow with red spot in center, late blooming.
• 'Jessica', salmon-pink, early blooming.
• 'Fidelio', purple-pink, blooms moderately early.
• 'Cordula', signal-light red, late blooming.
Baby Gladiolus *(Gladiolus nanus)*, like the large-flowered gladiolus, but with markedly smaller single flowers in loose racemes. Overall, more graceful

and elegant, June–July, about 16–24 in. (40–60 cm).
• 'Nymph', white, with red markings.
• 'Charm', violet-pink.
• 'Tropical Sunset', blood-red with dark center.
• 'Robinetta', fire-red.
Butterfly Gladioluses have somewhat smaller, always multicolored flowers with wavy edges. Early blooming, 32–40 in. (80–100 cm).
• 'Richmond', white, with red-orange center.
• 'Blackpool', yellow, with red spot.
• 'Arletta', peach-pink, with yellow spot.
Primulinus Hybrids have hood-shaped single flowers, smaller than the large-flowered gladiolus and in looser inflorescences, about 20–32 in. (50–80 cm).
• 'White City', white.
• 'Little Darling', pink.
• 'Carioca', orange.

Spanish Bluebell
Hyacinthoides hispanica

Hyacinthoides hispanica

May
H 8–12 in. (20–30 cm)

Spring bloomer for naturalizing beneath woody plants.
Flower: Medium-blue to violet-blue bell-shaped flowers in a conical panicle.
Leaf: Broad linear, grooved, bright grass-green.
Growth: One-stemmed bulbous plant that forms loose colonies by means of sowing seed and by brood bulbs.
Origin: Spain, Portugal, and North Africa. In woods and in the shade of rocks.
Site: Light shade to shade, cool. Soil well-drained to moist, humus, permeable.
Care: No care.
Propagation: By seed after seeds ripen, by removal of brood bulbs.
Use: Always in large numbers in woods-like areas, in the shade of walls.
Good Partners: *Galium, Pulmonaria, Waldsteinia*—azaleas.
Cultivars/Relatives:
• 'La Grandesse', white.
• 'Dainty Maid', old-rose.
• 'Excelsior', violet.
• *Hyacinthoides nonscripta,* English bluebell, indigenous, flowers tubular on shorter stems.

Hyacinth
Hyacinthus orientalis Hybrids

Hyacinthus orientalis hybrid 'Pink Pearl'

April–May
H 8–12 in. (20–30 cm)

Well-known bulbous plants.
Flower: Blue, violet, white, pink, crimson, apricot, rarely yellow, wonderfully scented. The single flowers are borne in dense terminal racemes on erect, leafless stems.
Leaf: Broad linear to lanceolate, stiff, fresh green, basal.
Growth: Low, one-stemmed bulbous plant that spreads slowly by means of brood bulbs.
Origin: Asia Minor to western Asia. In rocky settings.
Site: Sun, warm. Soil moderately dry to well-drained, very permeable.
Care: Plant in fall. No other procedures needed.
Propagation: By removal of brood bulbs.
Use: In sunny borders, in scented gardens, in front of south walls and woody plants. Let naturalize in terraced gardens.
Good Partners: In large groups with annuals like *Myosotis sylvestris, Viola wittrockiana* hybrids, as well as narcissuses and tulips. Alternatively, in small groups with gray-leaved perennials like *Stachys byzantina, Thymus,* and *Veronica spicata,* or with *Alyssum, Arabis, Iberis,* and wild tulips—beneath spring-blooming shrubs like shadbush and forsythia.
Cultivars/Relatives:
The more graceful wild form with loose racemes is not commercially available. If you leave the cultivars in the same site for years, they will lose their dense profusion of blooms. If you choose to do that, the blue and white cultivars are recommended for use.
• Blue: 'Bismarck', light blue; 'Ostara', bright blue.
• Blue-violet: 'Blue Jacket', 'Violet Pearl'.
• White: 'Carnegie', 'L'Innocence'.
• Pink: 'Lady Derby', light pink; 'Queen of the Pinks', medium pink; 'Pink Pearl', dark pink.
• Crimson: 'Amsterdam', 'Jan Bos'.
• Apricot: 'Gipsy Queen'.
• Yellow: 'City of Harlem', light yellow, not very lustrous.

Danford Iris
Iris danfordiae

Iris danfordiae

February–March ○
H 4–6 in. (10–15 cm)

Short-lived early spring bloomer.
Flower: Lustrous yellow, scented, on erect stems.
Leaf: Narrow linear, four-sided, grass-green, grows to full size only after the bloom.
Growth: One-stemmed bulbous plant. Short-lived; after the bloom the bulbs disintegrate into small pieces, which do not flower again for years.
Origin: Asia Minor. On barren mountainsides.
Site: Full sun, warm. Soil dry to moderately dry, highly permeable, sandy or stony. No wet sites!
Care: Plant in fall. Apply inorganic fertilizer occasionally during blooming season. Short-lived, so replace plants as needed.
Propagation: Difficult and protracted; not recommended.
Use: In small groups in rock gardens, in pebble beds, and in terraced gardens.
Good Partners: Mat- and cushion-forming perennials like *Aethionema, Dianthus gratianopolitanus, Sedum, Stachys byzantina*—*Iris reticulata* hybrids, squill.

Netted Iris
Iris reticulata

Iris reticulata hybrid

March–April ○
H 48 in. (10–20 cm)

Dainty herald of spring.
Flower: Bright violet-blue with contrasting orange-yellow markings, lightly scented.
Leaf: Basal, narrow linear, four-sided, grass-green.
Growth: Bulbous plant, forms small groups very slowly.
Origin: Near East and Caucasus. In rock debris and in thin bushes.
Site: Full sun, warm. Soil dry to moderately dry, very permeable, sandy or stony.
Care: Plant in fall. Apply inorganic fertilizer occasionally during blooming season. Cover with boughs in harsh winters.
Propagation: By removal of brood bulbs. Successful only in very warm regions.
Use: In small groups in rock gardens and terraced gardens and in beds of pebbles.
Good Partners: *Dianthus, Dryas, Sedum, Thymus*—low narcissuses and wild tulips.
Cultivars/Relatives:
• 'Cantab', light blue with orange-yellow markings.
• *Iris reticulata* hybrids:
• 'Pauline', purple-violet.
• 'Spring Time', blue-violet.
• 'Violet Beauty', dark violet.

Spring Snowflake
Leucojum vernum

Leucojum vernum

February–April
H 8–24 in. (20–60 cm)

Naturalized spring bloomer.
Flower: White with yellow-green spots at the tips, honey-scented, broad bell-shaped, nodding.
Leaf: Narrow linear, rich green, appearing during blooming season and dying back again in late spring.
Growth: One-stemmed bulbous plant, forms rather large stands by means of brood bulbs and self-sowing.
Origin: Europe. In woods with moist to well-drained soil.
Site: Out of sun, partial shade to shade, cool; with enough soil moisture also temporarily in sun. Soil vigorous and absolutely not dry, best are humus-rich, loamy soils, also clay soils. No extremely sandy soils!
Care: Feed from time to time, no other tending needed.
Propagation: By seed after seeds ripen, by removal of bulblets (daughter bulbs).
Use: Along edge of or beneath woody plants. Good in shade of house walls and near ponds.
Good Partners: Woodland perennials like *Epimedium, Helleborus, Hosta*—evergreen woodland grasses like *Carex pendula*, ferns.
Cultivars/Relatives:
• *Leucojum aestivum*, summer snowflake, less common because of the late bloom, late April to early June, 16 in. (40 cm).

Lilium LILIES

Asiatic hybrid lily 'Medaillon'

Lilies are among the most elegant and beautiful flowers in our gardens. They have to overcome a great many dangers—spring frosts, summer drought, botrytis, lily beetles, and voles—but when they finally bloom in summer, displaying their enchanting many-branched flower pyramids, their colors and scents are without equal.

Tips for Lily Lovers:

Shopping tip: Make sure that the roots at the bottom of the bulb are not dried up and that the bulbs are not shriveled or partly decayed.

The ideal site for lilies is sunny and sheltered from the wind; the roots, however, need a cool, shady environment. The soil should be permeable and humus-rich, but not likely to dry out. With heavy loam or clay soils, you need to add a drainage layer, because the bulbs will rot in waterlogged soil.

Drainage layer for heavy soils. Loosen the soil deeply and thoroughly, and place a 2 in. (5 cm) layer of sand or fine gravel at the bottom of the planting hole. Loosen the sides of the planting hole also. Mix the soil you've removed with sand, peat substitute, or perlite.

Tips on planting:
• The best planting time is fall, for late blooming lilies also spring.
• The specifications for the planting depth refer to the distance between the tip of the bulb and the surface of the soil.
• The later in the year lily bulbs are planted, the more important it is to add a mulch layer 2 to 4 in. (5–10 cm) deep to protect them from frost.

Tips on care:
• Cover the new growth to protect it from late frosts.
• Before the bloom, it is vital to water if dry. There is no need to keep watering faded lilies.

• After the initial growth, apply liquid compound fertilizer (one ounce per quart of water [20 ml/L]).
• Stake weak-stemmed cultivars.
• Remove the seeds before they mature, so that the plants save energy.

Propagation: Depending on the lily species, by seed, bulb scales, division, or removal of brood bulbs.

Cutting flowers: Leave parts of the stalk with leaves; never cut off stalks level with the ground.

209

Orange Lily, Bulbil Lily
Lilium bulbiferum

Madonna Lily, Bourbon Lily, White Lily, Annunciation Lily
Lilium candidum

David Lily
Lilium davidii

Lilium bulbiferum

Lilium candidum

Lilium davidii

June–July ◯ ◑	June–July ◯ ✂	July ◯
H 16–48 in. (40–120 cm)	H 32–48 in. (80–120 cm)	H 24–60 in. (60–150 cm)

Protected indigenous species.
Flower: Orange or red, with darker speckling inside, not scented. Bell- to saucer-shaped.
Leaf: Linear, fresh green.
Growth: Erect and one-stemmed, often with brood bulbs in the leaf axils.
Origin: Central Europe. Mountains, mountain meadows, and fringes of woods.
Site: Sun to light or partial shade, warm, damp in spring, dry in summer. Soil well-drained, nutrient-rich, sandy-loamy, also lime-rich. <u>No waterlogged soils</u>!
Care: Planting depth 8 in. (20 cm).
Propagation: By removal of brood bulbs and by seed.
Use: Among low plants, in natural gardens, at edge of woody plants.
Good Partners: *Campanula, Digitalis grandiflora, Polygonatum.*
Cultivars/Relatives:
• *Lilium bulbiferum* ssp. *croceum,* saffron lily, with yellow-orange, brown-speckled flowers, April. Leaf dull green.
• *Lilium maculatum* hybrids:
• 'Orange King', red-orange.
• 'Orange Dream', orange-red.
• 'Fireking', dark orange-red.

Old country-garden lily.
Flower: White, funnel-shaped, and strongly scented, five to 20 flowers on a stalk.
Leaf: Lanceolate, green.
Growth: Erect, one-stemmed, occasionally unstable. In September, a leaf rosette develops and remains all winter.
Origin: Mediterranean region, western Asia. Stony places, loose bushes, rock cliffs.
Site: Sun, warm, sheltered. Soil well-drained, nutrient- and lime-rich, best is sandy-loamy. <u>No wet sites</u>!
Care: Planting depth 1 in. (3 cm). Planting season July, at the latest September. Let grow undisturbed. With heavy frost, use winter protection.
Propagation: By bulb scales or by division of old bulb heaps. Rarely if ever sets seeds.
Use: In small groups among other plants in sunny beds.
Good Partners: *Delphinium* hybrids, *Lychnis*—nice with pink roses.
Cultivars/Relatives:
• *Lilium* x *testaceum,* Nankeen lily, light yellow, scented, July–August.

Ideal starter plant for lily novices.
Flower: Scarlet, spotted with darker shades, not scented, six to 20 or more flowers like Turk's caps in a loosely constructed inflorescence.
Leaf: Linear, dark green, over-arching.
Growth: Erect to arched and drooping, one-stemmed.
Origin: Western China. In mountain meadows and on limestone rocks.
Site: Sun, warm, if possible damp in spring. Soil moderately dry to well-drained; nutrient-rich, sandy-loamy, lime-rich.
Care: Planting depth 6–8 in. (15–20 cm), planting season October. Water in spring if dry.
Propagation: By seed.
Use: In beds with low partners.
Good Partners: *Geranium renardii, Inula ensifolia* 'Compacta'.
Cultivars/Relatives:
• *Lilium davidii* var. *willmottiae*, orange-red, black-spotted. Large- and many-flowered, in out-stretched, in some cases heavily drooping inflorescences, July–August, highly recommended.
• 'Maxwill', orange-red, very vigorous, up to 80 in. (200 cm) tall.

Tiger Lily
Lilium lancifolium

Lilium lancifolium var. *flaviflorum*

July–September
H 48–72 in. (120–180 cm)

Popular lily, easy to cultivate.
Flower: Orange-red, black-spotted, lacks scent. Inflorescence of 10 to 20 nodding flowers resembles Turk's cap.
Leaf: Linear, gray-green.
Growth: Erect, one-stemmed. In fall, brood bulbs appear in the leaf axils.
Origin: East Asia. In bushes and at edges of woodlands. Also grown for its edible bulbs.
Site: Sun, warm, root area in shade. Soil well-drained, mildly acid or neutral, nutrient-rich. No waterlogged soils!
Care: Planting depth 6 in. (15 cm). Planting season: fall. Unproblematic species.
Propagation: By removal of brood bulbs and daughter bulbs.
Use: In beds and at edge of woody plants, together with low perennials.
Good Partners: *Ceratostigma, Clematis* x *jouiniana, Euphorbia griffithii, Inula ensifolia.*
Cultivars/Relatives:
• *Lilium lancifolium* var. *flaviflorum,* yellow with brown dots, not very vigorous.
• 'Splendens', brilliant orange-red flowers, spotted with black-brown, large-flowered.

Martagon Lily, Turk's Cap Lily
Lilium martagon

Lilium martagon

June–July
H 24–48 in. (60–120 cm)

Woodland plant.
Flower: Purple-pink with wine-red dots, unpleasantly scented, with reflexed tips, three to 20 in inflorescence.
Leaf: Elliptical to lanceolate, dark green.
Growth: Erect, one-stemmed.
Origin: Europe to Siberia. Deciduous and mixed coniferous forests.
Site: Light to partial shade, warm; should not dry out. Soil well-drained, nutrient-rich, loamy and lime-rich.
Care: Planting season: fall. Planting depth 5 in. (12 cm). In winter, mulch with leaf mold.
Propagation: By seed, brood bulbs, and bulb scales.
Use: In natural gardens, at edge of woody plants, and in woodland meadows.
Good Partners: *Campanula latifolia*—grasses and ferns.
Cultivars/Relatives:
• *Lilium martagon* var. *album,* white, larger-flowered.
• *Lilium hansonii,* Hanson lily, four to 12 orange-yellow, brown-spotted flowers, June–July 24–60 in. (60–150 cm).
• *Lilium* x *marhan,* orange with yellow, spotted, June–July, 60–72 in. (150–180 cm).

Regal Lily
Lilium regale

Lilium regale

July
H 24–60 in. (60–150 cm)

Enchanting lily with sweetly scented, funnel-shaped flowers.
Flower: Inside white with yellow throat, outside brown-pink striped, with intense scent. The funnel-shaped flowers, in umbels of three to 20, are borne perpendicular to or nodding on the stalk.
Leaf: Linear, gray-green, numerous.
Growth: One-stemmed, erect to drooping bulbous plant. Some old bulbs can reach a diameter of 4–6 in. (10–15 cm).
Origin: China. Grassy mountain slopes.
Site: Sun, root area in shade, warm. Soil well-drained to moist, nutrient-rich, humus, also lime-rich.
Care: Planting depth 5–6 in. (12–15 cm). Initial growth is endangered by frost; it needs to be covered. Stake shoots that have an abundance of flowers. Mulch with leaf mold or compost.
Propagation: By seed, immediately after seeds ripen (germinates with difficulty).
Use: Among low perennials. Not too close to your house, as scent is quite strong.
Good Partners: *Astilbe, Campanula, Geranium.*
Cultivars/Relatives: As crossing partner, played a role in the development of the trumpet lilies.

Hybrid Lilies
Lilium Hybrids

Asiatic Hybrid Lilies
Midcentury Hybrids

Hybrid 'Tropper'

Hybrid 'Monte Rosa'

Hybrid 'La Rève'

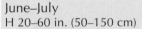

June–July
H 20–60 in. (50–150 cm)

Lilies, like tulips, now are available in thousands of different cultivars, to which new breeds in a host of colors and forms are added each year. Some of them, however, bloom only for one or two years, so it is advisable to buy new bulbs in late summer. The hybrids usually are arranged in eight groups that give amateur gardeners information about the origin and care of the plants. In catalogs, too, the cultivars are listed according to these groups. The boundaries between the groups, however, are becoming blurred by the continual development of new crosses.

Major Groups of Hybrid Lilies:

Asiatic Hybrids: Most important group, with a great many cultivars, which have saucer-shaped as well as Turk's-cap flower forms.

American Hybrids: Strains with special site requirements, in some cases difficult to cultivate.

Trumpet Hybrids: Magnificent, easy-to-grow cultivars with marvelous colors, pleasant scent, and huge, funnel-shaped flowers. The Aurelian hybrids also belong to this group (see page 213). The plants on the market usually have been raised from seed, rather than vegetatively propagated, and consequently may vary slightly in color.

Oriental Hybrids: Breeds mostly derived from Japanese wild species, usually with captivating, funnel-shaped flowers. In cool to moderate regions they can live several years in a garden; in harsher climates it is better to cultivate these beautiful plants in containers.

Splendidly colorful and problem-free lily breeds with saucer-shaped star flowers. Worthy of mention are the Midcentury Hybrids, which came on the market in 1949.
Flower: In numerous colors, saucer-shaped.
Leaf: Narrow, green.
Growth: Erect, one-stemmed.
Site: Sun, warm, "feet" in shade. Soil well-drained.
Care: Planting depth, see page 209.
Use: In beds.
Good Partners: Bedding perennials.
Cultivars/Relatives:
• 'Apeldoorn', orange, only 20 in. (50 cm) tall, strong-stemmed.
• 'Chinook', apricot, 32–40 in. (80–100 cm).
• 'Enchantment', orange-red.
• 'Golden Melody', golden-yellow, spotted, 28–40 in. (70–100 cm).
• Connecticut Hybrids: Pretty, saucer-shaped lilies. Flowers in pure colors. Otherwise similar to Midcentury Hybrids, but 28–48 in. (70–120 cm) tall:
• 'Connecticut King', lemon-yellow, free-flowering.
• 'Connecticut Yankee', salmon-orange.

Trumpet Hybrids
Aurelian Hybrids

Aurelian hybrid 'Stargazer'

July	○ ✂
H 48–80 in. (120–200 cm)	

Subgroup of the trumpet lilies with many cultivars, usually with widely opened, funnel-shaped flowers. The Latin name refers to Orleans, France, from where this group originated. The parents of these crosses are *Lilium regale, Lilium henryi,* and others. The Aurelian Hybrids are noted for their extremely far-reaching, intoxicatingly intense scent. When used as cut flowers or grown near a residence they are not to everyone's taste.

'Golden Splendour Strain'

Flower: Numerous colors, heavily scented. Funnel- or also saucer-shaped, in groups of 15 to 30 and more.
Leaf: Dark green, lanceolate.
Growth: One-stemmed, towering, depending on number of flowers more or less heavily bent.
Site: Sun, warm. Soil well-drained, loamy humus, permeable, also lime-rich.
Care: Planting depth 4–6 in. (10–15 cm). Initial growth is endangered by late frosts; protective covering is essential. Support tall flower stems. Protect from slug damage.
Use: In beds.
Good Partners: In some cases difficult to combine because of intense colors. It is best to plant suitable cultivars together.
Cultivars/Relatives:
• 'African Queen', yellow-orange, wide-open flowers, 60–72 in. (150–180 cm).
• 'Black Magic', inside white, outside bronze, funnel-shaped, 52–68 in. (130–170 cm).
• 'Golden Splendour', golden-yellow, orange-brown back stripe, trumpet-shaped, 56–72 in. (140–180 cm).
• 'Pink Perfection', crimson-pink, whitish median stripe, trumpet-shaped, 64–80 in. (160–200 cm). Best in light shade; in sun the color gets lighter.
• 'Royal Gold', golden yellow, back is yellow with lemony green, often trumpet-shaped, 52–60 in. (130–150 cm).

Armenian Grape Hyacinth
Muscari armeniacum

Muscari armeniacum

April–May	○ ✂ ☠
H 6–10 in. (15–25 cm)	

Extremely versatile.
Flower: Azure with white edge, scented.
Leaf: Linear, grass-green, evergreen, dies back in summer, puts forth again in fall.
Growth: Many-stemmed, in clumps. These long-lived plants are mat-forming.
Origin: Southeastern Europe to Asia Minor. Stony places.
Site: Full sun, warm. Soil moderately dry to well-drained.
Care: Plant in fall. Planting depth 2–3 in. (6–8 cm). Let the leaves die back after the bloom.
Propagation: By brood bulbs.
Use: With other early spring bloomers, in rock gardens, and to naturalize beneath shrubs.
Good Partners: *Primula vulgaris*— narcissuses and tulips.
Cultivars/Relatives:
• 'Blue Spike', brilliant blue, double, long- and free-flowering.
• *Muscari botryoides,* sky-blue, April–May, 4–8 in. (10–20 cm). Abundantly self-sowing.
• 'Alba', white.
• *Muscari comosum* 'Monstrosum', light violet in feathery racemes, May–June, 8–16 in. (20–40 cm).
Warning: The plants are poisonous!

213

Narcissus

NARCISSUSES

Spring meadow with large- and small-cupped narcissuses

The Major Narcissuses

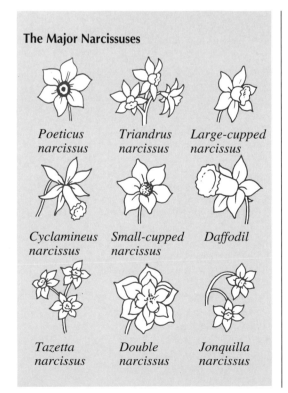

Poeticus narcissus　*Triandrus narcissus*　*Large-cupped narcissus*

Cyclamineus narcissus　*Small-cupped narcissus*　*Daffodil*

Tazetta narcissus　*Double narcissus*　*Jonquilla narcissus*

The enormous assortment is broken down into several groups that differ in flower form or origin (see drawing, left). The group names are also used in most garden catalogs.

Flower: Bipartite, divided into a star-shaped perianth and a trumpet- to plate-shaped corona or cup, often of a different color.

Leaf: Linear, dull green or gray-green. Appears early, dies back from June on.

Growth: Singular or multi-stemmed, from large bulbs.

Origin: Western and Central Europe to western Asia. In mountain meadows, pastures, and deciduous forests.

Site: Sun to partial shade. Soil moderately dry to moist, nutrient-rich, sandy to humus-rich loamy soils.

Care: Plant in fall, to a depth of 4–6 in. (10–15 cm). The later the bulbs go in the ground, the more tender they are the first winter.

In spring, water if dry; dryness in summer will do no harm. Occasionally feed shortly after initial growth. Cut off seed structures, leave foliage alone until it has died back.

Propagation: By secondary bulbs, best time: after blooming or in early fall.

Use: In borders among other perennials, in spring flower gardens, and in large colonies in meadows. As cut flowers.

Good Partners: Other spring bloomers and early blooming shrubs.

Warning: The entire plant is poisonous!

Daffodil, Trumpet Narcissus
Narcissus pseudonarcissus

Large-cupped Narcissuses
Small-cupped Narcissuses
Narcissus

Small-cupped narcissuses

Daffodils

March–April	◯ ◐ ☠
H 16–24 in. (40–60 cm)	

Along with crocuses and tulips, daffodils are part of the classic spring threesome. This group has been in cultivation for many years, and fascinating forms have arisen through various hybridizations and selections. In addition to traditional cultivars from the nineteenth century, we also have brand-new English, Dutch, or American breeds.
Flower: yellow, white, one-colored and bicolored, scented. Flowers solitary, large, with star-shaped perianth and trumpet-shaped corona.
Cultivars/Relatives:
One-colored Cultivars:
• 'Cantatrice', pure white.
• 'Mount Hood', creamy white.
• 'Exception', yellow, tall-growing, new cultivar, suitable for naturalizing beneath loosely planted groups of woody plants.
• 'Standard Value', yellow, late blooming.
• 'King Alfred', rich yellow, large-flowered, one of the oldest, most reliable cultivars.
• 'Dutch Master', golden yellow, flowers pointing slightly upward.

Double narcissus

Bicolored Cultivars:
• 'Bravour', perianth white, trumpet yellow.
• 'Magnet', perianth creamy white, trumpet yellow.
Double Narcissuses: Derived from trumpet narcissuses.
• 'White Lion', white.
• 'Van Sion', brilliant yellow, old cultivar with heavy blossom, not always stable, needs to be sheltered from wind.
• 'Tahiti', yellow-red, heavily doubled, almost ball-shaped, strong-stemmed and stable.

Large-cupped narcissuses

March–April	◯ ◐ ☠
H 12–16 in. (30–40 cm)	

Almost indispensable in gardens.
Flower: White, yellow, red, one-colored and bicolored. Single-flowered, scented. Large-cupped narcissus star-like with saucer-shaped corona. Small-cupped narcissus similar, but with shorter corona.

Large-cupped Narcissuses:
• 'Stainless', pure white.
• 'Carlton', light yellow.
• 'Ceylon', perianth golden yellow, cup orange.
• 'Satin Pink', perianth white, cup bright pink.

Small-cupped Narcissuses:
• 'Barret Browning', white, corona orange.
• 'Birma', perianth yellow, corona red-orange.

Triandrus, Cyclamineus, and Jonquilla Narcissuses
Narcissus

Narcissus cyclamineus

March–May	◯ ◐ ☠
H 4–20 in. (10–50 cm)	

Triandrus Narcissuses, Angels'-tears
Narcissus triandrus
Multiflowered narcissuses with intense scent. Perennial only in mild situations; in areas with harsher climate, cultivate in pots. Flower white, March–May. Curved perianth, cup-shaped corona. Sites with partial shade.
• 'Rippling Waters', pure white, three- to four-flowered.
• 'Liberty Bells', yellow.

Cyclamineus Narcissuses
Narcissus cyclamineus
Flower white, various yellow shades, March–April. For sites with sun to partial shade.
• 'February Silver', white.
• 'Peeping Tom', yellow.

Jonquilla Narcissuses, Jonquils
Narcissus jonquilla
Flower yellow, heavily scented, many-blossomed, small, April–May. Sites with full sun to partial shade. Moderately hardy.
• 'Suzy', perianth light yellow, corona orange.
• 'Tittle Tattle', one-colored, light yellow, late-blooming.
• 'Pipit', perianth lemon-yellow, corona white; rewarding cultivar.
• 'Trevithian', pale yellow.

Tazetta Narcissuses, Paper-whites
Narcissus tazetta

Cultivar 'Pride of Cornwall'

Cultivar 'Geranium'

April–May	◯ ◐ ☠
H 8–20 in. (20–50 cm)	

The tazettas are derived from *Narcissus tazetta,* which is native to the Mediterranean region. They are not always completely hardy; many cultivars thrive only in wine-growing climates.
Flower: Bicolored, white, yellow and orange shades, sweet-scented, multiflowered.
Cultivars/Relatives:
• 'Geranium', perianth white, corona orange, bowl-shaped, heavily scented, three- to five-flowered, May. More durable and robust than the other cultivars.
• 'Scarlet Gem', perianth yellow, corona red, three- to six-flowered.
• 'Silver Chimes', perianth white, corona creamy white to lemon-yellow, four- to six-flowered, enchanting but frost-tender, so plant near house.

Poeticus Narcissuses, Poet's Narcissuses
Narcissus poeticus

Narcissus poeticus

April–May	◯ ◐ ☠
H 12–20 in. (30–50 cm)	

The poeticus narcissuses occur throughout the Mediterranean area; for centuries they have been prized as garden flowers for their fragrance.
Flower: Perianth white, star-shaped, corona yellow with orange margin, bowl-shaped, heavily scented; one blossom per stem.
Use: Ideal for naturalizing. The plant is self-sowing.
Cultivars/Relatives:
• 'Actaea', perianth white, corona green-yellow with red margin, large-flowered, old cultivar.
• 'Cantabile', perianth white, corona greenish, margin red.
• 'Queen of Narcissi', perianth white, corona red, old, reliable cultivar.

BULBS/TUBERS

Common Star-of-Bethlehem
Ornithogalum umbellatum

Ornithogalum umbellatum

April–May
H 4–6 in. (10–25 cm)

The flowers are open only at midday ("11 o'clock flower").
Flower: White with green stripe on back, star-shaped, in umbel-like racemes.
Leaf: Grassy, grooved, green with whitish median vein, dies back after the bloom.
Growth: One-stemmed, loosely grassy, from densely crowded bulbs.
Origin: Mediterranean region to Near East. In meadows, on slopes, in vineyards.
Site: Sun to light shade, warm. Soil moderately dry to well-drained, any garden soil.
Care: Plant in fall, planting depth 3–4 in. (8–10 cm). No care required. Also tolerates mowing.
Use: In rock gardens, for naturalizing in flowery meadows and on park lawns.
Good Partners: *Nepeta, Origanum, Salvia, Thymus.*
Cultivars/Relatives:
• *Ornithogalum nutans,* nodding star-of-Bethlehem, nodding flowers on rigid stems, blooms at the same time. Leaves gray-green. For places with sun to partial shade, good for naturalizing.
Warning: The entire plant is poisonous.

Striped Squill, Lebanon Squill
Puschkinia scilloides var. *libanotica*

Puschkinia scilloides var. libanotica

March–April
H 4–6 in. (10–15 cm)

Trouble-free spring bloomer.
Flower: White to light blue, with blue back stripe, lightly scented. Bell-shaped in racemes, free-flowering.
Leaf: Grassy, short, and rigid, shiny green.
Growth: Long lived bulbous plant, grows loosely grassy and colonizes large areas.
Origin: Western Asia. Gravelly hillsides, thin woods.
Site: Sun to partial shade, warm, also hot. Soil dry to well-drained, any garden soil will do.
Care: Plant in fall, 2–3 in. (5–8 cm) deep. No other care needed.
Propagation: By removal of brood bulbs. Self-sowing.
Use: In rock gardens and for naturalizing in sparse grass beneath woody plants, where it can number in the thousands.
Good Partners: *Chionodoxa, Iris, Scilla.*

Siberian Squill
Scilla sibirica

Cultivar 'Spring Beauty'

March–May
H 4–6 in. (10–15 cm)

Gentian-blue spring bloomer.
Flower: Intensely blue star-shaped flowers in racemes having few blossoms.
Leaf: Broad linear, grass-green.
Growth: Two to three stems from egg-shaped bulbs.
Origin: Southeastern Europe to western Asia. In mixed deciduous forests.
Site: Sun to partial shade, bright in spring, warm. Soil moderately dry to well-drained, humus, in any garden soil.
Care: Plant in fall, to a depth of 2–3 in. (5–8 cm). Remove excess fallen leaves in spring. Cautious applications of organic fertilizer until the leaf flush.
Propagation: By removal of brood bulbs. Propagates itself without coaxing, by self-sowing.
Use: Always in largish colonies. In rock gardens, ideal for naturalizing at edge of woody plants or in sparse grass.
Good Partners: Narcissuses, tulips.
Cultivars/Relatives:
• 'Spring Beauty', splendid blue, all parts larger. Small, very crowded clumps. The plant produces daughter bulbs, but is not self-sowing, as it is sterile.
• *Scilla bifolia,* twinleaf squill, blue. Blooms somewhat earlier than *Scilla sibirica.* 4 in. (10 cm), sows its own seed heavily beneath thin stands of woody plants.

217

Tulipa TULIPS

White tulips and dark violet hyacinths

Tulips rank among the most popular bulbous plants for rock gardens and beds.

Classification of Tulips:
The countless cultivars are divided into classes:

Early Tulips:
Class 1: Single early tulips (see page 219).
Class 2: Double early tulips (see page 219).

Midseason Tulips:
Class 3: Triumph tulips (see page 219).
Class 4: Darwin Hybrid tulips (see page 219).

Late Tulips:
Class 5: Single late tulips (see page 219).
Class 6: Lily-flowered tulips (see page 219).
Class 7: Fringed or Crispa tulips (see page 220).
Class 8: Viridiflora tulips (see page 220).

Class 9: Rembrandt tulips.
Class 10: Parrot tulips (see page 220).
Class 11: Double late tulips (see page 219).

Botanical or Species Tulips:
Class 12: Kaufmanniana tulips (see page 220).
Class 13: Fosteriana tulips (see page 220).
Class 14: Greigii tulips (see page 220).
Class 15: True wild tulips.
• Multiflowered tulips (see page 221).
• Dwarf tulips (see page 221).
• Other wild species (see page 221).

Tips for Tulip Lovers:
Planting: Planting season September/October, planting depth about 4 in. (10 cm). Don't lift spent bulbs; they can stay in place for a long while.
Care: Feed during the leaf growth or right after blooming finishes, 1–2 oz. (30–50 g) per square yard [1 m^2]. It is essential to let leaves die back. Remove faded flowers or fruit structures at once. When cutting flowers for vases, leave one or two leaves untouched, to prevent the bulbs from starving.
Transplanting: Dig up only after leaves have died back—usually in June, once the leaves have turned brown. Then separate the primary bulb and the brood bulbs, and plant them elsewhere. If you reset them at the old site, they will become stunted.
Storing: Clean the bulbs and store them in a dark, dry place, but not in plastic bags or closed containers, where they will become moldy.

Early Tulips
Tulipa

'Diana', single-flowered

'Mansella', double-flowered

April
H 10–16 in. (25–40 cm)

Single Early Tulips:
Flower: White, yellow, orange, pink, and red, with slight scent. Cup-shaped, small.
Leaf: Gray-green, broad tongue-shaped.
Growth: Erect, short-stemmed.
Site: Full sun, bright in spring, warm. Soil moderately dry to well-drained, if possible sandy-loamy, humus-poor. <u>No wet soils</u>!
Use: In beds, troughs, and pots.
Cultivars/Relatives:
<u>Early blooming</u>:
• 'Diana', pure white.
• 'Joffre', yellow.
• 'Christmas Marvel', pink.
• 'Brilliant Star', scarlet.
<u>Midseason and late blooming</u>:
• 'Bellona', yellow, large-flowered.
• 'Princess Irene', orange, purple-mottled.
• 'Kaiserkrone', red with yellow.
Double Early Tulips:
Flowers resemble peonies, bloom longer than the single tulips, short-stemmed, 10–14 in. (25–35 cm).
Cultivars/Relatives:
• 'Schoonoord', pure white.
• 'Peach Blossom', pink.

Midseason Tulips
Tulipa

Darwin Hybrid 'Golden Parade'

April
H 16–24 in. (40–60 cm)

Darwin Hybrid Tulips:
They rank among the most magnificent tulips.
Flower: Usually yellow, orange, and red. Large, cup-shaped, brilliantly colored.
Leaf: Gray-green, broad tongue-shaped, erect.
Growth: Rigidly erect, large, with thick flower stems, 20–24 in. (50–60 cm).
Site: Sun to light shade. For any sandy-loamy garden soil.
Use: In beds.
Cultivars/Relatives:
• 'Golden Apeldoorn', yellow, black at base.
• 'Big Chief', pink with orange.
• 'Elizabeth Arden', salmon-pink with violet.
• 'Hollands Glory', brilliant orange-scarlet, large-flowered.
• 'Apeldoorn', orange-scarlet, black at base.

Triumph Tulips:
Strong-stemmed, commonly multicolored, 16–22 in. (40–55 cm) tall, for massed plantings.
Cultivars/Relatives:
• 'Pax', pure white.
• 'Golden Melody', golden yellow.
• 'Peerless Pink', pink.
• 'Cassini', blood-red.
• 'Negrita', purple.

Late Tulips
Tulipa

'Maytime', lily-flowered

'Bonanza', double-flowered

April–May
H 20–26 in. (50–65 cm)

Single Late Tulips:
Flower: Many colors, often multicolored, cup-shaped, early to late May.

Lily-flowered Tulips:
Flower: Elegant, slender, with tips curving outward.
Leaf: Broad tongue-shaped, gray-green.
Growth: Erect, not always stable.
Site: Sun. For any sandy-loamy garden soil.
Use: In beds.
Cultivars/Relatives:
• 'White Triumphator', white.
• 'Westpoint', light yellow.
• 'Queen of Sheba', blood-red with yellow margin.

Double Late Tulips:
Heavily doubled, weak-stemmed. For places sheltered from wind.

BULBS/TUBERS

219

Late Tulips
Tulipa

'Fancy Frills', fringed

Parrot tulip 'Flaming Parrot'

April–May ○ ✂
H 12–24 in. (30–60 cm)

Fringed or Crispa Tulips:
Unusual and increasingly popular.
Flower: Broad cup-shaped,
edges irregularly fringed.
Cultivars/Relatives:
• 'Fancy Frills', ivory-white, with
pink-and-white fringed edges.
• 'Hamilton', golden yellow.
• 'Arma', scarlet.

Viridiflora Tulips:
New breeds.
Flower: Bicolored, outside mot-
tled or striped with green.
Cultivars/Relatives:
• 'Spring Green', creamy white.
• 'Golden Artist', yellow.
• 'Eye Catcher', red.

Parrot Tulips:
Bizarre, reminiscent of a past era.
Flower: Intensely colored, with
fringed margins, opens wide in
sun.
Growth: Usually weak-
stemmed, stems curved.
Use: Sheltered from wind,
among supporting perennials.
Cultivars/Relatives:
• 'White Parrot', pure white.
• 'Red Champion', red.
• 'Blue Parrot', lilac-blue.

Botanical or Species Tulips
Tulipa

Tulipa kaufmanniana

March–April ○
H 6–16 in. (15–40 cm)

The botanical or species tulips
include forms that still conform
largely to the character of the
wild species.

Kaufmanniana Tulips:
Exceptionally early blooming. In
the sun the flowers open wide—
hence one of their names, water-
lily tulips.
Flower: Commonly bicolored
and tricolored. Star-shaped.
Leaf: Gray-green, occasionally
spotted with brownish red.
Growth: Short, compact stems.
Site: Sun, warm. Soil dry to
well-drained, any permeable garden soil.
Use: In rock gardens and in
beds.
Good Partners: Cushion-forming perennials and subshrubs.
Cultivars/Relatives:
• 'The First', ivory-white with
yellow base, margin light yellow,
outside crimson.
• 'Goldstuck', golden yellow,
margin yellow, outside scarlet.
• 'Daylight', orange-scarlet,
black at base.
• 'Shakespeare', pink with yellow base, margin salmon-pink,
outside crimson.

Tulipa greigii 'Plaisir'

Greigii Tulips:
Bloom later than the other
Botanical Tulips.
Flower: Bright, multicolored.
The blossoms open wide.
Leaf: Gray-green, with russet or
violet-red stripes.
Growth: Compact, slightly
rigid, one-stemmed.
Site: As for Kaufmanniana
tulips.
Use: In rock gardens.
Cultivars/Relatives:
• 'Yellow Dawn', yellow with
red base.
• 'Plaisir', creamy yellow with
red, base black.
• 'Ontario', inside apricot, base
black.

Fosteriana Tulips:
Very early blooming, usually
before the classic tulips.
Flower: Yellow, red, or white,
unusually large; in sun, they
open flat.
Leaf: Broad lanceolate, gray-
green, with faint reddish border.
Growth: Stem single and short.
Site: Full sun. Soil dry to well-
drained, must be permeable.
Use: In beds or in rock gardens,
in containers.
Good Partners: *Arabis, Iberis—
Muscari.*
Cultivars/Relatives:
• 'Purissima', white with yel-
low.
• 'Golden Emperor', golden yel-
low.
• 'Orange Emperor', orange.
• 'Red Emperor', brilliant scar-
let, base black.

True Wild Tulips, Multiflowered Tulips
Tulipa Species

Tulipa tarda

March–April ○
H 4–12 in. (10–30 cm)

We are familiar with the one-stemmed tulips we see in gardens and parks. Less familiar are the few wild species that bear several flowers per stalk.
Flower: In many colors. Small cup-shaped flowers, multiflowered.
Leaf: Linear, in various colors.
Growth: Dwarfed, one-stemmed, bulbs small, some species produce runners.
Origin: Central Asia. Steppes, stony mountain slopes.
Site: Full sun, warm, sheltered, damp in spring, dry in summer. Soil highly permeable, best is sandy-gravelly loam. No heavy soils!
Care: Planting season September/October, planting depth 3–4 in. (8–10 cm).
Propagation: By seed, by removal of daughter bulbs.
Use: In rock gardens and in gravel beds.
Cultivars/Relatives:
• *Tulipa praestans,* scarlet, two- to three-flowered, March–April, 10–12 in. (25–30 cm).
• 'Fuselier', brilliant orange-red.
• *Tulipa tarda,* yellow with white, three- to eight-flowered, March–April, 4–6 in. (10–15 cm). Produces runners, self-sowing.

True Wild Tulips, Dwarf Tulips
Tulipa Species

Tulipa violacea

March–April ○
H 2–6 in. (5–15 cm)

Miniature editions of tulips.
Flower: In many colors. Single, small cup-shaped blossoms.
Leaf: In a variety of colors. Narrow to broad linear.
Growth: Miniature.
Origin: Northern Persia and bordering regions. Steppes and stony mountain slopes.
Site: As for multiflowered tulips.
Care: Planting season September/October, planting depth 3–4 in. (8–10 cm).
Cultivars/Relatives:
• *Tulipa aucheriana,* dark pink, brown-yellow at base, star-shaped, April–May. A late blooming dwarf tulip, 2–4 in. (5–10 cm).
• *Tulipa bakeri* 'Lilac Wonder', purple-pink, yellow at base, March–April, 2–4 in. (5–10 cm).
• *Tulipa batalinii* 'Bright Gem', sulfur-yellow, April–May, 6 in. (15 cm).
• 'Red Jewel', brick-red, April–May, 6 in. (15 cm).
• *Tulipa pulchella,* violet, yellow at base, March–April, 2–4 in. (10 cm).
• *Tulipa schrenkii*, red, edged with orange, March–April, 3–4 in. (7–10 cm).
• *Tulipa violacea,* crimson-violet, blue-black at base, March, 6 in. (15 cm).

True Wild Tulips, Florentine Tulip
Tulipa sylvestris

Tulipa sylvestris

April–May ○ ◐
H 8–16 in. (20–40 cm)

The only tulip that occurs wild in more northern latitudes. Indigenous to the Mediterranean area, it has become naturalized in parts of Europe.
Flower: Golden yellow, scented. Flowers nodding, bell-shaped, opening to star shapes in warm weather.
Leaf: Lanceolate, gray-green.
Growth: Erect, stems thin but strong. Bulbs with runners, in some cases proliferating.
Origin: Europe. Along sandy-gravelly banks, in thin woods, preferably in vineyards.
Site: Sun to partial shade, warm, also hot. Soil moderately dry to well-drained, nutrient-rich, gravelly-loamy or sandy-loamy.
Care: Planting season September/October, planting depth 4–5 in. (10–12 cm), in heavy soils only 2–3 in. (6–8 cm).
Propagation: By seed right after seed collection, or by removal of runner bulbs.
Use: In gravel beds, pebble beds, or natural gardens. Let naturalize beneath thin bushes and at sunny edge of woods.
Good Partners: *Geranium, Iris.*

GRASSES AND FERNS—

Ferns used as ornamental foliage plants are nicely complemented by woodland perennials.

GREEN COMPANIONS

From the botanical point of view, grasses and ferns are in no way related; nevertheless, gardeners usually mention them in the same breath. They are plants that bloom either inconspicuously or not at all, but attract attention by their ornamental foliage and their shape. Both grasses and ferns can serve as a mediating link between diverse partners that are hard to combine. They provide the green frame for the colors of the blossoms.

Pennisetum alupecuroides

Ornamental Grasses

Although they are classed as flowering plants, their blossoms attract little attention, because they are pollinated by the wind. Not until this century did we discover that the ornamental grasses have great decorative potential in gardens. They played no role in historic garden design. Today more than 250 different species and forms are commercially available.

Ornamental grasses are appropriate for almost every part of the garden. The clumps contribute an elegant play of line and great beauty of form, and many species also enhance our gardens with their feather-like inflorescences and marvelously beautiful autumn colors.

Ferns

They are classified as a separate group of plants because they produce spores rather than flowers and seeds. The spores are borne in cases on the undersides of the fronds or on separate spore-bearing (fertile) fronds. In terms of their history of development, the ferns are far more ancient than the seed plants. The majority of the roughly 9,000 species are native to the tropics; only about 250 species are indigenous to this country.

Ferns are strictly ornamental foliage plants for light shade. They shun regions with dense shade, preferring the shifting, dappled light beneath trees and shrubs. A few species also thrive in crevices in walls.

Tip: Grasses and ferns are by no means the only plants with ornamental foliage. The perennials and the annuals also include quite a number of plants with extremely well-shaped leaves, such as hostas, cranesbill species, and lambs'-ears, the tobacco plant, and shrub marguerites.

Plant list:
① *Dryopteris borreri*
② *Campanula latifolia* var. *macrantha* 'Alba'

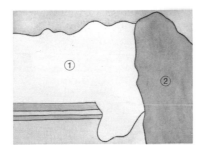

223

Reedgrass
Calamagrostis x *acutiflora* 'Karl Foerster'

Calamagrostis x *acutiflora* 'Karl Foerster'

June–July ◯ ◖
H 56–72 in. (140–180 cm)

Ornamental grass that remains decorative for months.
Flower: Creamy white, in feather-like outspread panicles. After the bloom the panicles draw together to form spikes and turn ocher in color, like the stems.
Leaf: Narrow linear, grows early.
Growth: In clumps, with rigidly erect culms.
Origin: Cultivated form.
Site: Sun to partial shade; the plant tolerates heat. Soil moderately dry to moist; any garden soil.
Care: Plant in spring. Cut back in early spring.
Propagation: By division.
Use: In borders.
Good Partners: *Aster dumosus, Aster novae-angliae, Chrysanthemum indicum* hybrids, *Helenium, Heliopsis, Rudbeckia fulgida.*

Morrow's Sedge
Carex morrowii 'Variegata'

Carex morrowii 'Variegata'

April ◖ ⬤ ✂
H 16–20 in. (40–50 cm)

One of the prettiest evergreen grasses.
Flower: Yellow, small, in spikes.
Leaf: Broad linear, downward-arching, firm, dark green with narrow creamy white stripe along margin, evergreen.
Growth: Shallow clumps, broader than tall when old.
Origin: The cultivated form is derived from the species from Japan. In woods.
Site: Light shade to shade, moderately warm to cool. Soil well-drained to moist, humus-rich, loamy. No wet soils or soils that dry out easily!
Care: Water in dry spells.
Propagation: By division in spring.
Use: In the shade of walls and in woodland plantings. Shady borders.
Good Partners: *Cardamine trifolia, Epimedium, Hosta, Pulmonaria, Tiarella, Waldsteinia.* Good companion plant for rhododendrons.
Cultivars/Relatives:
• *Carex pendula,* giant sedge. Inconspicuous, drooping spikes. Erect stems up to 60 in. (150 cm) tall. Leaves dark green, broad linear, with sharp margins, downward-arching, evergreen, in clumps 16–32 in. (40–80 cm) tall. Also for compacted or moist soils; no sandy soils!

Pampas Grass
Cortaderia selloana

Cortaderia selloana

September–October ◯ ✂
H 48–104 in. (120–260 cm)

Well-known, ornamental giant grass.
Flower: Silvery white, panicles up to more than 20 in. (50 cm) tall on stiff, erect stems.
Leaf: Long linear with sharp margins, gray-green.
Growth: Forms large clumps.
Origin: South America. On pampas.
Site: Full sun, warm, also briefly dry. Soil well-drained, permeable, nutrient-rich.
Care: Water in prolonged dry spells. Sensitive to wet winters; keep dry during winter—best done in late fall by tying the leaves together in a tuft and packing dry leaves and boughs around them.
Propagation: By division in spring.
Use: As solitary plant in gravel beds, in front of house walls.
Good Partners: *Anaphalis, Chrysanthemum indicum* hybrids, *Nepeta, Salvia.*
Cultivars/Relatives:
• 'Sunningdale Silver', with large, elegant panicles with a white, silky sheen, 80 in. (200 cm).
• 'Pumila', compact, 48 in. (120 cm).

Blue Fescue
Festuca cinerea

Festuca cinerea

June–July ○
H 12–24 in. (30–60 cm)

Small, blue-gray grass.
Flower: Gray-green, in loose panicles on erect stems, turns light brown after the bloom.
Leaf: Narrow linear, gray-green to steel-blue.
Growth: Hemispherical cushions.
Origin: Europe, Caucasus. On highland plateaus and in dry grass.
Site: Full sun, warm, also hot and dry. Soil moderately dry to dry, highly permeable, poor in humus and nutrients. No wet sites! Loses green color in nutrient-rich media.
Care: Tidy the clumps in spring. Cut back the panicles after the bloom.
Propagation: By division in spring. Self-sowing in congenial places.
Use: Alone or in small groups, never two-dimensionally, in rock and terraced gardens.
Good Partners: *Campanula, Cerastium tomentosum, Veronica spicata* ssp. *incana.*
Cultivars/Relatives:
• 'Frühlingsblau', steel-blue.
• 'Meerblau', showy blue.
• *Festuca ovina,* sheep's fescue, more vigorous and less sensitive to wet.
• 'Aprilgrün', sea-green.
• 'Superba', blue-green clumps, scarcely blooms at all.

Blue Oat Grass
Helictotrichon sempervirens

Helictotrichon sempervirens

July ○
H 44–64 in. (110–160 cm)

The largest of the blue ornamental grasses.
Flower: Gray-green, in slender, loose panicles on blades up to 60 in. (150 cm) tall.
Leaf: Narrow linear, gray-green to blue-gray.
Growth: Compact, multirayed clumps 12–20 in. (30–50 cm) tall, reaching almost 40 in. (1 m) across in suitable sites.
Origin: Western Mediterranean region and Alps. On slopes covered with rock debris up to altitudes of 1.5 miles (2400 m).
Site: Full sun, warm, also hot. Soil dry to moderately dry, permeable, nutrient-poor. No wet sites! The clumps fade in shade and in nutrient-rich soils.
Care: Plant only in spring. Cut off the panicles after the bloom. Cut back completely in spring.
Propagation: By division in spring.
Use: In all dry places in the garden. In sunny borders.
Good Partners: Gray-leaved perennials. *Anaphalis, Aster amellus, Nepeta, Scabiosa, Sedum.*

Wood Rush
Luzula sylvatica

Luzula sylvatica 'Hohe Tatra'

May–June ◐ ●
H 12–20 in. (30–50 cm)

Evergreen grass for shady areas of the garden.
Flower: Brownish, plain, star-shaped, in loose panicles.
Leaf: Broad linear, fresh green, evergreen, flushes early.
Growth: Loosely grassy, gradually forms mats by means of short runners.
Origin: Europe to Caucasus. In damp woods, usually in acid soils.
Site: Light shade to shade, cool, air humid. Soil well-drained to moist, humus-rich.
Care: Water in dry spells.
Propagation: Easily possible by division in spring.
Use: In small areas, in the shade of woody plants and walls.
Good Partners: *Epimedium, Symphytum grandiflorum, Tiarella, Vinca, Waldsteinia—*rhododendrons.
Cultivars/Relatives:
• 'Marginata', with white leaf margins.

Eulalia Grass
Miscanthus sinensis

Giant Moor Grass
Molinia arundinacea

Miscanthus sinensis 'Silberspinne'

Miscanthus sinensis 'Zebrinus'

Molinia arundinacea 'Windspiel'

September–October ○ ✄
H 40–108 in. (100–270 cm)

July–September ○ ◑
H 64–112 in. (160–280 cm)

Imposing, reedy grass with many differently shaped cultivars.
Flower: Depending on the cultivar, glossy silver, light brown to russet panicles on erect stems. Some cultivars do not bloom in colder climates. The fruit structures are visually striking throughout the winter, especially covered in frost and seen against the light.
Leaf: Broad to narrow linear, pendant, on bamboo-like stems, dark green with small, silvery stripes in the middle. Many cultivars with striking yellow or red fall colors.
Growth: Large, clump-like grass, flushes early, vigorous.
Origin: East Asia. In well-drained to damp meadows, on mountain slopes.
Site: Sun, warm. Soil well-drained to moist, any nutrient-rich garden soil.
Care: Cut back in spring; the grass is attractive all winter long. Feed adequately. Remove seedlings; they usually are less attractive than the cultivars.
Propagation: By division in spring. Self-sowing in suitable places.
Use: As solitary plant or keynote perennial. In borders.

Good Partners: *Alchemilla, Aster novi-belgii, Delphinium, Ligularia, Lythrum, Phlox.*
Cultivars/Relatives:
• 'Gracillimus', nonblooming cultivar 60–72 in. (140–180 cm) tall, with narrow linear, upward-arching leaves. Very pretty cultivar for cutting, evergreen in mild years.
• 'Kleine Fontäne', red-brown, free-flowering, 48 in. (120 cm).
• 'Malepartus', red-brown, early blooming, with stunning red fall color, 80 in. (200 cm).
• 'Silberfeder', creamy white panicles with silvery gleam, pretty yellow fall color, 92 in. (230 cm).
• 'Variegatus', with white-striped leaves, 80 in. (200 cm).
• 'Zebrinus', red-brown, leaves green with irregular, pale-yellow spots, 80 in. (200 cm).
• *Miscanthus giganteus* 'Aksel Olsen', giant eulalia grass, 120–160 in. (300–400 cm), with gorgeous, ocher fall color. Blooms rarely in northern latitudes.

Elegant grass with impressive fall colors.
Flower: Brownish, plain, branched panicles. Stems turn showy yellow in fall.
Leaf: Narrow linear, green, yellow in fall.
Growth: In clumps, leaf tufts 28–44 in. (70–110 cm).
Origin: Europe. In meadows, thin woods.
Site: Sun to partial shade, moderately warm. Soil moderately dry to moist, any garden soil.
Care: Water in dry spells. Remove seedlings.
Propagation: By division in spring. By self-sowing.
Use: In natural gardens and heath gardens. In borders.
Good Partners: Woody plants with fall colors. *Aster dumosus, Geranium, Hosta, Lysimachia.*
Cultivars/Relatives:
• 'Transparent', loosely drooping, 80 in. (200 cm).
• 'Windspiel', rigidly erect, 112 in. (280 cm).
• *Molinia caerulea,* July–September.
• 'Dauerstrahl', brilliant golden yellow fall color, 44 in. (110 cm).
• 'Variegata', leaves white-striped, 28 in. (70 cm).

Switch Grass
Panicum virgatum

Fountain Grass
Pennisetum alopecuroides

Panicum virgatum 'Rehbraun'

Pennisetum alopecuroides

August–September
H 44–60 in. (110–150 cm)

September–October
H 16–40 in. (40–100 cm)

Clumplike grass with fine-membered inflorescences.
Flower: Tiny, in very fine, veil-like panicles.
Leaf: Narrow linear, grass-green, erect to drooping, with ocher color in fall.
Growth: Compact clumps, erect, in some cases not stable; new leaves appear late.
Origin: North America to Central America. In tall grass prairies.
Site: Sun, warm. Soil moderately dry to moist, any garden soil.
Care: Water in dry spells. Feed occasionally. Cut back in spring.
Propagation: By division in spring.
Use: In borders.
Good Partners: *Aster, Chrysanthemum indicum* hybrids, *Solidago.*
Cultivars/Relatives:
• 'Rehbraun', copper switch grass, intense red fall color beginning in August, later glowing russet to golden yellow, 44 in. (110 cm).
• 'Strictum', erect, stable.

Ornamental grass that is immensely effective because long-lasting fruit structures keep their good looks well into winter. For gardens, choose the prettier cultivars over the species.
Flower: Light brown to reddish brown, tiny, long-bearded single flowers in dense terminal spikes like bottle brushes, on erect to bending stems.
Leaf: Narrow linear, drooping, rich green, golden yellow in fall.
Growth: Broad, tuft-like clumps.
Origin: East Asia to Australia. In damp meadows.
Site: Sun, warm. Soil moderately dry to moist. No very dry, compacted, or sandy soils, otherwise, any soil possible.
Care: Water in prolonged dry spells, feed occasionally. Cut back in spring.
Propagation: By division in spring.
Use: Alone or in threes, in sunny borders and on sunny slopes. Pretty in low mats of perennials and near woody plants with fall colors.
Good Partners: *Achillea, Aster, Chrysanthemum indicum* hybrids, *Solidago, Vernonia*—yellow roses.

Cultivars/Relatives:
• 'Hameln', free flowering, 24 in. (60 cm).
• 'Herbstzauber', with inflorescences clearly rising above leaf tufts, 32 in. (80 cm).
• *Pennisetum orientale,* Oriental fountain grass, gray, soft, hairy spikes with violet shimmer, July–September, dull gray-green foliage without fall color, 20 in. (50 cm). For dry, sunny places. Good with *Nepeta, Salvia, Stachys byzantina.*

American Maidenhair Fern
Adiantum pedatum

Adiantum pedatum

H 16–24 in. (40–60 cm)

Graceful, robust fern.
Leaf: Frond of eight to nine leaflets arranged in fan shapes on wiry stems.
Growth: Slowly creeping, forms broad clumps.
Origin: North America and East Asia. In well-drained woods.
Site: Light to partial shade, cool, air humid. The plant is endangered by late frosts. Soil moist to well-drained, permeable, humus-rich.
Care: Each year add roughly half an inch (1 cm) of leaf mold and dead needles. Restrict growth of vigorous neighbors. Let grow undisturbed.
Propagation: By division or from spores.
Use: In light shade and shifting shade of woody plants, with suitable soil also on the north side of walls.
Good Partners: *Cardamine trifolia, Epimedium, Saxifraga* x *urbium, Tiarella—Carex morrowii* 'Variegata'—rhododendrons.
Cultivars/Relatives:
• *Adiantum venustum,* Himalayan maidenhair fern, with fine-membered, conspicuously light green fronds, creeping, 8–12 in. (20–30 cm). Mostly evergreen. For sites with light shade, sheltered from winter sun.

Male Fern
Dryopteris filix-mas

Dryopteris filix-mas

H 20–44 in. (50–110 cm)

Undemanding fern.
Leaf: Pinnulate, dull green, slightly arched fronds.
Growth: Funnel-shaped clumps.
Origin: The entire northern hemisphere. In deciduous and coniferous forests, in tall perennial vegetation, and on slopes covered with rock debris.
Site: Light shade or partial shade, with enough soil moisture also sun, predominantly cool. Any well-drained to moist soil, also briefly dry.
Care: Water in dry spells. No other tending.
Propagation: By division or from spores. Propagates itself in congenial places.
Use: At edges of woody plants, in shady natural gardens.
Good Partners: *Astilbe, Bergenia, Campanula, Epimedium, Hosta, Waldsteinia—Carex.*
Cultivars/Relatives:
• *Athyrium filix-femina,* lady fern, with more delicately pinnate fronds, dull to brownish green, deciduous. Indigenous species, site and use as for male fern.

Ostrich Fern
Matteuccia struthiopteris

Matteuccia struthiopteris

H 24–56 in. (60–140 cm)

Impressive fern with regularly arranged fronds.
Leaf: Pinnulate, vivid green, deciduous, flushes early. The spores of the ostrich fern are borne on fronds resembling ostrich plumes, first olive-green, later black-brown.
Growth: Funnel-shaped, gradually spreading to cover surfaces by means of runners.
Origin: Northern hemisphere. In woods, on banks.
Site: Light shade, cool, air humid. Soil well-drained to moist, loose, humus-rich.
Care: Water sufficiently in dry spells; otherwise, the fronds wilt and no longer stand erect. If it spreads too much, prune by cutting off pieces.
Propagation: By removal of the runners.
Use: In shifting shade of woody plants and in light shade of walls. Only in sufficiently large areas, because of large numbers of runners.
Good Partners: Combine only with vigorous neighbors! *Campanula latifolia, Hosta, Rodgersia, Smilacina*—Rhododendrons.

Royal Fern
Osmunda regalis

Osmunda regalis

H 24–80 in.
(60–200 cm)

Largest indigenous fern.
Leaf: Large, pinnulate, with elongated to ovate single leaflets, vivid green with yellow fall color. Uppermost leaflets spore-bearing, brown in color.
Growth: In clumps, erect, funnel-shaped. Slow-growing.
Origin: Almost worldwide. In alder and willow groves, beside damp ditches.
Site: Light to partial shade, with wet soil also sun, mild in winter, air humid. Soil moist to wet, loose, humus-rich, acid.
Care: Improve planting site with peat. Water well. Apply humus occasionally.
Propagation: From spores, immediately after collection in June.
Use: In damp regions with woody plants, at shady edges of ponds.
Good Partners: *Aruncus, Caltha, Hosta, Lythrum, Rodgersia—Carex, Molinia.*
Cultivars/Relatives:
• 'Gracilis', dwarf royal fern, erect, 24 in. (60 cm).
• 'Purpurascens', purple royal fern, fronds purple during growth and in fall, 24–56 in. (60–140 cm)

Hart's-tongue Fern
Phyllitis scolopendrium

Phyllitis scolopendrium

H 8–16 in. (20–40 cm)

Unusual-looking fern.
Leaf: Entire, tongue-shaped, leathery, margins wavy, light green, shiny, evergreen.
Growth: Wide-set clumps.
Origin: Europe, Asia, and eastern North America. In mountain forests, beside rocks in damp, shady places.
Site: Light shade, cool, humid air, sheltered from wind. Soil well-drained to moist, permeable, humus-rich. No sites with strong sun or that dry out easily!
Care: Choosing the proper site is important for good growth. Water in dry spells. Occasionally apply leaf mold.
Propagation: By leaf stalk cuttings and from spores.
Use: In garden areas with light shade, sheltered from wind if possible. With suitable soils, also in shade of walls.
Good Partners: *Cardamine trifolia, Galium odoratum, Polygonatum, Saxifraga cortusifolia* var. *fortunei—Adiantum.*
Cultivars/Relatives:
• 'Crispa', with heavily wavy leaf margins.

Soft Shield Fern
Polystichum setiferum

Polystichum setiferum

H 14–24 in. (40–60 cm)

Fern with a great many forms.
Leaf: Large, pinnulate, finely divided, with densely overlapping leaflets, looks like terry cloth. Soft, dull green, evergreen.
Growth: Wide-set clumps.
Origin: Worldwide. In shady, damp woods, in regions with high precipitation and mild winters.
Site: Partial shade to shade, cool, air humid. Soil well drained to moist, loose, humus-rich.
Care: Water in dry spells.
Propagation: By division or from spores.
Use: In loose stands of woody plants. With sufficiently loose, humus-rich soils, also on the north side of walls.
Good Partners: *Cimicifuga, Epimedium, Tiarella.*
Cultivars/Relatives:
• 'Proliferum', with brood buds on the undersides of the fronds, which make them easy to propagate.
• 'Plumosum Densum', very finely pinnate, almost mossy, also with brood buds.
• 'Wollastonii', very vigorous cultivar.
• *Polystichum aculeatum*, hard shield fern, with strikingly glossy and leathery leaves. Unusual, 16–28 in. (40–70 cm).

INDEX

Numbers in **bold** indicate color photos and drawings
* Plant portraits.

INDEX

INDEX

INDEX

SOURCES

Further Reading

Books

Büneman, Otto and Jürgen Becker. *Roses*. Hauppauge, New York: Barron's Educational Series, Inc., 1994.

Catterall, E. *Growing Begonias*. Portland, Oregon: Timber Press, 1984.

Clarkson, Rosetta E. *Herbs: Their Culture and Uses*. New York: Macmillan Publishing Co., Inc., 1990.

_____. *Magic Gardens*. New York: Macmillian Publishing Co., Inc., 1992.

Cobb, Boughton A. *Field Guide to Ferns and Their Related Families: Northeastern and Central North America*. Boston: Houghton Mifflin Company, 1977.

Fell, Derek. *Essential Bulbs: The 100 Best for Design and Cultivation*. Avenal, New Jersey: Outlet Book Co., 1989.

_____. *Bulbs*. New York: Smithmark Publishers, Inc., 1993.

Freeman, Sally. *Herbs for All Seasons: Growing and Gathering Herbs for Flavor, Health, and Beauty*. New York: NAL-Dutton, 1991.

Haegeman, J. *Tuberous Begonias: Origin and Development*. Forestburgh, New York: Lubrecht and Cramer Ltd., 1979.

Hobhouse, Penelope. *Color in Your Garden*. Boston: Little, Brown, 1985.

_____. *Flower Gardens*. Boston: Little, Brown, 1991.

Loxton, Howard, ed. *The Garden: A Celebration*. Hauppauge, New York: Barron's Educational Series, Inc., 1991.

Randall, Harry and Alan Wren. *Growing Chrysanthemums*. Portland, Oregon: Timber Press, 1983.

Redoute, Pierre. *Lilies and Related Flowers*. New York: Overlook Press, 1982.

Van Brunt, Elizabeth R., ed. *Culinary Herbs*, Brooklyn, New York: Brooklyn Botanic Garden, 1989.

Verey, Rosemary. *The Art of Planting*. Boston: Little, Brown, 1990.

_____. *The Flower Arranger's Garden*. Boston: Little, Brown, 1989.

Vriends, Matthew. *Feeding and Sheltering Backyard Birds*, Hauppauge, New York: Barron's Educational Series, Inc., 1990.

Williams, Robin. *The Garden Planner*. Hauppauge, New York: Barron's Educational Series, Inc., 1990.

Yeo, Peter F. *Hardy Geraniums*. Portland, Oregon: Timber Press, 1985.

Zabar, Abbie. *The Potted Herb*. New York: Stewart, Tabori & Chang, Inc., 1988.

Journals

Fine Gardening

Green Scene, published by the Pennsylvania Horticultural Society.

Horticulture, published by Massachusetts Horticultural Association.

Organic Gardening

TLC...for plants (Canada)

Useful Addresses

Associations and Societies

American Begonia Society
P.O. Box 1129
Encinitas, CA 92024

American Fern Society
Pringle Herbarium
Department of Botany
University of Vermont
Burlington, VT 05495

American Horticultural Society
7931 E. Boulevard Drive
Alexandria, VA 22308

American Rock Garden Society
221 West 9th Street
Hastings, MN 55033

American Rose Society
P.O. Box 30,000
Shreveport, LA 71130

Associated Landscape
Contractors of America
12200 Sunrise Valley Drive
Suite 150
Reston, VA 22091

Cactus and Succulent Society of America
2631 Fairgreen Avenue
Arcadia, CA 91006

Californian Horticultural Society
1847 34th Avenue
San Francisco, CA 94122

Canadian Heritage Plants
(Conservation body)
Devonian Botanic Gardens
Edmonton, Alberta

Canadian Rose Society
686 Pharmacy Avenue
Scarborough, Ontario
M1L 3H8

The Garden Club of America
598 Madison Avenue
New York, NY 10022

Garden Clubs Canada
P.O. Box 7094
Ancaster, Ontario
L9G 3L3

The Garden Conservancy
P.O. Box 219
Cold Spring, NY 10516

Herb Society of America, Inc.
9019 Kirtland Chardon Road
Mentor, OH 44060

International Geranium Society
4610 Druid Street
Los Angeles, CA 90012

Massachusetts Horticultural
Association
300 Massachusetts Avenue
Boston, MA 02115

Men's Garden Clubs of
America, Inc.
P.O. Box 241
5560 Merle Hay Road
Johnston, IA 50131

National Chrysanthemum
Society
10107 Homer Pond Drive
Fairfax Station, VA 22039

National Council of State Garden
Clubs, Inc.
401 Magnolia Avenue
St. Louis, MO 63110

National Gardening Association
180 Flynn Avenue
Burlington, VT 05401

National Landscape Association
1250 I St. NW, Suite 500
Washington, DC 20005

National Wildflower Research
  Center
2600 FM 973 North
Austin, TX 78725

North American Lily Society
P.O. Box 476
Waukee, IA 50263

The Pennsylvania Horticultural
  Society
325 Walnut Street
Philadelphia, PA 19106

Perennial Plant Association
3383 Schirtzinger Road
Columbus, OH 43026

Primula Society
6730 West Mercer Way
Mercer Island, WA 98040

Mail Order Houses

Jackson & Perkins
1 Rose Lane
Medford, OR 97501-0701
1-800-292-4769

Wayside Gardens
1 Garden Lane
Hodges, SC 29695-0001
1-800-845-1124

CREDITS

Acknowledgments
The publishers and photographer
Marion Nickig thank the following garden owners, institutions,
and firms for their support:

Arends' Perennial Garden
  Center, Wuppertal, Germany
Mrs. M. Beuchert, Frankfurt
Botanical Garden, Munich,
  Germany
Caesar Family, Herten, Germany
Erfurt Seeds, Walluf-Rheingau,
  Germany
GRUGA Park, Essen, Germany
Herling Family, Dortmund,
  Germany
Hörsch Family, Uhingen,
  Germany
Kiepenkerl Plant Breeders,
  Münster, Germany
Mrs. I. Greve, Heerlen, Holland
Mrs. van Bennekom, Domburg,
  Holland
Palm Garden, Frankfurt,
  Germany
Rupp Family, Munich, Germany
Schmick Family, Hamburg,
  Germany
Weihenstephan Demonstration
  Garden, Freising, Germany
Westphalia Park, Dortmund,
  Germany
Countess Zeppelin's Perennial
  Garden Center, Laufen,
  Germany

Consultant
The editors thank Mrs. Karin
Greiner of the Botanical-
Ecological Advisory Institute for
valuable pertinent information.

The Photographers
All the photos in this book were
taken by Marion Nickig, with the
following exceptions:
Gärtner Pötschke: page 206
right; Hertle: page 221 center;
Kiermeier: pages 116 left, center,
133 left, 152 right, 195 center,
225 right, 227 left; Morell: page
183 center; Reinhard: pages 87
left, 156 left, 210 right, 225 center; Sammer: pages 171 right,
177 left, 188 left; SAVE/Pforr:
pages 60, 66; Seidl: pages 120
right, 133 right, 136 left, 163
left, 172 left, 208 left;
Silvestris/Brockhaus: page 7
center; Strauss: pages 175, 217
left.

Important Notes
This book deals with the care of garden flowers. Some of the species described are poisonous to varying degrees. In the plant portrait section (see pages 76 to 229), reference is made under the heading "**Warning**" to the toxicity of certain plants. Make absolutely sure that children and pets do not eat the plants. Some plants also exude skin irritants, and that fact is also mentioned under the heading "**Warning**" in the descriptions of the individual plants. Anyone who has sensitive skin or suffers from contact allergies should wear gloves when handling these plants.

If open injuries occur while you are handling soil, see a doctor at once for proper treatment. Ask whether immunization for tetanus is called for. Keep all fertilizers and plant-protective agents out of the reach of children and pets. For information on proper handling, see page 62. Consumption of these substances can be hazardous to your health. In addition, keep such substances away from your eyes. Secure relatively large liquid-fertilizer tanks with a grate or lid, so that small children cannot climb or fall in.

English translation © Copyright 1994 by Barron's Educational Series, Inc.
Published originally under the title *Gartenblumen* by Gräfe und Unzer Verlag GmbH, Munich, West Germany
Copyright ©1993 by Gräfe und Unzer Verlag GmbH, Munich, West Germany
Translated from the German by Kathleen Luft.

All inquiries should be addressed to:
Barron's Educational Series, Inc.
250 Wireless Boulevard
Hauppauge, NY 11788

Library of Congress Catalog Card No. 93-21323
International Standard Book No. 0-8120-6386-4

Library of Congress Cataloging-in-Publication Data
Hertle, Bernd.
    [Gartenblumen. English]
    Garden flowers : portraits of favorite garden flowers and ornamental grasses and ferns, with instructions for their care : with design ideas for large and small gardens / Bernd Hertle, Peter Kiermeier, Marion Nickig ; [translated from the German by Kathleen Luft].
        p.   cm.
    At head of title: You can have lovely plants and...
    Includes bibliographical references and index.
    ISBN 0-8120-6386-4
    1. Flowers. 2. Flower gardening. 3. Ornamental grasses. 4. Ferns, Ornamental. 5. Landscape gardening. 6. Flowers—Pictorial works. 7. Ornamental grasses—Pictorial works. 8. Ferns, Ornamental—Pictorial works. I. Kiermeier, Peter.   II. Nickig, Marion.   III. Title.
    SB407.H493513   1993   93-21323
    635.9—dc20   CIP

Printed in Hong Kong
4567   9955   098765432